Some Facets of *King Lear*

Edited by ROSALIE L. COLIE
and F.T. FLAHIFF

some
facets of
KING LEAR:
essays in
prismatic
criticism

UNIVERSITY OF TORONTO PRESS

© University of Toronto Press 1974
Toronto and Buffalo
Printed in Canada
ISBN 0-8020-1998-6
LC 73-81755

contents

preface

THE ESSAYS in this book form neither a casebook nor a 'perplex.' They were written because in each case their authors wanted to understand something specific about a very complicated play, *King Lear*. Though the different contributors have occasionally influenced one another's readings of the play, these essays were written independently of one another: that they are in some cases so mutually supportive is the result, we like to think, of the play's central insistence on its own primary meaning, visible from whatever perspective[1] a serious reader may take. The term 'prismatic criticism' is a deliberate metaphor: the editors wish to suggest by it their conviction that a work of art is whole, even though it presents more than one face or facet; that, depending upon the particular cut of the glass and the angle of the light playing upon it, the work of art may produce different effects; that because a work of art has many faces, one person cannot see it 'all' from one perspective – but also, that he may move around the work of art, or may move it in relation to the source of light. Most of all, the term seeks to evoke a prism's way of breaking up light to produce spectra that colour whatever they fall upon – a prism's radiance.

Methodological and theoretical assumptions underlie the metaphor, too. The image of the prism, with its multiple refractions, offers some sense of the inexhaustible variety of a work of art. Like a prism, *King Lear* is attractive; like a prism, it is a multiply shaped thing; like a prism, it is an object of admiration, as well as an instrument of analysis. Certainly, like a prism, a work of art such as this one may also prove hypnotic, rapture- or stupor-producing: it may then seem beyond criticism. Even Newton, we know, was temporarily enraptured in his dark chamber as he contemplated his prism – but Newton was Newton, so that his rapture was bound to be creative for optics and, indirectly, for poetry as well.[2] The contributors to this book have tried not to lose consciousness before the brilliance of their prismatic subject, *King Lear*, but to recognize that the play makes claims as itself, not merely as an hallucinogenic object on which any critic's imagination, fantasy, and self-analysis may play at will. For the authors writing here, the play exists in a meaningful environment, as the prism exists in a significant environment of light: its existence in time and place, the culture from which it and its author sprang, are factors in *King Lear*'s remarkable radiance.

In other words, these essays deal with many different topics as if they were in fact facets of a prism, cut in a particular way, to refract light. The topics are, like the facets of the prism, 'in' the play, cut into it, to make its particular shape; they are part of its art, and therefore of its meaning. The way the playwright managed the topics, cut the faces of his work, confirms the 'whole' that the play is. The title figure insists, then, that this prismatic play is a pluralist work of art, but that its many sides are not separate, detachable, or arbitrary. The spectra cast by the faces of a prism are, after all, alike; no one face, according to the textbook definition, annuls the effect of another. So, we hope, these essays do not annul one another – certainly, as they came to the editors they seemed to confirm that the many identifiable 'elements' of *King Lear*, however disparate, all worked toward a single great result.

One good thing about a prism is that it cannot be reduced to just one of its faces: so with the play, which resists simplifications to one or another reading (Christian tragedy, crypto-sceptical argument, a tissue of commonplaces, a study of disordered natural hierarchy, of wrath, of existential bleakness, etc.). Nor does a prism permit diffusion; it refracts light, makes radiance visible, but not foggy. Concentration on the facets and consideration of the sources of light in each particular case can, then, help us guard against the diffuseness to which a work at once so vast and so detailed as *King Lear* has tempted so many of its critics.

Though he is unaware of the fact, Maynard Mack's *'King Lear' in Our Time*[3] is grand- or godfather to many of these studies, which seek to work out in detail some of the many suggestions he made about the play. Like Mack's book, these essays honour the shaping and the shapedness of *King Lear*, honour its playwright as artisan and as maker, as *banausos* and as *demiourgos* too. Throughout, our emphasis is on Shakespeare's consciousness of his craft, on his critical use of the materials, notions, and devices available to him – on the play (prism-like) as an instrument of analysis. We can understand something of the mystery of ordinary light, by which we see anything we see, by the act of perceiving the serried brilliance that makes it up. So with the play, which tells us not just about itself but also about making itself, about the meanings of its language and of language in general, about the significance of the many different *schemata* turned to its particular uses. W.H. Auden has a lien on Shakespeare's beautiful image for himself as artist, 'the dyer's hand': this collection deals with that hand, with the dyes it used, and with the patterns – the master-pattern that resulted here.

If one believes in the genuine pluralism of a work of art such as *King Lear*, then what is the justification for limiting the perspectives, as they are limited here, to historical ones? The question is, again, one of validity: the authors have tried not to read anything *into* the play which could not be read *out* of it. Light must come from the right angle to strike spectra from a prism. The heuristic devices for these essays are not, as some critics think all heuristic devices should be, expendable; they are intrinsic, the authors think, to the play, to the means by which the play refers to its own created world and to the world outside itself, the means by which that larger world is drawn into the play. In a real sense, these essays deal with *King Lear* in *its* time, with its time as part of its meaning.[4]

The play is a shaped thing, made from materials and by tools available to the playwright, not by systems or insights to which he could have had no access. If Shakespeare can turn out to have been proto-Freudian, proto-existentialist, or absurdist, the attribution of such schemes to him measures the emotional and intellectual appeal of his work to legatees who live by systems other than his, as well as, we have no doubt, his remarkable powers of insight. What he was, though, was something quite simple: the child of parents who (according to T.P.R. Laslett[5]) could not write; he was grammar-school educated and alert to the literary habits, new and old, of his lifetime, habits by which his practice was formed and received, and which his practice altered, analysed, and enlarged. This is not to say that Shakespeare's plays are merely collections of the conventions, traditions, devices, schemes, and formulae available for his choosing: these essays do not suggest that genetics alone can substitute for criticism of any man's work, particularly not of *King Lear*. In so far as these essays are source-studies, they are so in a special sense, directed to the poet's active craftsmanship rather than to his derivativeness. Similarly, though they deal with 'forms' literary, intellectual, moral, and social, the essays are not concerned with formalist identification and categorization: rather, they present Shakespeare as a poet-critic, constantly testing the sources and resources of his craft, seeking out new sources, new forms as yet unincorporated into that craft; as a man exploring meaning, including the formal and ideational implications of the forms and conventions he used, and presenting and representing the meanings so found within the terms of dramatic literary expression. No claim is made that Shakespeare's work can be understood *only* in relation to his time and place, when it has so clearly spoken to other cultures, other sensibilities, ever since it first appeared; but the claim is put forth that Shakespeare's shaping art, if not the ultimate significances of his work, *can* be better understood against the possibilities that his times offered his craft. For many of us, Claudio Guillén's book, *Literature as System*, has legitimated the theory behind literary history, so long regarded as anti-theoretical. Behind Guillén's work looms that of E.H. Gombrich, whose exemplary *Art and Illusion*[6] offers justifications both brilliant and commonsensical for the study of the arts, works of art, and artists – the study, really, of any formulation – in their perceptual contexts.

A last word about this collection: only one of the essays has appeared in print before, and it has been considerably reworked for this volume; the other essays were all conceived by or coaxed from diffident authors for this enterprise, which testifies as a whole to the values of collective and co-operative scholarship, as against the exclusivism so often implied by separate publication. Here, at least, polemic is not merely conventional; the authors have attempted, in as workmanlike a fashion as each could, to present particular facets of the play in hopes of sharing the common angles on which light breaks into colour. If this book carried a dedication, it would be to Millar MacLure, whose understanding of analysis, synthesis, and co-operative endeavour has been significant for many of its authors.

R.L.C.

Unless otherwise indicated, all references to *King Lear* are to the Arden edition, edited by Kenneth Muir (London 1964).

This book has been published with the help of a grant from the Humanities Research Council of Canada, using funds provided by the Canada Council. I am grateful to my fellow contributors for their kindness and co-operation, indebted to Professor Sheldon Zitner and other friends for their assistance, and thankful to Miss Jean Jamieson of the University of Toronto Press for her patience and concern.

F.T.F.

NOTES

1 After considerable thought and discussion, the editors decided that they meant 'prismatics' and not 'perspectivism,' because they did not want to imply the shimmering, elusive aspect of the play *King Lear* so much as its solidity and radiance. It is true that it is possible to think of these essays as offering 'perspectives' upon the play – but the essays do not imply that the play exploits the kind of relativism that, say, the pastoral perspectivism of *As You Like It* forces upon the reader, or *Don Quixote* insists upon. For more on perspectivism, see Leo Spitzer *Linguistics and Literary History* (New York 1962), and Claudio Guillén *Literature as System* (Princeton 1971).

2 For this, see Marjorie Hope Nicholson's classic study of Newton's influence upon poetics and poetic practice, *Newton Commands the Muse* (Princeton 1946).

3 Berkeley 1965

4 For a responsible presentation of the premises on which this paragraph is based, see E.D. Hirsch, jr *Validity in Interpretation* (New Haven 1966).

5 Verbal communication from T.P.R. Laslett of Trinity College, Cambridge, who is now working on literacy and illiteracy in early modern England

6 London and New York 1960

Some Facets of *King Lear*

SHELDON P. ZITNER

King Lear and its language

IS IT AN ACCIDENT that a play so intense in feeling should end with Edgar's injunction to 'Speak what we feel, not what we ought to say'? Is it an accident that Lear's incoherence should convey his insight and Kent's rudeness his nobility, Cordelia's chilly plainness her devotion, Gloucester's courtliness his dereliction, and the play's central negations and affirmations be expressed less often in decorous soliloquy or set speech than in cries or silence? And how can we explain less obvious verbal anomalies: Kent's and Edgar's sudden adoption of folk or dialect speech in their encounters with Oswald, Edgar's bravura scene-painting during the grotesque mock-suicide, and the continually defeating flatness of sententious utterance? Possible answers to such questions are the burden of what follows – an argument that the language of *King Lear* has not only an opportune excellence but a design, that its language is not only the vehicle for *King Lear*'s questions, but one of them, and that the uses of language are as intended and systematic a motif as the uses of love.

Those who doubt the Folio assignment of the final speech to

Edgar often do so (as did Halliwell) on the ground of decorum, 'Albany being the person of greatest authority in the scene.' And even Theobald, arguing for the Folio attribution, sees it – 'in spite of decorum' – as given to Edgar only because his part was played by 'a more favourite actor.'[1] But how indecorous the speech is, and how indecorous the speeches that prompt it! A king, and such a king, dead without farewell apostrophe or clamour of regret; Britain lopped, and those who should sustain it resigning awkwardly from power; the only ceremonial unison the muffled drums of what the curtainless stage made an obligatory dead march. The passage itself is a conscious defiance of conventions. It is not, as Halliwell suggests, 'a gentle reproof to Kent's despairing speech, telling him that "the weight of this sad time we must obey." ' Rather, Edgar agrees with Kent and with Albany as well; they must say what they feel: Albany drawing back from his horrid image of the 'gor'd state'; Kent, his loyalties still centred on Lear, drawing back from a duty to the state, in favour of a spectral duty to the dead; Edgar, by his youth and special experience, the natural inheritor of the future, his thoughts fixed on a retrospect that wilts all his royal prospects. The scene is a paradigm of the unconventional and Edgar's speech is its rationale. All the theatrical 'oughts': apostrophe, lament, sentence, the grand futurity, even simple aesthetic closure, are rejected in a monosyllabic flatness that rebukes the shallowness of their big rhetoric, rejected in favour of speaking what one feels, which that very flatness hints language is ill equipped to do. Perhaps Edgar has learned something since the smugly pat formulation,

> The dark and vicious place where thee he got
> Cost him his eyes, (5.3.172–3)

which he applied to his father, that other Lear. More likely, the contrast between this and the rejection of formula in his final speech is less a piece of characterization than Shakespeare's prohibition of nice pieties at the end of the play. Even the conventional cry 'The king is dead; long live the king!' is forestalled in Edgar's final words, 'We that are young / Shall never see so much, nor live so long.'

Lear ends with a stroke of art that exposes – rather than conceals – art. It suggests that the demands of form and decorum in language may lead to untruths. With a paradoxy that the passage shares with much else in the play,[2] language as literature, therefore language at the top of its bent, declares itself inadequate for the task it has just performed.

Important speeches in King Lear seem at times to break off as if through such inadequacy; others are brought up short by enforced silences. Something can be made of these meaningful 'rests,' the emblems of the play's motif of nothingness, but silence is not the only alternative to the decorous speech that we, and criticism, conventionally presume is best. We can, as Edgar urges at the play's end, also 'Speak what we feel, not what we ought to say,' striving for a language to satisfy Troilus' demand for 'matter from the heart,' rather than 'words, words, words.' Such a language *Lear* provides in the obscurity or 'impertinency' of the heath scenes, in the uncouthness of Edgar's dialect and in Kent's 'plainness.' Together they form a counter-system of language, subversive of the inadequate system of decorum and reasonable discourse. Yet the considerations that lead away from decorum (proper words in proper places) must subvert any and every kind of language. The spectrum of propositions running from 'words are inadequate' to 'words lie' is the universal form of the Cretan liar paradox. It makes liars of us all, even as we proclaim our dearest truth: that life is not an affair of words. This contrast between word and deed is a perennial observation among artists, whom no achievement fails to disappoint. However, there are specifically contemporary reasons for Shakespeare's concern with the inadequacy of language. One is the impact of social change, of 'Antiquity forgot, custom not known, / The ratifiers, and props of every word' (*Hamlet* 4.5.104–5). An exchange in *Twelfth Night*, written at about the same time as *Hamlet* and full of significant parallels to it,[3] illuminates this passage. 'Indeed,' says the Clown of *Twelfth Night*, 'words are very rascals since bonds disgraced them' (3.1.19ff). The Clown's irony centres on the commercial and moral meanings of the word 'bond.' 'Thy reason, man?' the disguised Viola asks him. And the Clown continues, 'Troth, sir, I can yield you none without words, and words are grown so false I am loath to prove reason with them.' Shakespeare is sensitive to semantic change (see 2 *Henry* IV 2.4.129ff for example) arising from the growth of commercial enterprise and the cash nexus. He is fascinated by words like 'occupy' and 'commodity.' He doodles with the lingo of getting and spending in sonnet 30. The language of Goneril and Regan is full of the counter and the counting house. Their terminology of 'possession and calculation'[4] taints as it pre-empts Cordelia's language of service and mutuality, of 'bond' and 'cause.' Language thus far disgraced, says the Clown of *Twelfth Night*, is unfit even to think in.

But whatever Shakespeare's other reasons for it, his emphasis on the deceptiveness and frailties of utterance is wholly in keeping with his playing off of the pragmatic and the humane in *Lear*. This concern with the deceptiveness of language takes the form of a contrast of decorum with its alternatives, and of false speech with true seeing. These contrasts are, I think, the most important uses of language as motif in the play. They represent a culmination of Shakespeare's encounter with the deficienices of the verbal medium, an encounter important in plays as different as *Love's Labour's Lost* and *Much Ado about Nothing*. In such earlier plays Shakespeare's primary linguistic targets were the most prescriptive and best-articulated varieties of verbal decorum, the two forms of 'high' style, formal eloquence and courtly wit. But in *Lear* the 'attack' on decorous language is more pervasive and more intimately related to social and ethical themes.

If one takes decorum at its most thoroughgoing, one can hardly have dramatic literature at all, only décor – verbal tableaux with men fixed in their stations: kings pronouncing as kings, clowns as clowns. But Shakespearian tragedy is precisely indecorum: improper persons in proper places – clown as king, the pelican daughter battening on her father's breast. The world of *Lear* is so disordered it rarely generates decorum narrowly defined. At its head is a king and no king, a 'Nuncle' who, in the Fool's words, made his daughters his mothers, his subjects victims or dispensers of justice, his courtiers exiles, himself a fool and madman. Such contexts must transform the high style to pathos, deception, or irony. Thus, in the first act of the play there is a surface appropriateness of manner to station in the regal eloquence of Lear and in the cavalier sprightliness of Gloucester's wordplay on 'blush'd' and 'braz'd' when he refers to Edmund's bastardy. But their contexts and content make such passages indecorous for governors and fathers, and their surface of court rhetoric becomes a bitter irony. Occasionally, as in Kent's speeches before Lear's entrance in the first scene, or on the heath (see 3.2.42–8 for example), or in his counsel with a gentleman in the French camp near Dover (4.3), matter briefly answers to a courtly manner. Even in this latter scene, however, the gentleman's description of Cordelia's grief (4.3.11–33) suggests the emptiness of the high style in a pasteboard prettiness that anticipates the descriptions of royal sentiment in the last act of *The Winter's Tale*. But for the most part 'high' utterance comes under the rubric of 'that glib and oily art / To speak and purpose not.' Edmund's decorous reticence in the first scene is something other than a well-mannered dutifulness; Gloucester's courtly wordplay something other than proper paternal affection; the 'appropriate' sententiousness of Goneril and Regan something other than daughterly devotion; Burgundy's speeches something other than princely prudence. Only France's acceptance of Cordelia rings true. His is the language of sonnet and romance. And at the moment he accepts his undowered bride, France is authentically a romance figure and may truly speak proper romance words in their proper places. Yet the other courtly speeches are only superficially appropriate to their speaker's station. The decorum of the high or court style, then, is undercut in a variety of ways. Its magniloquence cloaks Lear's self-indulgence, its *copia* the sisters' disloyalty, its nimbleness Gloucester's sin, its descriptive elegance the gentleman's shallow sentiment. It is at best with Kent a brief convenience – a cachet to undo the impression of his dress and situation when he encounters a gentleman ally. One looks vainly in *King Lear* for set speeches or dialogue in which the courtly style finds answerable matter.

Kent states the principle on which the high style becomes evil utterance when he defends Cordelia's silence and his own plain-speaking against Lear's wrath:

> be Kent unmannerly,
> When Lear is mad. What would'st thou do, old man?
> Think'st thou that duty shall have dread to speak
> When power to flattery bows? To plainness honour's bound
> When majesty falls to folly. (1.1.145–9)

Kent's 'plainness' is one alternative to the decorum of speech to station. Cordelia employs a less extreme form of it, beginning with silence, then proceeding to the heartfelt but 'inappropriate' directness of a twice repeated 'Nothing' in answer to Lear's demand for verbal 'proofs' of love. 'Let pride, which she calls plainness, marry her,' is Lear's response. We are perhaps so influenced by our sense of what is owed by subjects and daughters that we are ready to accuse Cordelia of a virginal coldness in not humouring the old man. But this is to substitute modern 'realistic' deductions about personality for inductions from the design of language. Corderlia's silence, like her plainness, is the response that 'honour's bound [to] / When majesty falls to folly.' It is part of a verbal pattern, and not to be judged according to the implications of such responses in 'real' life. Nor is Cordelia reduced to plainness or to silence by the 'psychological' effect of her sisters' protestations of affection. She points out, of course, that their deeds belie their words:

> Why have my sisters husbands, if they say
> They love you all? (1.1.99–100)

But for her, the relation between thing and word is such that 'what I well intend, / I'll do't before I speak' (1.1.225–6). This harbours a more thoroughgoing objection to speaking the expected than a shame at contending with her sisters' hypocrisy. There is something of Feste's reply to Viola here; words are now too 'disgraced' to reason in. They can become valid only when they follow deeds that define them. By asking for words only, and by making words the test and matter of his own words, 'Which of you shall we *say* doth love us most?' (1.1.51), Lear makes Cordelia's silence inevitable and just. Indeed, the words of Goneril and Regan, and Lear's own words, too, have as little to do with Lear's actual deeds as with his daughters'. He has already divided his kingdom. His own words in the first scene are speaking that purposes not. Amid such speech Cordelia must be silent.

The logic of the references to language in the first scene prepares us for that silence. 'I love you more than word can wield the matter'; 'A love that makes breath poor and speech unable,' so Goneril decorously puts her case, using the expected *topoi* (1.1.55,60). But since Cordelia's love is indeed 'More ponderous than my tongue,' she cannot heave her heart into her mouth. In some contexts proper words in proper places fail, and language must acknowledge its inadequacy by silence or by reductive, self-deprecating plainness.

Yet the idea of decorum is not simple or monolithic; there is a decorum of occasion as well as a decorum of status, and only in the narrowest sense is decorum so prescriptive as to preclude the eloquence of servants or the vulgarity of crowned heads. Sometimes Shakespeare deliberately breaks with this decorum of occasion, shaping language to emphasize the contradiction between occasion and word. The opening speech of *1 Henry* IV and Claudius' public explanation of his marriage are instances in which the labour and exactness of the high style are meant to convey attitudes that are false or unlikely. But Kent and Cordelia strive to avoid such contradictions. Their plainness carries with it no negative self-reference; it aims to be wholly substantive, devoid of profession, or of insistence on 'place.' 'Sir,' Kent says to Cornwall, ' 'tis my occupation to be plain' (2.2.93). But there is no easy escape from the reflexiveness of language. Plainness can also be a mere style, as Cornwall, a military man, recognizes:

> This is some fellow,
> Who, having been prais'd for bluntness, doth affect
> A saucy roughness, and constrains the garb
> Quite from his nature.   (2.2.96–9)

The play's master-metaphor of clothing for all that is superficial and deceitful is here – in the word 'garb' – punningly applied to styles of speech:

> he cannot flatter, he,
> An honest mind and plain, he must speak truth:
> And they will take it, so; if not, he's plain.
> These kind of knaves I know, which in this plainness
> Harbour more craft and more corrupter ends
> Than twenty silly-ducking observants,
> That stretch their duties nicely.   (2.2.99–105)

This attack of Cornwall's is what we expect of his cynical and villainous nature. Yet it also carries on the play's consideration of utterance, of 'the slander that lies in tongues.' And Cornwall is right; Kent *is* garbed. Kent's only defence of his plainness is a counter-attack on courtly decorum. He responds to Cornwall by parodying the absurdities of the high style. In Kent's speech, beginning with those redundant protestations of truth, 'Sir, in good faith, in sincere verity' (2.2.106), scholars have detected an unflattering allusion to the ornate 'Epistle Dedicatory' of Florio's *A Worlde of Wordes*.[5] Perhaps Shakespeare is playing off plain, bluff English (Kent's speeches are a sociological coda, now elevated, now dialectal and folkish) against fashionable Italianate verbal artifice. But Cornwall's rejection of 'plainness,' while it is unjust to Kent, is finally just; language is a garb, not the thing itself. Kent can only respond that courtly verbal niceties are a worse cloak still, can only protest that 'I know, sir, I am no flatterer.' He is forced to grant that 'he that beguil'd you in a plain accent was a plain knave.' Finally, no verbal style is self-validating. Yet the play does distinguish between glib and oily propriety and the relative truthfulness of silence and plainness.

Two variants of plainness in *King Lear* are dialect and folkish speech. Their use follows, again, from the idea that when majesty wears motley the high style is a form of concealment or sophistication. Like Lear's unbuttoning and his interest in Tom o' Bedlam and the poor, dialect and folk speech are reductions to the primitive and the predecorous in a search for authenticity. The two characters who employ dialect or folk speech most extensively are Kent and Edgar, less Edgar as Tom o' Bedlam, than Edgar after he has thrown off his disguise. As early as 4.6, Edgar's 'voice is alter'd,' as the blind Gloucester tells him, and he is 'better spoken.' Edgar no longer needs the pseudo-mad speech of Tom o' Bedlam, part of his defence and evasion. Having suffered and learned with both Lear and his father, he can become his proper self. Yet when he tells Gloucester, 'You're much deceiv'd; in nothing am I chang'd / But in my garments' (4.6.9–10), he is being both truthful and equivocal. Edgar has indeed altered his dress from Tom's rags to the peasant clothing given him by the Old Man (4.1.49–50). His language as Tom was also a garb, and as Edgar leads his father, he removes that verbal 'daub' as well, declaring truthfully, and in his own voice, that he is

> A most poor man, made tame to Fortune's blows;
> Who, by the art of known and feeling sorrows,
> Am pregnant to good pity.   (4.6.222–4)

Yet a moment later, when Oswald discovers Gloucester and attempts to take him as a 'proclaim'd prize,' Edgar affects the Devonshire stage dialect that Shakespeare's company apparently used in such plays as The London Prodigal (1605).[6] There does not seem any prudential reason for 'daubing it further' here. Oswald's cry, 'the sword is out / That must destroy thee,' makes it clear that disguise can serve no purpose. At first Edgar seems trying to avoid a struggle with Oswald:

> Good gentleman, go your gait, and let poor volk pass.

Yet his very next words,

> And 'chud ha' bin zwagger'd out of my life, 'twould
> not ha'bin zo long as 'tis by a vortnight,   (4.6.236–41)

are provocative, not defensive. What releases Edgar's dialect manner is Oswald's courtly one, his succession of coldly turned phrases, the loftiness of his epithets, 'bold peasant,' 'slave,' 'dunghill.' That Gloucester shows no surprise when Edgar suddenly drops into dialect is one of Bradley's list of oddities in the play.[7] But realism here would only have blunted the encounter between styles, and indeed what explanation could Edgar have given for his dialect? As it is, the contrast of the courtly and the crude articulates the motif of the validity of language.

Something like this scene had taken place before in Oswald's clashes with Kent in 2.2, and earlier still in 1.4, when Kent undertook to teach the insolent Oswald 'differences.' In 2.2 Oswald's manner again prompts Kent to administer a lesson in 'differences.' Before drawing his sword, however, Kent lashes Oswald, not with lofty invective, but with billingsgate and worse, rich in folkish allusion (2.2.13ff). This lesson in 'differences' continues after Cornwall has arrived, with the result that the teacher is put in the stocks. In reply to Cornwall's rebuke of Kent's language, his lack of 'reverence' or decorum, Kent states that 'anger hath a privilege.' That privilege is plainness, here mixed with dialect and folkishness.

> Smoile you my speeches, as I were a Fool?
> Goose, if I had you upon Sarum plain,
> I'd drive ye cackling home to Camelot.   (2.2.83–5)

'Smoile' is dialectal, and the country references, still imperfectly explicated, are buried in their native soil, the rich aphorisms of rural folk.

Once again, the metaphor of clothing accompanies the concern with language. For Kent, Oswald is a man made by a tailor; for Cornwall, Kent's plainness is a garb. The language of the two confrontations with Oswald underlines the role of courtly speech as deception. Kent's lesson in 'differences' relates the theme of language to the themes of superfluity and charity. In the ideal kingdom it is as fatuous to go gorgeous in epithet as in furs. The doctrine of decorum of station suggests that style is what we owe ourselves; the plainness and dialect of Kent and Edgar tell us that style is what we owe to others. Thus Cornwall's rebellious servant can defy him with a pungent simplicity, and Kent can address the apparently loyal Edmund (in 1.1) and the truly loyal Gentleman in 4.3 with a courtly elegance of phrase. Utterance, we perceive, ought not to be framed according to the mere fact of station, but according to one's bonds, no more nor less.

A second alternative to the high style is obscurity. In the cryptic speeches of Lear and the disguised Edgar, the play tries to discover another authentic language. Lear's obscurity is the language he can use only after he has been reduced from court eloquence, reduced first by the silence of Cordelia, which denies him occasions for the magniloquence of 'our grace, our love, our benison' (1.1.265), reduced then by the illtreatment of his daughters, which causes his choking fit of *hysterica passio*, and leads him to tell Regan, 'I can scarce speak to thee' (2.4.137) and, in his defeated rage, to tell Goneril 'I'll not chide thee ... I can be patient' (2.4.227, 232). This process of silencing his high style ends shortly before his 'wits begin to turn,' in the lines:

> No, I will be the pattern of all patience;
> I will say nothing.   (3.2.37–8)

Edgar's language, too, is a language that comes after deracination. But in Lear's speech the languages of the play are gathered up in a progression that suggests the implications of each: the glib and oily art of eloquence by which a man may irresponsibly speak and purpose not, the indecorous plainness of anger that authentically states what one feels at the moment, the silence that falls when speech is no longer adequate, the obscure broken speech and the raw wordless howl that expose one's inmost state of being, and at last the innocent plainness of self-recognition that leaves almost everything to be conveyed by context, tone, and gesture. This progression is something like a trial of language in which decorum and its alternatives, though they are not equally falsifications, are yet convicted of some inadequacy.

Obscurity is the most adequate exposition (if not expression) of Lear in anguish. The art of his necessities is indeed strange, making 'impertinency' fitter than propriety. The obscurity of Lear's mad speech is a stage in the reduction of primitivizing of style, a verbal imitation of the act of unbuttoning. Lear's obscurity is language desocialized, a removal of the logical syntax, the immediate denotation, and the direct address in which we clothe and conventionalize thought and feeling to make them recognizable, instrumental, and acceptable to others. But Lear's obscurity – like all primitivizing – is also an effort at clarifying and simplifying, and, as we shall see later on, it can be readily decoded.

If, in order to define it, we contrast the madness of Lear with that of the Fool and Tom o' Bedlam, we must also contrast the kinds of obscure speech that convey it. The Fool is sometimes referred to as clinically mad, as having a 'maimed but agile mind,' perhaps because we too easily equate decorum with sanity. But the Fool is a model court Fool: a sage without laurels, obscuring, trivializing, and blunting home truths in order to forestall the blows that are their traditional reward. The logic of his defenceless loyalty is this: the more telling his insight the more quirky its statement. In the Fool obscurity is the guarantee of truthful or 'clear' utterance; it is not ornamental or merely attractively riddling, but a balance of defensiveness and aggression. There is good reason for the Fool's defensiveness, not only in the vulnerability of his station, but in the aggressiveness of his truth-telling. As much as Kent, the Fool rebels against and clings to a King who denies his kingship. His obscurities are ironic, for irony is a way of being at once angry and kind. Even as he guides Lear through the storm, he tells him:

> O Nuncle, court holy-water in a dry house is better than this rainwater out o' door. Good Nuncle, in, ask thy daughters blessing; here's a night pities neither wise men nor Fools.   (3.2.10–13)

There is kindness in the action, kindness in the sympathy of the first sentence, in the first exhortation of the second, in the empathy of the last clause; and one must expect that the actor will convey sympathy in the whole speech by voice and gesture. Yet the first sentence clearly relates the painful effects of Lear's thirst for flattery with their cause, and the Fool's religious reference in 'court holy-water' is mordant. The suggestion that Lear ask his 'daughters blessing' is another keen thrust, recalling the earlier allusion to his daughters' flattery, and to the benediction Lear refused Cordelia, so mistakenly conferring it on Goneril and Regan. This obscurely aggressive truth-telling is the primary content of the Fool's speeches. When the mad and anguished Lear falls exhausted, his last words are the pathetic 'We'll go to supper i' th' morning.' The Fool's comment is 'And I'll go to bed at noon.' The speeches that precede it suggest the meaning of this disputed line.[8] In his hallucinations, Lear often conducts himself as though his situation were unchanged. 'You, sir,' he says to Tom o' Bedlam, 'I entertain for one of my hundred;' but you must change your livery to serve me. And when at last he lies down, he commands:

> Make no noise, make no noise; draw the curtains:
> so, so. We'll go to supper i' th' morning.   (3.6.85–7)

It is as though a king, surrounded by his Gentlemen of the Bedchamber, should give assurance that, though he is wearied by some single untoward occasion, the ceremony of dinner will be only postponed. For all Lear's self-abandonment, there runs through the hovel scene a pathetic clinging to the habitual, an inability to encounter the whole truth of his situation. 'And I'll go to bed at noon' is the Fool's irony directed against Lear's illusions. It declares that polite formulas cannot cover the great revolutions in Lear's condition. There will be as much supper in the morning as bedtimes at noon. I will be as much deceived, says the Fool, as you. This ironic empathy is small but prophetic, for at last Lear will be as undeceived as his Fool.

The Fool directs his veiled truth-telling not only at Lear's but at the world's illusions. As the Fool enters for the first time, Lear has just said to Kent: 'Now, my friendly knave, I thank thee: there's earnest of thy service,' and has given him money. 'Let me hire him too: here's my coxcomb' (1.4.98–100), says the Fool. So much for Lear's illusion that one buys and sells loyalties. It is also true that Lear's folly (*his* coxcomb) does 'hire' Kent's loyalty, but this is not 'hire and salary.'

If the Fool can burst Lear's illusion and the world's, he can also understand Edgar's. In the mock-trial scene Lear, thinking of vengeance on Goneril and Regan, cries: 'To have a thousand with red burning spits / Come hizzing in upon 'em–' and Edgar counters: 'The foul fiend bites my back.' To these cries of revenge and self-pity the Fool replies: 'He's mad that trusts in the tameness of a wolf, a horse's health, a boy's love, or a whore's oath' (3.6.15–19). The Fool does not, of course, know Edgar or his situation, but he does know that the desire to persecute and the sense of being persecuted arise from the same foolish trust in the world's appearances. Such aggressive truth-telling by the Fool underlines one kind of connection between obscurity and validity of statement.

Yet the Fool is more than a truth-teller. In Lear's mad mock trial, it is Tom o' Bedlam who is the 'man of justice'; the Fool is 'his yoke-fellow of equity.' In the fashion of equity, he comments obscurely not only on immediate cases but on the general circumstances, such as human cupidity and sexuality, to which they must be related. Hence his codpiece song, with its radical insistence on all self-indulgence as essentially sexual. Further still, he is a figure of mercy, bearing with his master's madness, attempting to lead him to understanding and, despite his refusal to abate his criticism, able to minister with his antics and cry 'Whoop, Jug! I love thee.'

Essentially the Fool's obscurity, like the silence and plainness of Cordelia and Kent, is an instrument employed by weakness to counter folly. This is the psychological rationale for the Fool's obscurity. But it has a thematic and theatrical rationale as well. When 'truth' appears in conventional stage guise – as the unobscure didactic aphorism, the couplet *sententia* – it is often not truth at all, but empty formula that denies either the complexity or the intensity of the play or both. *Lear* offers no cause in nature that breeds hard hearts or explains blinding and execution. For example, Edgar's sententious view of his father's blindness as punishment for fornication is simplistic. On the theatrical side, what contrasts with the play's violence and anguish is not the lofty QED of aphorism, but the quiet of Lear's self-recognition, 'I am a very foolish fond old man,' and the modest ellipsis of Cordelia's 'no cause.' The play's conventional wisdom is, as the critics observe, 'detached' from the play, 'essay material,' 'inappropriate,' 'flat,' or 'thin.'[9] In a play so paradoxical, so problematic, such truths as can be hazarded must be enveloped in ironic verbal textures: snatches of song, riddle, burlesque prophecy, and quip. Having little application, conventional wisdom is relegated to the merely rhetorical artifice in which *sentence* began. In this way the play's languange again undoes decorum.

In the speech of Edgar as mad Tom other motives lead to obscurity. Edgar's suddenly altered situation has left him almost without plain truths to tell: 'Edgar I nothing am.' But even unaccommodated man has an 'interest,' and much of his gibberish is intended simply to frighten intruders from his hovel. Edgar's aggressive comments on what he sees and hears about him are self-interested in other ways as well. When Lear says: 'Death, traitor! nothing could have subdu'd nature / To such a lowness but his unkind daughters' (3.4.70–1), Edgar replies: 'Pillicock sat on Pillicock hill: / Alow, alow, loo, loo!' The reference is perhaps to the rhyme:

> Pillycock, Pillycock sat on a hill;
> If he's not gone, he sits there still.

In any case 'Pillicock' is both a term of endearment and a euphemism for the penis. It is as though Edgar, unjustly persecuted by his father, were to speak for all sons, declaring that their begetting is the fruit of indulgence, not of love or kindness. Pillicock sits on the hill (the *mons veneris?*), sits there still, responds still to the hunting call, 'Alow, alow, loo, loo.' And if unkind daughters result from the exploits of Pillicock, parents must take their chances. Fathers have no cause to complain; let them know that sons also have been outraged, and that the filial bond is an illusion; as daughters live by appetite so do fathers. Edgar's obscure comment returns us to Gloucester's earlier discussion of his sexual prowess and to the Fool's codpiece song. If the Variorum editor's suggestion (189, n74) is correct and 'Alow, alow, loo, loo' is not a hunting cry but a cock-crow, the reduction of paternity to barnyard pride could not have been made more clearly. This strain in Tom o' Bedlam's obscure speech answers Lear's lament of the fathers with Edgar's lament of the sons.

But the themes of *Lear*, unlike those of *Hamlet*, require avoidance of the idea of simple generational conflict; if *Hamlet* is the tragedy of youth seen in prospect, *Lear* is the tragedy, not of age, but of the whole condition of man in retrospect. Lear's first words to Tom are the question, 'Didst thou give all to thy daughters?' And Edgar's reply is the counter-question, 'Who gives any thing to poor Tom?' Implicit in the exchange is Edgar's later formula of understanding, 'He childed as I father'd.' But self-pity and aggressiveness keep Edgar from the fullness of that understanding and dictate his obscurity here. There follows Edgar's surreal self-pitying speech: the 'foul fiend' has given him nothing – save a path through physical hardship (bog and quagmire), through imagined conspiracy and violence (knives under his pillow, rats-bane by his porridge). These two motifs of hardship and imagined betrayal are brought together in the last clauses of the breathless sentence which makes up most of the speech (3.4.50–62): 'on a bay trotting-horse,' a horse trained for aristocratic ceremony and display, Edgar must manœuvre dangerous paths ('four-inch'd bridges'), seeking the treachery ascribed by his father to his proud traitor's heart. For all the knowledge of his innocence, perhaps because of it, Edgar is still self-accusing. The image of a leisured past is displaced as in nightmare into the horrible present caused by his father's suspicions. The speech ends in self-pity ('Do poor Tom some charity, whom the foul fiend vexes') and in an ambiguous miming of revenge ('There could I have him now, and there, and there again, and there'). The speech gives us one set of violent gestures, but directed both against himself and against the foul fiend. It is a convenience to reserve the theme of Edgar's self-flagellation and continue for a moment with his relation to his father. For Lear 'the fiend' must be 'his daughters.' But not for Edgar. When Gloucester enters, his torch lighting up both its bearer and the hovel, Edgar speaks at once: 'This is the foul Flibbertigibbet.' Edgar goes on to ascribe to Gloucester all the blights of nature and the traits of a soul in purgatory. When Gloucester asks, 'Your names?' Edgar replies with the catalogue of his hardships, directing attention as in the bay-mare-traitor imagery to the *de casibus* story of poor Tom 'who hath had three suits to his back, six shirts to his body,' but now must eat the swimming frog as he flees or is whipped, stocked and imprisoned. He concludes with threat and propitiation: 'Beware my follower ... peace, thou fiend!' again expressing the mental division that leads both to the innocent's desire for revenge, and the guilty man's plea for forbearance. In short, Edgar's obscurity here comes from his confused sentiments of innocence and guilt, his confused aggressiveness and self-pity.

Edgar provides us with further obscure and even more aggressive comment on his own case when Gloucester is appalled that his king has no better company than the likes of Tom o' Bedlam. 'The Prince of Darkness,' Edgar volunteers, 'is a gentleman; Modo he's called, and Mahu.' But in this reply Edgar has, though less than Lear in his concern for 'Poor naked wretches,' also taken a step toward humanity, by asserting the moral irrelevance of social distinctions. Though he strikes out at his father's tainted proprieties, Edgar is also telling us here something about the emptiness of social decorums.

Edgar's obscure speech also echoes Lear's moral and physical terror, but it is more than stage-set or chorus. It is a verbal mortification. Are we to imagine the stage-figure as indeed one of those Bedlam beggars

> who, with roaring voices,
> Strike in their numb'd and mortified bare arms
> Pins, wooden pricks, nails, sprigs of rosemary?   (2.3.14–16)

It would be useful to know in detail how the first Edgar was actually costumed, and how much emphasis the costuming put on mortification. Edgar probably did 'grime [his face] with filth, / Blanket [his] loins, elf all [his] hair in knots, / And with presented naked-ness outface / The winds and persecution of the sky.' Perhaps Edgar's disguise was suggested by the Paphlagonian king of Sidney's *Arcadia*, who was forced to exist on alms, but the self-flagellation is Shakespeare's invention. Edgar's language is a verbal extension of it. His obscure self-indictments answer to his mortifications of the flesh. Man unaccommodated is man self-accused and self-punished. But the accommodations for lack of which Edgar is Tom o' Bedlam are spiritual ones for which his physical distress and his costume of mortification are a metaphor. The absence of fatherliness and brotherly feeling leads to fear and self-rejection, and these are expressed in a language whose obscurity comes largely from imperfect reference. Tom is outside the bonds of society and hence beyond coherence. Once accommodated, capable of pity and love, he drops his disguises of rag and ellipsis and enters humanity again. Yet Edgar as Tom, despite his feigning, *is* the thing itself – man seen in and of himself, torn from the human fabric. His affected mad speech, then, is a form of truth-telling since it exposes, at its outset at any rate, the crude self-interest that the oily decorums of the sisters and the sensible businesslike language of Cornwall cloak so well. In Edgar's mad speech the motifs of mortification and persecution and the ambiguity of reference are the verbal form of self-destructive lovelessness, that absence of human bond concealed in the decorous language of the sisters but exhibited in their behaviour. Edgar's obscurity is the language of bondless man.

In addition to his accusations against his father and his self-flagellation, there is another motif in Edgar's obscurity, one closely related to the two others. Typical of this strain in Edgar's speech is his response to the Fool's comment that 'This cold night will turn us all to fools and madmen.' Edgar replies with a version of the Commandments: 'Obey thy parents; keep thy word's justice; swear not; commit not with man's sworn spouse.' He concludes with the self-pitying 'Tom's a-cold' (3.4.80ff). These are the conventional cries of religious mania, with their biblical echoes and their implication that human wretchedness is solely the wages of sin. This implication relates Tom's statements to his guilty self-punishment and to his accusations against his father. But passages of this sort lead in the direction of

> The Gods are just, and of our pleasant vices
> Make instruments to plague us;
> The dark and vicious place where thee he got
> Cost him his eyes. (5.3.170–3)

Whatever one's private beliefs on the doctrine of this passage, 'poetic justice' is notoriously ill-served by the play, as Johnson's famous reluctance to re-read the death of Cordelia testifies. Not only the death of Cordelia and the blinding of Gloucester, but the anguish of Lear himself record the excess of punshment over crime in the play. Tom o' Bedlam's obscure warped commandments – like his later warped aphorism – alert us to the ethical import of the action before us. And by their formulaic inadequacy they insist that we cannot view Lear's fate or his own as cautionary tales.

Like his brother taking 'villanous melancholy' as his cue, Edgar as Tom is, paradoxically, what he pretends to be. His madness, however, is feigned. Lear's, on the other hand, is not. But to say this is only to begin making necessary distinctions. In the heath scenes Edgar's speeches are largely defensive; they centre on his private ills; they are knowingly addressed to persons actually on the stage – and they reflect Edgar's movement from self-pity to empathy with Lear, to an understanding of Lear's situation, to a rejection of self-pity and, at last, to a self-mastery that brings him back into society. Lear's speeches, on the other hand, are more self-exploratory than defensive; they move back and forth between private and public ills; they are addressed less to actual persons than to powers or symbols of powers on a universal and spiritual plane; and they do not progress toward self-sufficiency (as do Edgar's) but circle, returning in 'kill, kill, kill, kill, kill, kill,' (4.6.189) to the angry 'Crack Nature's moulds, all germens spill at once,' that began the sequence (3.2.8).

Though Lear is mad and Edgar only feigning madness, both speak in a way that strikes us as authentic. A useful foil for understanding Shakespeare's method in their madness is Zabina's speech in 5.2 in the first part of Marlowe's *Tamburlaine*. Informed of the death of Bajazeth, the Queen goes abruptly from highly rhetorical blank verse to:

> Give him his liquor? Not I. Bring milk and fire, and my blood I bring him again. Tear me in pieces. Give me the sword with a ball of wild-fire upon it. Down with him! Down with him! Go to, my child. Away, away, away! Ah, save that infant! Save him, save him! I, even I, speak to her. The sun was down – streamers white, red, black. Here, here, here! Fling the meat in his face! Tamburlaine, Tamburlaine! Let the soldiers be buried. Hell, death, Tamburlaine, hell! Make ready my coach, my chair, my jewels. I come, I come, I come![10]   (5.2.246–55)

Whereupon the distraught Zabina 'runs against the cage and brains herself.' This is effective theatre, and perhaps as much as Marlowe needed to do at this point. But the redundancy and arbitrariness of the details, their infrequent ethical import and their shallow evocation of other materials in the play, their relatively infrequent generation of particular stage gesture, suggest that Marlowe is concentrating on pathos and realism, on 'mere' madness, and depending too heavily on the physical presence of the actor. In short, the virtues of the passage are narrowly theatrical. It is spoken only to us, but in the madness of both Lear and Edgar there is more matter, almost no 'impertinency' whatever.

It is best to demonstrate this relative absence of the merely theatrical by referring to passages thought to be the most 'incoherent' ones in the play. The pervasiveness of central themes and the 'stage business' supporting these passages should – if we take Shakespeare's devotion to clarity seriously – lead us to see them as accessible to a theatre audience. When Lear enters *'fantastically dressed with wild flowers'* at 4.6.80, we are to take it as a cue that his statements: 'Nature's above art' and 'I am the king himself' relate to some effort to act out an authentic 'natural' self. And in what follows Lear does become in fantasy the authentic king, a commander and a dispenser of mercy and justice. He denies that he can be accused of counterfeiting either currency or kingship. We must see him giving imagined coins to imagined troops; encouraging and supervising their training; piteously stooping to offer cheese to a mouse, with the cry, 'Peace, peace' that humanizes and thus validates his warlike sternness; throwing down his gauntlet and asserting the honour of his word even against a giant; once again moving his archers (Edgar? Gloucester?) to their correct position; being recalled by the marjoram password – allusion to his madness – and by the voice of Gloucester to a sense of his immediate situation; and then declaring justly that adversity has reduced him to recognize the viciousness of his daughters' natures and the frailty of his own. But Lear's responses to Gloucester after line 105 veer off in the opposite direction. Self-pity distorts his mercy to cynical indulgence as both commander and 'justicer.' He exhausts himself in self-disgust and disgust with the world, declaring 'I'll not love.' The rest of his speeches in the scene build toward the violence that ends with the six times repeated resolution to 'kill.' The impression of incoherence in this scene arises from the illusion of discreteness in its materials. While it may be useful to point to the 'nature' materials in 'crow-keeper,' 'mouse,' 'bills,' 'bird,' and so on, there is something awkward in a critical method whose concentration on the realms of discourse from which images are drawn can also lead us to the ludicrous sequence 'clothier's yard,' 'gauntlet,' 'bills,' and 'clout.' In any case, there is no need for it. Recollections of earlier themes and a sense of stage gesture supply the connections among the 'incoherent' words. The passage (as the rest of the heath scene) gives us two Lears: an idealized king of mercy and command, and a self-indulgent violent cynic. Both of these contending Lears are – despite Lear's madness – more clearly verbalized here than else-where, in part because they are abstracted from the flow of the action, introspected as in dramatic monologue. In these scenes, the respite from communication and decorum allows Lear to act out the dividedness that he feels and is.

Yet in the mixed prose and verse which Shakespeare assigns Lear in his worst anguish, a logical, even an oratorical, organization per-sists. One can outline the 'every inch a king' speech as a pupil of Mulcaster might outline Cicero. Propostion: there is no need to punish adultery. Arguments: first, adultery is the norm of nature, viz., the wren and the fly; second, adultery has better effects than does lawful intercourse, viz., the 'loyalty' of Edmund, the 'treach-ery' of Edgar; third, kings need soldiers; fourth and fifth, amplifi-cations of the first, adultery is the law of human life, viz., yon 'simp'ring dame,' and woman's centaur nature. And all the argu-ments are enclosed in the consciousness that they are products of an imagination gone sour, for which, good apothecary, an ounce of civet. Lear's obscurities are very nearly transparent; only his courtly speeches were opaque.

In items 293 and 304 of his *Philosophical Investigations* Witt-genstein asserts that if we construe the grammar of the expression of sensation and other private experiences on the model of 'object and name,' the object drops out of consideration and such experi-ences become incommunicable. Perhaps. But in the heath scenes such experiences *are* expressed. They provide the opportunity for circumventing the limitations of syntax, direct address, and surface coherence that decorous or conventional language imposes.

Edgar's language of assumed madness enables him both to speak what he feels and to feel what he speaks. 'Bless thy five wits,' Edgar says to Lear and then, in an aside to the audience:

> My tears begin to take his part so much,
> They mar my counterfeiting.   (3.6.60–1)

And mar his counterfeiting they do. It becomes emotionally impos-sible for him to sustain the alienation of disguise and hence un-necessary to the plot for him to do so. Feeling what he has spoken liberates Edgar from his self-ignorance. But on yet another exemplary occasion Edgar will speak what he does not, even cannot, feel. Perhaps the most memorable 'poetic' speech of the play is a summary and paradigm of its critique of language.

This virtuoso instance of the emptiness of persuasive speech occurs at the cliffs of Dover.[11] What we see is an old blind man falling after a 'jump' on level ground. What we hear is a convincing account of suicide thwarted by miracle. I am far from proposing a complete explanation for this endlessly troubling scene. For one thing its negative, even comic, treatment of suicide is demanded by the themes of the play. But if we are correct in thinking that Shakespeare is concerned in *Lear* with the uses of language, it is difficult not to view this scene as also a culmination of his comments on the art of words. In any case, the illusory suicide stands as an exemplum of the virtuosity of language, at once a delight and a warning. Verbal excellence has its own uses, but at the top of its bent that excellence lies, however convincing lies may be to the blind.

One could go further in specifying such warnings. Sometimes the inadequacy of language is conveyed by ellipsis, as in

> No, you unnatural hags,
> I will have such revenges on you both
> That all the world shall – I will do such things,
> What they are, yet I know not, but they shall be
> The terrors of the earth.   (2.4.280–4)

Both Lear's revenges and the world's reactions to them are literally unspeakable. And when they are spoken as in 'Howl, howl, howl,' and the obsessively iterated 'kill,' it is not the words that are expressive, but the repetitions. The words alone are inadequate. But throughout *Lear*, who really listens to anyone else; whom do words alter or persuade?

> A man may see how this world goes with no eyes. Look with thine ears: see how yond justice rails upon yond simple thief. Hark, in thine ear: change places, and, handy-dandy, which is the justice, which the thief?   (4.6.151–6)

Bottom's confusion is Lear's wisdom. To 'look with one's ears' finally does lead to a realization that words are only words. Unlike deeds or bonds (which they badly reflect), they are interchangeable among all sorts and conditions of men, and hence of uncertain moral significance. To learn this emptiness of words is to learn a great deal; it is to 'see how this world goes' – this world whose authority we feel even as we listen, for, being beyond the grasp of language, it beggars description.

NOTES

1 Both Halliwell and Theobald are cited in the Variorum *King Lear* ed. H.H. Furness (Philadelphia 1880) 349n.
2 See on this point Rosalie L. Colie *Paradoxia Epidemica* (Princeton 1966) chap 15.
3 On the relation between *Twelfth Night* and *King Lear*, see Julian Markels, 'Shakespeare's Confluence of Tragedy and Comedy,' *Shakespeare Quarterly* xv (1964) 75–88.
4 See Wolfgang Clemen *The Development of Shakespeare's Imagery* (London 1951) 135.
5 New Arden *King Lear* 75n
6 New Arden *King Lear* 185n
7 A.C. Bradley *Shakespearean Tragedy* (London 1956) 207
8 The line is explicated in quite a different way in Hilda Hulme *Explorations in Shakespeare's Language* (London 1962) 70–2.
9 B.I. Evans *The Language of Shakespeare's Plays* (London 1966) 172
10 The text is that of *The Complete Plays of Christopher Marlowe* ed. Irving Ribner (New York 1963) 106.
11 See Sigurd Burckhardt *Shakespearean Meanings* (Princeton 1968) 276–7, for a related but quite different interpretation. Burckhardt's considerations of *Lear* (237ff) are suggestive.

TWO

BRIDGET GELLERT LYONS # the subplot as simplification in king lear

LEAR'S WORDS just before his death have always eluded the attempts of critics to label what he sees, does, or feels at the moment that he utters them:

Pray you, undo this button: thank you, Sir.
Do you see this? Look on her, look, her lips,
Look there, look there! [*Dies*   (5.3.309–11)

If we are rigorous in our analysis of this passage, we reject speculations like Bradley's about whether the king is dying of joy or grief: 'this' in line 310 lacks an antecedent and is therefore unclear. But there are other grounds for hesitating to fill in the gaps of Lear's fragmented requests and exclamations, and these grounds are related to the very different way in which we have learned of Gloucester's death shortly before. This event is narrated by Edgar and is not seen by the audience at all:

and in this habit
Met I my father with his bleeding rings,

> Their precious stones new lost; became his guide,
> Led him, begg'd for him, sav'd him from despair;
> Never – O fault! – reveal'd myself unto him,
> Until some half-hour past, when I was arm'd;
> Not sure, though hoping, of this good success,
> I ask'd his blessing, and from first to last
> Told him my pilgrimage: but his flaw'd heart,
> Alack, too weak the conflict to support!
> 'Twixt two extremes of passion, joy and grief,
> Burst smilingly.   (5.3.188–99)

What this account lacks in immediacy it gains in coherence. We see Gloucester's death through the mediation of a narrator who structures the event in terms of known forms by which life and literature pattern themselves ('List a brief tale' in 5.3.181; 'my pilgrimage'), and who cannot speak of eyes without expressing their analogical value. Motives and moral evaluations are clearly spelled out, and there is no mystery about the death itself: the allusion to the conflict of passions which literally broke Gloucester's heart assumes the interlocking systems – moral, physiological, psychological – by which people of the Renaissance conventionally interpreted behaviour.[1] The passage's ornate figures ('Their precious stones new lost,' 'Burst smilingly') are also heightened expressions of its intelligibility.

Edgar's account, understandable in the way Bradley wanted Lear's death to be, points to some of the most characteristic differences between plot and subplot in the play. The Gloucester story intensifies our experience of the central action by supplying a sequence of parallels, impressed upon us by frequent commentary by the characters themselves:

GLOU. This villain of mine comes under the prediction; there's son
against father: the King falls from bias of nature; there's father
against child. We have seen the best of our time ...   (1.2.114–18)
EDG. How light and portable my pain seems now,
When that which makes me bend makes the king bow;
He childed as I father'd!   (3.6.111–13)
LEAR Let copulation thrive; for Gloucester's bastard son
Was kinder to his father than my daughters
Got 'tween the lawful sheets.   (4.6.117–19)

But repetition alone cannot supply dramatic interest, and the characters' consciousness of the existence of a mirror does not mean that the reflection is exact. Hamlet too sees Laertes as a 'foil,' but the audience is as much aware of the differences between the responses of the two characters as of the analogous situations that provoke those responses. The same point has been cogently made by Sigurd Burckhardt about the double plot in *King Lear*:

> I submit that Shakespeare, in this tragedy and in no other, constructed parallel plots of considerable rigor, and that we must assume that he meant something by this structure. He cannot have meant the plots to be merely parallel, one reinforcing the other; for then the subplot would become a mere redundancy, and if ever an action needed no reinforcement of its impact, it is Lear's. There is every reason to think that the apparent similarity of the two plots is like that of controlled experiments, and that the meaning of both lies in the one element which accounts for the difference.[2]

The element of difference on which I would like to concentrate lies in the way the subplot simplifies the central action, translating its concerns into familiar (and therefore easily apprehensible) verbal and visual patterns. The subplot is easier to grasp because its characters tend to account for their sufferings in traditional moral language; it also pictorializes the main action, supplying interpreted visual emblems for some of the play's important themes. The clarity of the subplot and its didacticism are related, furthermore, to the old-fashioned literary forms, like the morality play and the chivalric romance, through which it represents experience.[3] These give expression to the idea of convention, and therefore to a world of recognizably structured perceptions and values – the very opposite of dislocation and madness. But the verbal and visual simplifications of the subplot do not merely provide a contrast with what goes on elsewhere in the play; they help to reveal the nature of Lear's experience by being so obviously inadequate to it. Lear's sufferings are heroic because they cannot be accommodated by traditional formulas, moral or literary, and the subplot exists partly to establish that fact.

The simplifications of the subplot can be seen first of all in its method of defining character. The behaviour of Edmund the Bastard, for example, is more comprehensible than that of Lear's bad daughters because his depravity is largely explained by his illegitimacy. He is what so-called 'natural' children were supposed to be; and his definition of 'nature' as circumventing law, custom, and order is in keeping with the application of the word 'natural' to children who were born outside of society's laws and excluded from its benefits. Legal treatises of the later Middle Ages, often compendia of commonplace morality, demonstrate the extent to which traditional moral thinking made the bastard susceptible of emblematic treatment. In Sir John Fortescue's commendation of the English laws of the fifteenth century, for example, he particularly praises their intransigence towards illegitimate children (their exclusion from inheritance even if their parents eventually married) as being in accord with biblical examples. He goes on to explain that bastards are actually contaminated by the sinful circumstances of their begetting: they have more than their share of the sin that all inherit, and nature brands them 'by setting as it were a natural mark or blemish on the natural children, though secretly impressed upon the mind.'[4] Gloucester's initial action in disinheriting the bastard son whom by his own admission he loves as much as his legitimate son is entirely in accord with this legal notion of justice: bastards were living emblems of their parents' sin in begetting them.

Moral and legal ideas about bastards had already been translated into dramatic conventions by the time *King Lear* appeared on the stage, and Edmund's behaviour was recognizable also in terms of a dramatic tradition. The Elizabethan stage abounds with bastards (Shakespeare's Don John in *Much Ado about Nothing* and Tourneur's Spurio in *The Revenger's Tragedy* are examples) who are envious and villainous because they are dispossessed and whose actions reveal the 'secret blemish' of their minds.[5] The important contrast in *King Lear* is between Edmund's conventionally explicable villainy and the seemingly incomprehensible evil of Goneril and Regan. The two daughters, who have been given 'all,' must remain the subject of unanswered questions about what in nature breeds such 'hard hearts.' Their behaviour is as much of a mystery as Cordelia's goodness, defying explanation in terms of natural causes like heredity:

> KENT It is the stars,
> The stars above us, govern our conditions;
> Else one self mate and make could not beget
> Such different issues. (4.3.33–6)

Lear twice attempts to explain his older daughters' nature on the grounds of their bastardy and their consequent lack of kinship with him (1.4.262–3; 2.4.130–4); Edmund, though his father's son, does what he does because he acts in accordance with a well-established moral and dramatic tradition.

Edgar too illustrates how the conventionality of the subplot's roles expresses the more clearly defined nature of its concerns. Undeveloped at the beginning except in his function as a virtuous dupe, he later purposefully assumes a disguise as a Bedlam lunatic which is in direct contrast with Lear's uncontrolled, real madness. The difference between the two kinds of madness is expressed through dramatic roles: Edgar's pose is an imitative one whose stereotyped nature has been alluded to earlier by Edmund ('my cue is villanous melancholy, with a sigh like Tom o' Bedlam,' 1.2.142–3), and for which there were prescribed costumes and gestures:

> The country gives me proof and precedent
> Of Bedlam beggars, who, with roaring voices,
> Strike in their numb'd and mortified bare arms
> Pins, wooden pricks, nails, sprigs of rosemary;
> And with this horrible object, from low farms,
> Poor pelting villages, sheep-cotes, and mills,
> Sometime with lunatic bans, sometime with prayers,
> Enforce their charity. (2.3.13–20)

While the king wildly imagines a variety of impossible roles for himself, from that of the avenging fury to being the 'pattern of all patience,' Edgar's mad pose is one for which there was 'proof and precedent' in the social and dramatic world. His conscious control of all the roles that he chooses is embodied in their stereotyped, fixed quality – Bedlam, rustic with a typical stage dialect, knight.

Closely related to the greater conventionality of the subplot's characters are two of its other most striking features: its pictorial nature and its archaism. First, the subplot often provides emblems, or pictures with clearly stated meanings, for the benefit of the audience as well as for Lear and the Fool. The appearance of Edgar on the heath as a poor and naked Bedlam beggar, for example, supplies the physical actuality of the poverty and nakedness that preoccupy Lear, stripped of his retinue and position:

> Is man no more than this? Consider him well. Thou ow'st the worm no
> silk, the beast no hide, the sheep no wool, the cat no perfume. Ha!
> here's three on 's are sophisticated; thou art the thing itself;
> unaccommodated man is no more but such a poor, bare, forked animal
> as thou art. (3.4.105–11)

While Lear soon tries to imitate Edgar and act out the metaphor of nakedness, it is Edgar who serves as a living example and a lesson, a subject for meditation ('Consider him well'). Gloucester's entrance with a torch immediately afterwards inspires the Fool to similar emblematic imaginations on a different subject:

> Now a little fire in a wild field were like an old lecher's heart; a small
> spark, all the rest on 's body cold. Look! here comes a walking fire.
> (3.4.114–17)

Later, when the mad king meets the blinded Gloucester at Dover, Lear uses him as a source of emblems: the blind man is 'blind Cupid' (4.6.138) and 'Goneril, with a white beard' (4.6.97), in each case a picture that we associate, in its context in the play, with lust. These images prompted by Gloucester also become assimilated to Lear's vision of injustice:

> Get thee glass eyes;
> And, like a scurvy politician, seem
> To see the things thou dost not.   (4.6.172–4)

The function of emblems, with their detachable meanings, whether conventional or assigned, is to clarify and to teach; this was the aim of many of the numerous emblem books of the period. But emblems were often excessively ingenious, even arbitrary, in creating pictorial embodiments of moral truths on figures of speech, and therefore the continuously emblematic nature of Lear's imaginings becomes a sign of their insanity, even while they suggest a higher order of insight. His emblems portray the obsessive moral imagination of the character who creates them and at the same time they provide physical analogues for some of the play's important themes – nakedness, appetite, injustice. Edgar and Gloucester, in the examples cited, constitute the pictorial parts of the emblems for which Lear supplies the text.

The pictorial simplifications of the subplot contribute to the particular nature of its archaic quality: it often evokes a medieval legal morality, with its direct translation into codes of justice of biblical injunctions and metaphors. The blindness of Gloucester, a physical representation of a lack of moral perception, also illustrates the tendency of the subplot to lend itself to old-fashioned moral simplicities. In the early Middle Ages, biblical notions of justice and redemption, that an eye should be exacted for an eye, or that an offending eye or limb should be removed if it was an obstacle to salvation, were physically acted out. For example, blinding (as well as castration) was a penalty for rape, justified on the grounds of exact and literal retribution: 'Let him thus lose his eyes which gave him sight of the maiden's beauty.'[6]

Gloucester's blinding lends itself to this sort of construction by the characters involved in a way that Lear's sufferings never do. While the actual mutilation first strikes any audience or reader as a dreadful display of brutality, Edgar and Gloucester later interpret the experience as having some sort of connection with justice, forcing us to redefine our response to its physical horror. Edgar speaks sententiously to Edmund of the blinding in terms of legalistic notions of punishment for lust:

> The Gods are just, and of our pleasant vices
> Make instruments to plague us;
> The dark and vicious place where thee he got
> Cost him his eyes.   (5.3.170–3)

Even Gloucester himself defines his blindness as the appropriate expression or symbol of his previous errors of judgment, and perhaps also as an inadvertent blessing:

> I stumbled when I saw. Full oft 'tis seen,
> Our means secure us, and our mere defects
> Prove our commodities.   (4.1.19–21)

Gloucester's blindness pictorializes his sin and his folly because the significance of the eyeless man's presence on the stage is clarified for us, by himself and Edgar, in moralized language.

Sententious language most obviously reflects the tendency towards stereotype in the characters of the subplot; Edmund's kinship with his brother and father is evident in the way in which he moralizes his own end: 'The wheel is come full circle; I am here' (5.3.174). The contrast between Edgar's stock of formulations and the language of Lear's visions in their respective madnesses is as striking as the general difference which we have already observed between an imitated role and an involuntary condition. As a madman, Edgar invokes the most familiar moral formulas, the seven deadly sins and the ten commandments,[7] both in his self-characterization and in the advice he dispenses:

EDG. Take heed o' th' foul fiend. Obey thy parents; keep thy word's
       justice; swear not; commit not with man's sworn spouse; set not
       thy sweet heart on proud array. Tom's a-cold.
LEAR What hast thou been?
EDG. A servingman, proud in heart and mind; that curl'd my hair, wore
       gloves in my cap, serv'd the lust of my mistress' heart, and did the
       act of darkness with her; swore as many oaths as I spake words,
       and broke them in the sweet face of Heaven; one that slept in the
       contriving of lust, and wak'd to do it. Wine lov'd I deeply, dice
       dearly, and in woman out-paramour'd the Turk: false of heart, light
       of ear, bloody of hand; hog in sloth, fox in stealth, wolf in
       greediness, dog in madness, lion in prey.   (3.4.80–95)

Edgar's picture of himself as a madman and epitome of sinfulness is conveyed in terms of unmistakably traditional categories and emblems ('hog in sloth,' etc.). Structurally, both of the speeches quoted above are organized in syntactic series that emphasize the formulaic nature of their content, despite the supposed madness of the character who utters them.

Lear's mad visions differ substantively and structurally from Edgar's 'lunacy,' as well as from Gloucester's sanity. Lear alludes, for example, to the sin of adultery in such a way as to undermine it as a moral category and associate it with a general vision of lechery:

> I pardon that man's life. What was thy cause?
> Adultery?
> Thou shalt not die: die for adultery! No:
> The wren goes to 't, and the small gilded fly
> Does lecher in my sight.   (4.6. 112–16)

Contrary to the formal structure of Edgar's syntactic series and parallels, Lear's hypothetical interrogation of an offender sounds spontaneous and becomes a spoken dialogue in his own mind: 'Thou shalt not die: die for adultery! No.' Furthermore, the small animals that Lear evokes do not illustrate exemplary couplings, as in Edgar's case; they are animated sources of his visions.

Gloucester's most striking simile about his sufferings – 'As flies to wanton boys, are we to th' Gods; / They kill us for their sport' (4.1.36–7) – offers another kind of contrast with Lear's mad language. Gloucester's figure sets up an exact proportion between the terms of comparison, clearly limiting itself as a figure of speech. Lear's visions, on the other hand, are characterized by a confusion of the general and the particular that gives excessive (and obsessive) personal concreteness to abstractions ('I tax you not, you elements, with unkindness; / I never gave you kingdom, call'd you children' [3.2.16–17]), or creates universalizing emblems out of personal particulars:

> Dost thou squiny at me?
> No, do thy worst, blind Cupid; I'll not love.   (4.6.138–9)

Whereas sententious speech tends to submerge individual feelings in known formulas, Lear's language does the opposite, stressing the personal motivation behind each generalization. The mistake of quoting Gloucester's observation about the malignancy of the gods as an objective statement about life could therefore hardly be made with Lear's speeches, which through their disproportions insist upon themselves too strongly as personal, motivated utterances, even while they discuss the nature of the world or the universe.

The distinctive features of the subplot characters and their language – didactic, sententious, occasionally archaic, and pictorially clarifying – extend to entire episodes. The scene on what Gloucester takes to be Dover cliff, for example, can be perceived as an enactment of Regan's earlier words to Lear:[8]

> O, Sir! you are old;
> Nature in you stands on the very verge
> Of her confine; you should be rul'd and led
> By some discretion that discerns your state
> Better than you yourself. (2.4.147–51)

Edgar later makes the imaginary cliff visually intelligible, organizing it spatially like a painting which self-consciously makes sense of mere sight:

> Come on, sir; here's the place: stand still. How fearful
> And dizzy 'tis to cast one's eyes so low!
> The crows and choughs that wing the midway air
> Show scarce so gross as beetles; half way down
> Hangs one that gathers sampire, dreadful trade!
> Methinks he seems no bigger than his head.
> The fishermen that walk upon the beach
> Appear like mice, and yond tall anchoring bark
> Diminish'd to her cock, her cock a buoy
> Almost too small for sight. (4.6.11–20)

The unseeing old man, obviously 'led' by Edgar, is also metaphorically 'ruled' by him, brought to believe in the steep cliff of which he stands near the 'extreme verge' (4.6.26), and in its moral significance.

But the abortive leap from the 'cliff,' like the blinding of Gloucester, is the physical enactment of a larger metaphor as well. Levin has observed that Gloucester's fall suggests the fall of man, or the kind of fall that is central to tragedy.[9] It may be even more precise to see it as a rendering of the 'fortunate fall,' the Christian paradox whereby man's original fall was interpreted as happy because it enabled him to receive more grace and be redeemed.[10] Gloucester's attempt to kill himself is deflected in dramatic terms by Edgar into what could be comedy or farce (a man's falling flat on his face when he has other expectations); but whereas the joke is usually that one who is pompously upright is unexpectedly brought low, here the man who had already been humbled (he takes the plunge from his knees), and who expects to fall, by his own wish, even more catastrophically, is prevented from doing so. Gloucester's 'fall' is interpreted by Edgar, who has arranged the whole scene, as miraculous ('Thy life's a miracle,' 4.6.55); the suicide attempt leads Gloucester to the resolution that he must bear his life.

The moral emphasis of the scene, its function as a lesson, is closely connected with its formal evocations of the morality play. Edgar externalizes Gloucester's suicidal intentions, suggesting that it was a fiend who led him to the edge of the cliff, and that the 'clearest Gods' have preserved him from the mad beggar who was really a fantastic devil:

> As I stood here below methought his eyes
> Were two full moons; he had a thousand noses,
> Horns whelk'd and wav'd like the enridged sea:
> It was some fiend ...   (4.6.69–72)

The imaginative mode of the moralities appears as a simplification of experience because of the discrepancy between Edgar's presentation of the scene and Gloucester's reception of it. Edgar's performance – his exploitation of his disguise as a fiend-haunted Bedlam, his minute descriptions and rapid changes of voice – draws attention to itself as invention and fantasy, exuberant and almost superfluous in the exactness of its details. But Gloucester accepts it simply and literally, in the spirit of the moralities, which literalized abstractions. This artistic deception is as successful as the creation of the cliff itself:

> I do remember now; henceforth I'll bear
> Affliction till it do cry out itself
> 'Enough, enough,' and die. That thing you speak of
> I took it for a man; often 'twould say
> 'The Fiend, the Fiend': he led me to that place.   (4.6.75–9)

When Gloucester prays later ('Let not my worser spirit tempt me again / To die before you please,' 4.6.219–20), his language shows that the impact of the lessons he has had is inseparable from his imaginative apprehension of it as a morality play.

The self-consciously archaic artistry of the subplot, as well as its more limited scope, can be seen even more clearly in the presentation of its climactic episode, the duel between Edgar and Edmund. Like the curious scene on Dover cliff, the combat – chivalric and medieval – is out of keeping with the main story of *King Lear*. In this scene the idea of justice is rendered in the archaic mode of the romances. The duel proves not only that Edgar is the stronger, but also that his claim is right, his assertion, formally delivered, of Edmund's treachery, true.

The trial by combat portrays the idea of law in its perfect form: ideally the just man won because of the rightness of his cause,[11] just as in earlier primitive trials like the ordeal, a suppurating wound became infected only if the defendant was guilty. In the play, the stylized battle therefore gives form to an archaic conception of the way in which divine justice manifested itself in human affairs. It is contrasted not only with Lear's visions of the inadequacy of existing forms of justice to the world's radical evils (his mad parodies of arraignments and assizes), but also with the sacrifice of justice to power by Cornwall and Goneril. Cornwall explicitly associates his power with 'wrath' rather than with justice when he blinds Gloucester:

> Though well we may not pass upon his life
> Without the form of justice, yet our power
> Shall do a court'sy to our wrath, which men
> May blame but not control. (3.7.24–7)

Goneril's response to Edmund's fall in the duel is just as outspokenly Machiavellian: she is willing to take advantage of the law if it favours or protects her interests, but otherwise she disregards it. When Edmund falls she invokes the minutiae of the rules governing duels to prove that he was not really defeated:

> This is practice, Gloucester:
> By th' law of war thou wast not bound to answer
> An unknown opposite; thou art not vanquish'd,
> But cozen'd and beguil'd. (5.3.151–4)

But when Albany confronts her immediately afterwards with the proof of her own treachery, she asserts that she is above the law:

> the laws are mine, not thine:
> Who can arraign me for't? (5.3.158–9)

Her claim to be a ruler who is outside the law is exactly opposite to the idea of rule-under-law for a medieval monarch, whose conception of justice is evoked by the trial by combat. Her despotic definition of privileges, more primitive and more modern, is reminiscent of her father's original ascription of power to his own word – his arbitrary division of his kingdom, or his denial, by kingly fiat, of

Cordelia's filial 'bond.' The ceremony by which justice is celebrated in the duel scene, on the other hand, is an expression of custom and tradition.

Trial by battle was supposed to demonstrate not only the identity of law and justice; it rested also on the belief that word and ritual reflected reality. The form of the challenge was exactly prescribed and had to be returned verbatim by the defendant,[12] as Edmund makes a show of doing when he first returns Albany's challenge and then Edgar's. The whole procedure is appropriately formalized in the play: Albany's challenge and the exchange of gloves, the herald and three trumpets that summon Edgar as champion, Edgar's elaborate diction in his challenge (5.3.126–41). The vindication of ceremony in the duel, the consonance of appearance with reality, is set in contrast not only with the play's first scene, where verbal show proves deceptive, but also with the substance of Lear's visions later in the play. He is obsessed, in his arraignments of evil and injustice, by the discrepancy between appearance and reality that he discounted earlier:

> hide thee, thou bloody hand,
> Thou perjur'd, and thou simular of virtue
> That art incestuous; caitiff, to pieces shake,
> That under covert and convenient seeming
> Has practis'd on man's life ...   (3.2.53–7)

> Behold yond simp'ring dame,
> Whose face between her forks presages snow ...
> The fitchew nor the soiled horse goes to't
> With a more riotous appetite.   (4.6.120–5)

Forms of justice bear no relation to the truth, according to Lear's vision, in a world where the judge is indistinguishable from the thief (4.6.151–6). There could not be a greater contrast when Edgar, the anonymous but noble-looking and well-spoken champion (5.3.142–3), fulfils the expectations of any real or literary audience:

> ALB. Methought thy very gait did prophesy
>   A royal nobleness.   (5.3.175–6)

The formal expression of Edgar's triumph contrasts with the fragmented form of Lear's visions, as well as with their substance. In what is perhaps the king's maddest moment in the fourth act, the ingredients of the trial by battle become grotesque in his imagination. The gauntlet and the formal challenge are qualified first of all by being associated with much less romantic images of war:

There's your press-money. That fellow handles his bow like a crow-keeper: draw me a clothier's yard. Look, look! a mouse. Peace, peace! this piece of toasted cheese will do't. There's my gauntlet; I'll prove it on a giant. Bring up the brown bills. O! well flown bird ...

(4.6.86–92)

The stylized combat, its meaningful language and its symmetry, are distorted in a series of associations that work by arbitrary similarities of sound (peace/piece) and by sheer incongruity: the formidable gigantic opponent is a mouse, and the challenging gauntlet is a piece of toasted cheese. A little later the idea of the incongruous and ineffective challenge is developed even further:

LEAR Read thou this challenge; mark but the penning of it.
GLOU. Were all thy letters suns, I could not see. (4.6.140–1)

A madman's challenge is delivered to a blind man who cannot read it. Although the allusion to the challenge is not developed, it gives the impression of being connected with the vision of perverted justice that follows, as if Lear (somewhat less explicitly at this point than Titus Andronicus with his mad letters to the gods) were ineffectively challenging the order of things.

The chivalric duel in the last act, then, reminds us of the possibility of a more orderly world by ritualizing what is distorted in Lear's imagination and experience. But its placement in the play, following the defeat of Lear and Cordelia's forces and preceding the even more appalling catastrophe of Cordelia's hanging and Lear's death, points also to the limitations of the order that it suggests. The main action complicates the subplot in various ways, and shows the inadequacies, in a truly tragic situation, of its moral and literary formulas. After the Dover cliff episode, for example, the sight of the dishevelled, mad king modifies our response to Gloucester's cure. Lear's frantic efforts to evade his benevolent captors, whose prisoner he finally regards himself, and the uncompromising nature of his visions, which defy 'sweetening,' make Gloucester's submission, physical and imaginative, to Edgar's 'rule' seem very simple. At the end of the play we see how Edgar, who exhorted his blind father to 'look up' after his fall and succeeded in a spiritual sense, is unable to change anything with the same injunction to Lear (5.3.312).[13] Lear's sufferings outweigh any optimistic or encouraging words, whether Edgar's or Albany's, and they are told by Kent that pain should be allowed to end in death.

Albany's language at the end of the play becomes even more ineffectually formulaic than Edgar's, and this suggests a final important if obvious point about the subplot: its language (like its action) overlaps with that of the main plot, even while it is partly distinct. Albany has been inclined towards pious optimism in his interpretation of earlier events:

> This shows you are above,
> You justicers, that these our nether crimes
> So speedily can venge! (4.2.78–80)

As the play's ranking figure just before Lear's death, he speaks a conclusion appropriate to one of the Dukes of the comedies:

> for us, we will resign,
> During the life of this old Majesty,
> To him our absolute power: [*To Edgar and Kent*]
>   you, to your rights,
> With boot and such addition as your honours
> Have more than merited. All friends shall taste
> The wages of their virtue, and all foes
> The cup of their deservings. O! see, see! (5.3.298–304)

The formula is destroyed by actuality: the sight of the king's sufferings, his insistence on the lifelessness of Cordelia, and his death. The simplifications that are so obviously concentrated in the subplot, its suggestions of non-tragic forms, extend to the language of minor characters like Albany in the main plot as well, because the two actions are never entirely separate – it is Edgar who finally declares that we must 'Speak what we feel, not what we ought to say' (5.3.324). Contrary to a play like Middleton and Rowley's *The Changeling*, whose two plots seem to present imaginative worlds that are distinct despite the verbal and thematic connections between them, the two actions of *King Lear* never become remote from each other, even if they have different emphases.

The analogous stories in *King Lear*, then, illuminate each other by offering related but contrasting ways of structuring experience. The subplot functions partly as didactic illustration. Though it never transposes the concerns of the main action into a radically different, archaic style (as the Gonzago play does in *Hamlet*), it evokes old-fashioned literary modes – the romance of chivalry, the medieval morality play – that asserted the intelligibility and purposefulness of action. Characters like the Bastard show the relation between simple dramatic conventions and intelligibility: he is a machiavel, while Lear's older daughters, mysteriously, are Machiavellian. Furthermore, the language, moral and circumscribed, of Edgar, Gloucester, and at the end, of Edmund, contributes to the effect of the subplot as limited and apprehensible in its moral meanings. Its didactic emphasis colours our view of the main plot as well, inviting us repeatedly to impose its patterns on Lear's experience. Our sense of the redemptive value of Lear's sufferings comes not only from the pity that he feels on the heath for the poor, but from the similarities between his situation and Gloucester's. The eyeless man is a physical image, an emblem, of Lear's condition also. Because Gloucester says that he stumbled when he saw, we are more likely to assume that Lear's recognition that he is old and foolish (even though this was originally Regan and Goneril's contention) represents a positive apprehension of truth.

The formulations of the subplot, however, are somewhat oversimplified even on their own terms. Gloucester's sententious observations after his eyes are put out are not adequate to the horror of that event, and the ordered world of the duel, where ritual reflects reality and power is joined to virtue, is an archaic one. The main action shows up such simplifications even more pointedly; for better and for worse, Lear's experience cannot be accounted for in the way that Gloucester's is. On the one hand, the king's agonies are incommensurate with any evil that he may have committed, irreducible, by himself and others, to notions of justice. He is more sinned against than sinning; he and Cordelia are 'not the first / Who, with best meaning, have incurr'd the worst' (5.3.3–4). Where Edgar can see some kind of justice in his father's blinding, Cordelia refuses to consider the nature of Lear's crimes or mistakes at all, let alone any idea of retribution: 'No cause, no cause!' But the corollary to this transcendence of commonplace or legalistic judgment is that the patterns by which Gloucester's destiny is ordered and given meaning do not apply to Lear. Neither his sufferings nor the nature of his children are explicable, as Gloucester's are, by dramatic stereotype and moral aphorism, for in the two plots, formal devices and substantive material are fused. Lear's experience is truly tragic and heroic not merely because he suffers – Gloucester suffers too – but because the literary forms that avoid tragedy are so clearly inadequate to express what he goes through.

NOTES

1 See for example the discussion of the dangers of excessive or contradictory passions in Peter de la Primaudaye *The French Academy* tr. T.B. (London 1594) 33.

2 'King Lear: The Quality of Nothing,' in *Shakespearean Meanings* (Princeton 1968) 238

3 See Maynard Mack's suggestion that the relation of subplot to plot is not dramatic so much as 'homiletic,' 'King Lear' in Our Time (Berkeley 1965) 7. See also Alvin B. Kernan, 'Formalism and Realism in Elizabethan Drama: The Miracles in King Lear,' Renaissance Drama IX (1966) 59–66, for an interpretation of the Dover cliff scene as a morality play.

4 De Laudibus Angliae: A Treatise in Commendation of the Laws of England tr. Francis Gregor (Cincinnati 1874) 156 and 150ff

5 A rare exception is the Bastard in King John, who had all the potential for villainy, being a 'man of the time' and a corrosive scoffer at custom, but who is placed in a world where these attributes become virtues. For an interesting analysis of this character and his contrast to Edmund, see John F. Danby Shakespeare's Doctrine of Nature: A Study of 'King Lear' (London 1959) 57ff. It is worth noting that treatment of aristocratic bastards, at least, was radically ameliorated during the sixteenth century in England.

6 Bracton De Legibus et Consuetudinibus Angliae ed. G.E. Woodbine, tr. S.E. Thorne (Cambridge, Mass. 1968) 414–15

7 Mack, in 'King Lear' in Our Time 61, comments on this and likens Edgar to the fallen hero of the morality plays.

8 On this connection, and on the scene in general, see Harry Levin, 'The Heights and the Depths: A Scene from King Lear,' in More Talking of Shakespeare ed. John Garrett (London 1959) 87–103, and Kernan, 'Formalism and Realism.'

9 'The Heights and the Depths,' 100

10 The background of the 'felix culpa' tradition is described by Arthur O. Lovejoy, 'Milton and the Paradox of the Fortunate Fall,' Essays in the History of Ideas (Baltimore 1948) 277–95.

11 '[The trial by combat] was instituted upon this reason, that in respect the Tenant had lost his Evidence, or that the same were burnt or imbezeled, or that his witnesses were dead, the Law permitted him to try it by combat between his Champion and the Champion of the Demandant, hoping that God would give the victory to him that right had ...' (Coke's commentary on Fortescue, quoted in John Beames A Translation of Glanville [Washington 1900] 35n). In the play, Edgar must have recourse to the duel because the very evidence of his identity, his name, has been usurped by Edmund (5.3.119–22).

12 See for instance Beames A Translation of Glanville 36: if the duel is accepted, the defendant 'must deny the right of the Demandant, word for word as the Demandant has set it forth.'

13 See Levin, 'The Heights and the Depths,' 103.

THREE

JOHN REIBETANZ # Theatrical emblems in King Lear

'ALL DARK AND COMFORTLESS,' the blinding of Gloucester is not only the most horrible act of physical retribution in Shakespearean tragedy; it is also the most emblematic. Coming toward the end of act 3, it catches up the many previous examples of Gloucester's 'blindness' and crystallizes them in an unforgettable pictorial image. The stage action becomes a dramatic emblem, a highly symbolic visualization of one of the play's most important themes. One could even find a motto which captures the outrage of this punishment in Regan's earlier words to Gloucester: 'O! Sir, to wilful men, / The injuries that they themselves procure / Must be their schoolmasters' (2.4.304–6). But no motto is necessary; the picture says all that needs to be said.

Gloucester's is one of many such pictures in King Lear. With notable frequency, the play's characters arrange themselves into fleeting but memorable tableaux, pictorial realizations of abstract themes. The first scene of act 4 ends with one of these groupings: paradox leaps to life when Edgar, supposedly mad but really the sanest man in the play, leads out a blind Gloucester who has finally gained a clearer vision of himself. No iconographer could portray it more concisely. Lear calls our attention to an equally symbolic tableau in act 2. Fleeing from Goneril's ingratitude, he has arrived for a visit with Regan; but even as he complains of the treatment that brought him, Goneril enters. Regan immediately shows where her allegiance lies, as Lear's shocked exclamation indicates: 'O Regan! will you take her by the hand?' (2.4.196). By holding hands, the two sisters provide us with an unmistakable emblem of their affinity, and of Lear's folly in thinking that they would be different. The gesture is focused on for its emblematic implications and exists primarily in terms of them.

Shakespeare was not the only Elizabethan dramatist to employ this technique. His theatrical emblems are rooted in the dramatic traditions of his time; and in order to discuss theatrical emblems in *King Lear*, I should briefly suggest how those traditions defined themselves.

When *King Lear* was first performed at the Globe in c. 1606, the greatest theatrical rivalry of the age had been in full swing for about six years. This rivalry was between the public theatres – huge, open-air structures situated in the London suburbs – and the private theatres, fully enclosed buildings located in the heart of the city and accommodating much smaller audiences.[1] Each type of theatre had its devotees: the public theatres attracted a wide audience that was representative of the whole spectrum of Elizabethan society, while the private theatres (which charged six times as much and therefore had considerable snob appeal) catered to a more exclusive and sophisticated upper-class audience. Each type of theatre attracted its own circle of playwrights as well: Dekker, Heywood, and Tourneur were some of those who were committed to the public theatres, while plays were written for the private theatres' child actors by such figures as Marston, Middleton, Chapman, Beaumont, and Fletcher.[2] Most important, each type of theatre evolved its own style of playwriting. Since private-theatre drama was written largely in reaction to the practices and conventions of the public stage, public-theatre playwriting demands consideration first.

The two cornerstones of public-theatre drama were its mainly narrative structure and its emphatic character presentation. Some public-theatre genres emphasized one aspect more than the other: chronicle histories such as *Sir John Oldcastle* or *The Valiant Welshman* stressed narrative detail, while domestic dramas such as *A Woman Killed with Kindness* cultivated a naturalistic focus on personal relations. But the two usually fitted in together: playwrights built up moral and emotional sympathy for (or against) characters by depicting them in a series of developmental scenes. And most public-theatre plays shared a propensity to sacrifice individual dramatic exhibitions to a cumulative development, in much the same way as narrative fiction. Departing from this form, private-theatre dramatists consistently emphasized the strong, self-sufficient scene; rather than involving the audience empathetically in characters' fortunes, they tended to elicit a more detached appreciation of technical virtuosity. In very early works like *Histriomastix* and *The Maid's Metamorphosis* the highly wrought metre and frequent songs accent individual moments rather than uniform movement: action gives way to ornament, and the plays tend to become series of set pieces. This propensity, combined with the boy actors' probable inability to sustain close imitation at length, fostered a dramatic structure which underplayed continuous progression. Later private-theatre playwrights turned this tendency to advantage by further accentuating the individual scenes and allowing each strong scene to dramatize a distinct perspective on the play's basic situation; almost any play by Chapman or Marston consists of a series of such disjunctive scenes. The characters who populate these scenes are treated by private-theatre playwrights as variables rather than constants: dramatists from Chapman to Beaumont and Fletcher manipulate them to achieve the most volatile effect, usually with little regard for the kind of consistency that invites an emphatic response. Our appreciation of verbal and theatrical fireworks takes precedence over our involvement.[3]

King Lear was written for a public theatre and shares many of its characteristics with other public-theatre plays. But Shakespeare's art was always an eclectic one, open to influences from private-theatre drama as well. In *King Lear* the two theatres merge. Shakespeare adopts aspects of both theatrical traditions and weaves them into the fabric of a new vision, distinct from either. This paper will focus on one aspect of that fabric, its theatrical emblems.[4]

Before we turn to particular emblems in *King Lear*, however, one further differentiation needs to be made. In his illuminating article on 'Emblems in English Renaissance Drama,'[5] Dieter Mehl distinguishes three types of dramatic emblems: direct borrowings or quotations from emblem books; full allegorical scenes that comment on a play's action (for example, dumb shows); and significant combinations of verbal and pictorial expression in the course of a scene. It will be evident that the theatrical emblems that this discussion distinguishes in *King Lear* bear closest resemblance to Mehl's third type, in that we will not be concerned with direct borrowings or full allegorical scenes. But an important distinction must still be made between his third type of emblems and those which I shall discuss in relation to *King Lear* and the drama of Shakespeare's contemporaries. In every example adduced by Mehl, it is the characters in a scene who give full emblematic interpretations to objects or relationships around them. They give the impression of having themselves read emblem books. Our interest will be directed primarily towards those scenes where it is only the audience who perceives such emblematic meaning. These scenes are so constructed as to encourage *us* to trace emblematic figures, while the characters are unaware of them and are engaged in other activities. There is thus a fundamental difference in the relation of audience to play: Mehl's emblems have been worked into the surface of the play, so we experience them through the characters even as we continue to be involved in the unwinding dramatic action; the emblems we shall cite in *King Lear* and other Jacobean plays tend to exist as emblems apart from any characters' consciousness, and require us to stand momentarily back from the action in order to perceive their outlines and their significance.[6] Like set pieces, they briefly interrupt our involvement in the flow of events in order to foster a more profound involvement in the world of the play.

At the opening of this essay, we looked at three tableaux from different parts of *King Lear* and found that they shared a tendency to underline the symbolic nature of the pictures that they presented to us. We may now trace this same tendency through a series of emblematic entrances in *King Lear*, noticing also how the entrances resonate with irony because the characters involved in them do not perceive the emblems. The first occurs when Lear unconsciously follows the stage direction 'Enter ALBANY' with a proverb that he utters in response to his own condition, but that provides the picture of Albany with a bitterly prophetic motto: 'Woe, that too late repents' (1.4.266). Lear then unconsciously drives the point home as he wakes up to Albany's presence and continues: 'O! Sir, are you come?' In contrast, the next emblematic entrance takes place with lightning speed and effect, as motto precedes illustration. Getting much the worst of his scuffle with Kent, Oswald cries for assistance: 'Help, ho! murther! murther!' (2.2.43). Immediately there enters a true type of the allegorical figures he has invoked, as the stage direction indicates: 'Enter EDMUND, *with his rapier drawn.*' The end of this scene brings yet another emblematic combination of word and picture. Kent settles in for his night in the stocks by calling for benevolence from another allegorical presence: 'Fortune, good night; smile once more; turn thy wheel!' The wheel turns, but again in a downward direction appropriate to the play's increasingly tragic world, as Edgar enters breathless, hunted, and desperate, resembling one of those illuminated manuscript figures at the bottom of Fortune's wheel. In this world, characters must tolerate 'false Fortune's frown' (5.3.6) rather than bask in her smile. The most cutting of the play's emblematic entrances literally lights up the storm scenes. The Fool, chilled to the bone, is appalled by Lear's nakedness and resorts to a simile to express his feelings: 'Now a little fire in a wild field were like an old lecher's heart; a small spark, all the rest on 's body cold' (3.4.114–6). As if on cue ('Look! here comes a walking fire'), in comes the old lecher whose moral blindness will soon be translated into agonizing physical terms: '*Enter* GLOUCESTER, *with a torch.*' The emblematic prop of Gloucester here, like that of Edmund in his entrance, helps to rivet our attention on the picture's symbolic nature, even as it fulfils its more usual dramatic function.

Such emblematic tableaux were most characteristic of private-theatre drama, where the emphasis on both theatrical artifice and self-sufficient scenes fostered this kind of display. Chapman, for instance, uses the technique to image his hero's isolation in act 4 of *Byron's Tragedy*: as the outcast Byron stands at centre stage with a single confidant, other nobles enter and walk around him in couples, whispering together but refraining from communication with him. The result is an emblem of alienation, as effective as the emblem of affinity observed between Regan and Goneril in *King Lear*. Similarly, the moving tableau at the end of Shakespeare's play – where Lear and Cordelia form a kind of pre-Christian *Pietà* – has its private-theatre analogues. The body of Marston's heroine is borne in to her final presence chamber and decorated, in the gruesome last scene of *Sophonisba*, to show the price that this 'wonder of women' has paid for freedom; and the famous ending of *Bussy D'Ambois* presents us with another 'Roman statue,' this one in a more martial pose than Shakespeare's. The final scenes of all three plays gain in impact by being both dramatically and graphically striking.

Shakespeare also uses costuming for emblematic effect. As R.B. Heilman has noted,[7] clothes symbolism is an important leit-motif in *King Lear*; and it achieves stage realization through the gestures of many characters. When Kent accuses Oswald of being made by a tailor, he opens our eyes to the visual proof of Oswald's concern with other than inner worth. The opposite concern is visible in the nakedness of Edgar and Lear on the heath, where Shakespeare follows the practice of Renaissance iconographers in depicting Truth without clothes. Lear's madness comes to life in the same way: Cordelia first sketches him as 'Crown'd with rank fumiter and

furrow-weeds, / With hardocks, hemlock, nettles, cuckoo-flowers'
(4.4.3–4) – noxious weeds, some associated with death and insanity; shortly afterwards, Lear completes the picture by appearing on
stage in this very costume (4.6.81). On the private-theatre stage,
Chapman had anticipated this effect in the first act of *Bussy D'Ambois*. First, Bussy enters dressed in tatters, and proclaims that 'Fortune, not Reason, rules the state of things'; then, later in act 1,
Henry states that his French court is a mirror of confusion, while
the foppery of the English court masks an inner worth which the
French do not possess. At that moment, Bussy enters dressed in
fantastic court attire (1.2.56),[8] and the emblem's meaning is plain:
besides showing at once that he has accepted Fortune rather than
Reason, the clothes associate him with the outer affectation and
inner worth of the English court.

Even in those scenes that are not tableaux of abstract themes,
Shakespeare often manages to create pictorial vividness and emblematic effect by juxtaposing the same kind of action in two different scenes. In the play's first scene, Lear's mercenary conduct
and imagery demonstrate a zeal for quantifying which recoils back
on him in the 'retainers' incident of act 2, when Regan and Goneril
treat him to a bold rehearsal of his own values. A more immediate
juxtaposition emerges in act 3; when Cornwall gives orders to apprehend Gloucester, Edmund's reaction comes in an aside: 'If I find
him comforting the King, it will stuff his suspicion more fully'
(3.5.20–1). In the next scene Edgar, busy comforting the King, also
voices his reaction in an aside: 'My tears begin to take his part so
much, / They mar my counterfeiting' (3.6.60–1). The contrast between the two brothers could not be sharper: they appear like
back-to-back pictures of Vice and Virtue in an emblem book. Conversely, Shakespeare forges an unmistakable link between Gloucester and Edmund in act 1: no sooner has Edmund finished his defiant
soliloquy on Nature ('Why bastard? Wherefore base?'), than Gloucester enters and immediately picks up the same questioning caden-
ces: 'Kent banished thus? and France in choler parted? / And the
King gone tonight?' (1.2.23–4).[9] Such juxtaposition of similar or
contrasting actions is also characteristic of private-theatre dramaturgy, as may be seen in Jonson's *Epicoene*. Tom Otter and his wife
open act 3 with a terrific argument, during which he is reduced to
timid monosyllables under his wife's continuous barrage of exple-
tives; neither is aware that the argument is being observed by
Truewit, Clerimont, and Dauphine. The scene finds its counterpart
in act 4, when the three gallants feed Tom's courage with alcohol,
and watch as he explodes into an equally fierce denunciation of

Mistress Otter; unfortunately for Tom, the hidden observer this time is Mistress Otter herself. The two scenes are mirror images, and the second one picks up immense theatrical vitality from this kind of paralleling.[10]

Shakespeare's eclecticism is nowhere more evident than in his use of these mainly private-theatre techniques, the symbolic tableau and the juxtaposed action, to buttress a basic structure which is typical of public-theatre drama – the plot-subplot configuration. This configuration was developed long before private productions began at the turn of the century and is found in every public-theatre form – chronicle histories, domestic dramas, comedies, and tragedies. Its occurrence is much rarer in private-theatre drama, where playwrights tended to confine themselves to developing aspects of a single situation or intrigue. In *King Lear* we can see the two theatres coalescing in the third scene of act 2, where an emblematic stage action establishes connections between plot and subplot. As the scene opens,[11] Kent is in the stocks and sleeps in the background; he is wearing the disguise he assumed after Lear banished him, and has just read a letter from Cordelia, the other outcast. Now Edgar enters:

> I heard myself proclaim'd;
> And by the happy hollow of a tree
> Escap'd the hunt. (2.3.1–3)

>   and am bethought
> To take the basest and most poorest shape ... (6,7)

>   Poor Turlygod! poor Tom!
> That's something yet: Edgar I nothing am. (20–1)

Like Kent and Cordelia, Edgar is now an outcast; and even as Kent sits behind him, he too resolves to disguise himself. As if these plot-subplot parallels were not enough, to fill out the emblem Shakespeare reinforces them with a verbal echo: Edgar's 'nothing' repeats Cordelia's unfortunate answer to Lear.

Actually, Cordelia's reply has echoed in the subplot long before this. When Gloucester asks Edmund what letter he is hiding, Edmund repeats the same original phrase: 'Nothing, my Lord' (1.2.31). The second scene of *King Lear* is in fact a mirror image of the first, with the roles of Regan and Goneril played by Edmund, Lear by Gloucester, and Cordelia by Edgar. The foolish old man is again taken in by a 'play' of deception, and the worthy child again falls into disfavour. Edmund's reply here confirms him as Cordelia's antithesis, a villain who masquerades in innocuous words; and it paves the way for our association of Edgar with Cordelia in their respective plots. Like the emblematic tableau in act 2, the juxtaposition of this second scene against the first crystallizes those elements that the subplot has in common with the main action. Shakespeare also underlines the connection in several related set-speeches, given by plot and subplot characters who have been manoeuvered into similar situations. The blind Gloucester's speech on how 'distribution should undo excess' (4.1.66–70) repeats, in essence, the short speech with which Lear follows up his admission 'I have ta'en / Too little care of this' (3.4.32–6); and Edmund's defence of bastardy (1.2.6–15) is echoed in Lear's defence of adultery, where an allusion to Edmund calls attention to the parallel: 'Gloucester's bastard son / Was kinder to his father than my daughters / Got 'tween the lawful sheets' (4.6.117–19). Similar pronounced counterpointing of scenes and speeches frequently obtains in those private-theatre plays which have subplots.[12] On the other hand, the plot-subplot contours of public-theatre plays are almost always defined by similarities that emerge as each plot unfolds independently.[13]

In addition to the solitary or juxtaposed tableau, more complex kinds of emblematic patterning are woven into the fabric of *King Lear*. Several of these patterns are reiterative: an abstract concept will be brought to life in one scene, and then later scenes will turn variations on this initial figure. For example, the first scene of *King Lear* unfolds as an emblematic test or trial, and its outlines reappear in numerous other places: the 'trial' and condemnation of Edgar by Gloucester and Edmund; Kent's expulsion of Oswald (and its reversal, the censure of Kent by Cornwall); the Fool's satiric rehearsal of the opening scene with Lear; the successive trials of Lear by Goneril and Regan, culminating in his self-exile to the heath; Lear's mad mock-trial of his daughters; Cornwall's inquisition and punishment of Gloucester, and Gloucester's self-exile to the Dover cliffs; Edmund's sentencing of Lear and Cordelia; the trial of Edmund by Albany and Edgar; and the final 'judgment of the heavens' in the last scene. Similar structural patterning characterizes many private-theatre plays, including *Epicoene*, *A Chaste Maid in Cheapside*, *Amends for Ladies*, and *Bussy D'Ambois*. As L.A. Beaurline has written of *Epicoene*, 'Much of the play is like the working out of a series of permutations with a fixed number of constants and two variables.'[14] The variables consist of character and situation, and the playwright places them in a sequence of related combinations. As in a fugue, elements of a given initial statement are recombined to form successive later versions. In *King Lear* the trial pattern is of primary thematic importance and is responsible for much of the play's emotional impact: the first trial unleashes a harsh, primitive justice which relentlessly reverberates in characters and actions until all of the fatal permutations have been worked out.

Another reiterative pattern illustrates the reciprocal obligations attendant upon man's social existence. As Maynard Mack observes of *King Lear*, 'Shakespeare's imagination appears to have been ... fully oriented toward presenting human reality as a web of ties commutual.'[15] Seen in this light, Lear's love-test is a symbolic violation of a commutual bond, and its enormity is driven home to us by the succession of other perspectives on the 'web of ties.' One of these is the servant-master relation, a perspective first displayed by Kent and Lear in the opening scene. Kent speaks out against his master's conduct at the risk of his own welfare, demonstrating the selfless dedication that the relation can involve. Later incidents reveal that it can also involve a whole spectrum of very different reactions: after the initial statement, Shakespeare provides illuminating variations on it in the relations of Oswald and Goneril, the Fool and Lear, the First Servant and Cornwall, the Old Man and Gloucester, and the Captain and Edmund. A series of juxtaposed opposites also dramatizes the commutual bond: the opening scene pits France's generosity against Burgundy's materialism; later scenes hold up Kent's selfless loyalty against Oswald's selfish sycophancy; and towards the end of the play the guileless husband, Albany, is opposed to the scheming adulterer, Cornwall. With the complete consort before us, we recognize virtue as a matter of necessity, not choice; without it, unaccommodated man is nothing more than an animal.

Similar to these reiterative patterns is one which presents us with an abstract statement and then proceeds to illuminate it with a series of theatrical illustrations, each one lighting up a part of the statement. So Gloucester's speech about 'These late eclipses of the sun and moon' (1.2.107–20) points us to several abstract statements, biblical descriptions of the discords auguring the end of the world. The descriptions in Mark 13 are especially relevant because they almost form a synopsis of later scenes:

> Tell us, when shall these things be? and what shall be the sign when all these things shall be fulfilled? And Jesus answering them began to say, Take heed ... ye shall hear of wars and rumours of wars ... For nation shall rise against nation, and kingdom against kingdom ... Now the brother shall betray the brother to death, and the father the son; and children shall rise up against their parents, and shall cause them to be put to death ... then let them that be in Judaea flee to the mountains ... And pray that your flight be not in the winter ... But in those days, after that tribulation, the sun shall be darkened, and the moon shall not give her light.

Each of these abstract statements finds its realization in a later scene. The whole teleological chain reaction that Lear has set off culminates in the last scene when trumpets sound and characters ask, 'Is this the promis'd end?' 'Or image of that horror?' as the 'judgment of the heavens' fulfils itself. Our sense of a pattern fulfilling itself is heightened by the marked pictorial similarity which the last scene bears to the first. For the first time in the play, most of the main characters from that opening court scene are together again on stage. As Lear tragically experiences the immeasurable love that he was blind to in the beginning, the others are all grouped around him once more, the quick and the dead.[16]

Edmund has foretold it all, right from the beginning. In the second scene, when Edgar asks him what he is contemplating, he lies and answers: 'I am thinking, brother, of a prediction I read this other day, what should follow these eclipses.' He then enlarges upon the lie with these words:

> I promise you the effects he writes of succeed unhappily; as of
> unnaturalness between the child and the parent; death, dearth,
> dissolutions of ancient amities; divisions in state; menaces and
> maledictions against King and nobles; needless diffidences,
> banishment of friends, dissipation of cohorts, nuptial breaches, and
> I know not what.   (1.2.150–6)

The effects succeed very unhappily, and every disaster that Edmund mentions actually comes about. It is as if the play were designed to illustrate the elements of this general statement, with characters and situations manipulated to meet its pre-imposed conditions. R.B. Heilman observed that a similar technique is employed, on a smaller scale, following Edmund's soliloquy at the start of this scene: 'Now, the announcement of his plan follows immediately upon his exposition of Nature, and it is connnected with the statement of his nature theory by the word *then* – precisely as if his scheme followed as a logical projection of the theory into action.'[17] As Edmund effects a realization of his theory, so Shakespeare projects his own abstract statements into dramatic realities in the course of *King Lear*. It is a technique originated by neither Edmund nor Shakespeare, and found in many private-theatre plays.[18]

King Lear opens with what turns out to be an emblematic set piece: the conversation of Kent, Gloucester, and Edmund is as pivotal for the rest of the play as the abstracts just mentioned, and is related to private-theatre dramaturgy in several ways. To begin with, the gathering of lesser nobility is an opening which Beaumont and Fletcher were soon to employ in many of their tragedies and tragicomedies; they apparently found it especially appropriate for private-theatre drama. In a standard opening scene, several nobles await the entrance of royalty – the main protagonists – for a festival or state occasion. This is how *Philaster, Cupid's Revenge,* and *The Maid's Tragedy* open. The nobles sketch the characters of their superiors, and enumerate details of the basic situation in which the main characters will next appear. In *King Lear* as in the Beaumont and Fletcher plays, the brief scene serves as a prologue or induction, creating a 'mental set' in the audience for what will follow. However, Shakespeare's scene is related to the rest of the play in a more emblematic and tangential way: where Beaumont and Fletcher present the play's basic issues quite explicitly, Shakespeare only hints at these.[19] It is only in retrospect that the allusions to deceptive appearances and to acknowledgment of paternity, the concern with 'proper' conduct, and the use of words like 'weigh'd' and 'division' carry their full weight of meaning. Thus the initial scene emerges in retrospect as an abstract of major themes. This use of a preliminary incident has no parallel in public-theatre drama, but it does resemble the opening scenes of several private-theatre plays.[20]

In the last two acts, Shakespeare creates an emblematic pattern that conveys the perversity of the *Lear* world – a place where intentions are unremittingly thwarted. A series of incidents, all involving Edgar, counterpoints abstract statements with theatrical tableaux that negate rather than fulfil the statements: in each case, the emblem contradicts its motto. At the start of act 4, for instance, Edgar accepts his poor lot: he has experienced the worst possible buffetings, he says, and owes nothing to Fortune. Immediately Gloucester enters, blinded and bleeding. The wretched tableau shows Edgar that 'the worst is not / So long as we can say "This is the worst"' (4.1.27–8). Then, after he saves Gloucester from suicide in scene 6, he gives his father this stoical advice: 'Bear free and patient thoughts' (4.6.80). Mad Lear enters at once, decked in wild flowers, and the apparition forces Edgar to betray his own injunction: 'O thou side-piercing sight!' When Lear has finished his pitiful spectacle, Edgar volunteers to lead his father to shelter. 'Hearty thanks,' Gloucester replies, 'The bounty and the benison of Heaven / To boot, and boot!' (4.6.225–7). Oswald enters immediately and, with sword drawn, follows up Gloucester's wish for 'bounty' with an ironic counterpoint: 'A proclaim'd prize! Most happy!' Finally, during the battle in act 5, Edgar leaves Gloucester with these words: 'If ever I return to you again. / I'll bring you comfort' (5.2.3–4). He returns almost at once, a picture of apprehension: 'Away, old man! give me thy hand: away! / King Lear hath lost, he and his daughter ta'en.' Behind this pitting of an emblem against its motto stands a private-theatre convention: many private-theatre plays feature scenes which abrasively counterpoint philosophical positions with conflicting dramatic action, though in a less emblematic way than *King Lear*. Marston's *The Dutch Courtesan* is structured in this way, as is part of Barry's *Ram-Alley*: Boucher, like Malheureux in *The Dutch Courtesan*, meets passion with speeches of extreme puritan confidence and strictness, which are defeated by a probative situation. When the coquettish widow Taffeta makes advances to him, he proudly affirms:

> I yet am free and reason keepes her seate,
> Aboue all fond affections, yet is she fayre.[21]

'Yet' – like Malheureux, he is only passionate man in his slight play, and in this scene he turns to putty in the widow's able hands. More serious variations on the technique are executed in the tragedies of Chapman and of Marston; but no private-theatre playwright realizes its formidable thematic implications. In *King Lear*, the series of contradicted emblems becomes itself emblematic of the play's perspective: the metaphor becomes the meaning.

All of the tableaux and emblematic patterns that Shakespeare weaves into *King Lear* have this in common: like bas-relief details on a plane composition, they do not quite yield up their individuation to the whole of which they are parts. Each tableau fosters an awareness of the singularity of the light it sheds on the main situation, instead of completely subsuming that light to a single cumulative impression. Furthermore, they all either ignore or resist the forward-moving impetus of a developing sequence of events: the solitary tableau stands apart from such an impetus, briefly motionless, while the juxtaposed or patterned emblem encourages a retrospective view of the action. Instead of keeping our attention fixed only on an unbroken line of development, Shakespeare calls also for an awareness of dramatic structure as an object of static or retrospective contemplation. This structural emphasis is a pronounced departure from the public-theatre practices outlined at the start of this paper: like the self-sufficient scenes of private-theatre drama, Shakespeare's emblems stand in contrast to those typical public-theatre scenes that subordinated their articulation to a steady progress. His emblematic technique predicates a structure which incorporates the emphases of private-theatre drama.

In fact, the structure of *King Lear* masterfully fuses basic attributes of both theatrical traditions. As in public-theatre plays dating all the way back to the early Marlowe, structure issues from the central character and serves to illuminate him for us. Lear's first-scene blunder opens the floodgates, and the tide that rushes in carries us through a series of perspectives on his purgatory. The chaotic incidents that follow all relate directly to him – betrayals, folly, madness, the storm; even Gloucester (was ever subplot more like the main action?) is an alter ego. All these applications are critical commonplaces, and do not demand further consideration here. Yet within this character-centred structure so typical of public-theatre drama, the private-theatre influence is strong. *King Lear* conveys the impression that each scene projects its own drama, depicting only that minute when the essential nature of a character or situation manifests itself. Cordelia's 'No cause, no cause,' may be applied to the play's structure: there is no gradual accumulation of causes, no careful supplying of connectives, and not even a thorough elaboration of consequences. Actions break upon us in a rather inchoate manner; their unfolding is as nebulous as the settings that contain them; and progression from one incident to the next is often marked by the kind of sequential discontinuity that characterizes our dreams rather than our waking moments. We have trouble making connections, fitting the parts into the whole, even after we have just seen or read it. If one opens the play at random to any scene after act 2, when the storm takes over, one finds it nearly impossible to say just what actions come immediately before or after. The first scene of act 5 is typical. Edmund, Regan, and their retinue enter with drum and colours. We do not know where they have come from or where they are going, and no attempt is made to enlighten us. Instead, Edmund and Regan discuss whether or not he has made love to Goneril. Two scenes have elapsed since Regan's last appearance, and five since Edmund's, with no indications that they were together so long and intimately as their present conduct implies. The primary concern of this scene is completely different from those of the two previous ones, which centred on Gloucester's suicide attempt and Lear's cure. Edgar, last on stage in the scene before last, is the only character from either previous scene to appear here, and he disappears again in the space of ten lines. Every scene in *King Lear* absorbs us as completely as this one does.

By evolving a structure of such moments, Shakespeare achieves great immediacy. Each scene involves us directly in yet another upheaval, and its force is undiminished by the need to subsume the individual effect into a cumulative progression. As a result of this private-theatre approach, we find ourselves adrift in a world lacking the usual reassurances of narrative continuity. The vagueness of locale is partially responsible for our unease, with no distinct places where we can get a foothold; but the main gadfly to our sense of cumulative sequence in *King Lear* is the self-sufficient nature of its scenes. Like Lear, we tend to lose our bearings. The experience of the spectator approximates in a minor way that of the hero, and his disorientation becomes more compelling as we experience a lesser version of it. What Shakespeare has done, then, is to employ elements of the disjunctive private-theatre structure to reinforce the empathic effect of a conventional structure associated with public-theatre drama. The structure is therefore a perfect vehicle for both the dramatic and the emblematic aspects of Shakespeare's art; since it is both tumultuous and recurrently fixed, it satisfies both needs at once.

The characters who bring life to the self-sufficient scenes and emblematic patterns of *King Lear* owe much of their peculiar nature to these aspects of the play, for Shakespeare presents his characters to us in terms of them. The powerful scenes of *King Lear* are constructed not only to be dramatically dynamic, but also to be vehicles of acute insight into the characters. At the core of each situation are those moments when the inner man is translated into perfectly representative action. This is true of Lear's conduct in the opening scene, of Gloucester's during Edmund's ruse, and of every other character who is put to the test (and all are, eventually). The process is itself an emblematic one: the artist arranges each scene to represent the essence of those involved in it. It follows, then, that the 'inner man' must of necessity be a creature whose nature *can* be delineated in this emblematic way. The basic outlines of his character must be writ large and bold, its essential attributes easily defined by such quick brush strokes. And in a play that depicts an intense moral struggle, the characters' affinity to one pole or the other must be unmistakable, gargantuan. The characters of *King Lear* are in fact extreme with a vengeance: when they are good, they are very good, and when they are bad they are unspeakable. Cordelia 'redeems nature from the general curse,' while Goneril has a 'marble-hearted fiend' within her; Edgar is 'a brother noble, / Whose nature is so far from doing harms / That he suspects none' (1.2.186–8), while Edmund is an absolute bastard; and so on. Polarization begins immediately, with the first act pitting Cordelia, Kent, Edgar, and the Fool against Regan, Goneril, Edmund, and Oswald. Every later incident brings a further definition of the lines of battle, until the polarity is all-encompassing. Lear, Gloucester, and Albany stand at first in the middle, more deluded than depraved; but by the last act, they too have shown their colours and won our sympathy through their suffering and the wider awareness they gain from it. Shakespeare's conception of character in *King Lear*, and the economy with which it is realized, are reminiscent of Aristotle's observations on tragic characterization: 'Character is that which reveals moral purpose, showing what kind of things a man chooses or avoids. Speeches, therefore, which do not make this manifest, or in which the speaker does not choose or avoid anything whatever, are not expressive of character.'[22] Every gesture in *King Lear* is expressive of character in this sense.

The roots of this kind of character presentation may be found in public-theatre dramaturgy, and characterization is the aspect of *King Lear* that most resembles public-theatre practice. Conventional presentation of characters on the public stage involved a definite initial establishment of the characters' moral positions, and dictated that later appearances would reinforce those initial impressions; as each play unfolds, characters act precisely as we would expect them to on the basis of these *données*. The entire process was designed to produce either positive or negative empathy through moral approval or disapproval. It is based on the concept that, in Muriel Bradbrook's words, 'characters did not develop,'[23] and on the assumption that the most important (and sometimes the only) information that a dramatist could present about a character was whether that character was good or evil. Good characters exhibit their election (as in *King Lear*) by being noble, which means that they are chaste, charitable, or courageous. Evil characters have wider scope, for they display their wickedness by subverting good in a variety of ingenious ways. Whichever colours they show, their conduct does not usually invite our examination or analysis; it is exemplary.[24]

Shakespeare makes the exemplary more dramatic in *King Lear* by staging frequent encounters between characters whose natures are so antithetical that they turn any meeting into a radical confrontation of opposites. These meetings occur in almost every scene; act 1 features Cordelia *versus* Regan and Goneril, France *versus* Burgundy, Edgar *versus* Edmund, and Kent *versus* Oswald. The effect of such character juxtaposition, as with the juxtaposed actions mentioned earlier in this paper, is emblematic: thanks to the extreme nature of the characters, we feel in each case that we are looking at illustrated exempla representing both sides of a moral question. This effect is most pronounced in the polarity that exists between Lear's daughters, especially as portrayed in the opening scene. With its ceremonial setting and patterned dialogue, the scene is extremely stylized: in a recitative-and-aria pattern of parallel speeches, Lear questions and rewards each daughter in turn, going from eldest to youngest. The basic moral antipathy is conveyed in equally formal terms, as Cordelia follows up each of her false sisters' performances with a similar aside. After Goneril's parade of empty mouthings, Cordelia turns to us in genuine panic: 'What shall Cordelia speak? Love, and be silent' (1.1.62). The contrast between her and her sister could not be more striking, and Cordelia's aside gains our immediate sympathy. Public-theatre playwrights frequently used the aside in this manner, to create a bond between an admirable character and the audience. Here, Shakespeare strengthens the bond and the artifice by giving Cordelia a second aside following Regan's speech: 'Then poor Cordelia! / And yet not so; since I am sure my love's / More ponderous than my tongue' (1.1.76–8). The parallel 'mottoes' undercut the tableaux in which they appear (each aside is sandwiched between a sister's hollow oath and their father's blind reward), and crystallize this polarity in an altogether fitting way. For Edgar and Edmund may be morally antithetical, but Cordelia and her sisters stand throughout the play as moral types of the angelic and the demonic. Perhaps this is Shakespeare's most emblematic touch, and the aspect of *King Lear* for which the un-naturalistic opening encounter is a most necessary preparation.

Cordelia, in particular, exists as a dramatized emblem. There is never any question of this Cordelia's being romantically repelled (as in *King Leir*) or attracted (as in Tate's play) by anybody. Unlike Desdemona or even Ophelia, Cordelia has none of the dimensions of the romantic heroine. It is her nature to be singular. She behaves less as a naturalistic character than as Shelley described his Prometheus, 'the type of the highest perfection ... impelled by the purest and the truest motives to the best and noblest ends.' Because she is so emblematically conceived, her motives and her ends will not brook questioning; we cannot imitate Lear or ask Cordelia to justify herself. That would be like probing *The Faerie Queene* in search of local colour. We must accept this emblem, and wait for our faith to be confirmed later in the play when an anonymous Gentleman reaffirms her symbolic nature – 'There she shook / The holy water from her heavenly eyes' (4.3.30–1) – or when he – or another – cries to Lear:

> Thou hast one daughter,
> Who redeems nature from the general curse
> Which twain have brought her to.   (4.6.206–8)

Or when Shakespeare gives these words to Cordelia herself: 'O dear father! / It is thy business that I go about' (4.4.23–4). Alone among the characters in *King Lear*, Cordelia carries much of the play's Christian symbolism; she brings an otherworldly light to the sun-less *Lear* world. And her conduct in the opening scene is a perfect introduction to her. As Russell Fraser has written, her muteness there 'is not so much a reflection of character as it is the embodiment of an idea.'[25] The emblematic and motiveless conduct associated with Cordelia in the opening tableau, with its roots in private-theatre artifice and public-theatre characterization, provides a key to the nature of her character throughout the play.

Yet no key opens every lock. No theatrical heritage can account for the overwhelming power of this or any other emblem in *King Lear*. The private-theatre drama that stands behind much of the play cultivates and rewards a delight in technical artifice, but Shakespeare touches deeper chords and sees theatrical technique as a means rather than an end. Though *King Lear* displays more pronounced patterning than any other Shakespearean tragedy, the pattern does not intrude; it serves to reinforce rather than infringe upon our profound but less definable emotional experience. The two theatres gave Shakespeare a stage, a platform from which he could project an emblem of reality that is in the end as compelling as it is unfathomable.

NOTES

1 Further information on theatres and audiences may be found in Alfred Harbage *Shakespeare and the Rival Traditions* (New York 1952), which first established that there were indeed 'two traditions' of Elizabethan drama. Harbage's study is more concerned with Elizabethan morality than with dramatic form, however. See also Arthur C. Kirsch, '*Cymbeline* and Coterie Dramaturgy,' *English Literary History* 34 (1967) 285–306.

2 The private theatres were the exclusive preserve of child actors until about 1610, when the King's Men (Shakespeare's company) began regular performances with adult actors at Blackfriars.

3 A much fuller treatment of dramatic form in the two theatres may be found in the author's doctoral dissertation, 'The Two Theatres: Dramatic Structure and Convention in English Public and Private Plays, 1599–1613' (Princeton University 1968), now being prepared for publication. The dissertation deals solely with non-Shakespearean drama.

4 Other aspects of the relation between *King Lear* and the two theatres are explored in a full-length study on the subject, which the author hopes soon to publish.

5 *Renaissance Drama* n.s.2 (1969) 39–57

6 This is not to say that *King Lear* contains no emblems of the kind that Mehl describes. Henry Green noticed some of the first type a century ago in his *Shakespeare and the Emblem Writers* (London 1870); see especially

his list on p. 540. Those of the third type also occur: Kent, the 'good man' in the stocks at 2.2.157; Lear kneeling at 2.4.156; blind Gloucester epitomizing the world's 'strange mutations' for Edgar at 4.1.11; and poor Tom, pointed to by Lear ('Is man no more than this? Consider him well'), at 3.4.105–6. Granville-Barker recognized the emblematic quality of this last scene when he wrote of it: 'Here is a volume of argument epitomized as only drama can epitomize it, flashed on us by word and action combined,' in *Prefaces to Shakespeare* (Princeton 1946, reprinted 1965) II 33.

7 See *This Great Stage: Image and Structure in 'King Lear'* (Baton Rouge 1948, reprinted Seattle 1963) 67–87. In particular, Heilman shows how Lear's redemptive experience is manifested in a succession of tableaux relating to Lear's headgear: the king goes from crown to bare head to crown of weeds (or thorns).

8 Revels edition, ed. Nicholas Brooke (London 1964)

9 I use the Folio reading here, rather than Muir's in the Arden edition.

10 See also Edward Sharpham *The Fleer* (1606), where the opening scenes of act 3 present the parallel actions of several characters in even closer juxtaposition. Earlier, Marston had used the technique to emphasize a turning point in the action of *Antonio's Revenge* (1600). When Antonio enters in scene 5 of act 3, he forms a tableau that reveals his absolute commitment to violence: his arms are bloodied, and he stands with a torch in one hand and a dagger in the other. The emblem is the more telling because it exactly duplicates the entrance of the villainous Piero at the start of act 1.

11 Kenneth Muir notes at this point in the Arden edition that the Folio has no scene division, and that presumably Kent remained on stage during Edgar's speech.

12 To take only one example, in Marston's *The Dutch Courtesan* Cocledemoy's praise of bawds (1.2.29–54) closely echoes Freevill's praise of prostitutes in the previous scene (1.1.92–127) ed M.L. Wine (London 1965). See also Chapman's *Monsieur D'Olive*, Field's *A Woman is a Weathercock*, and just about any comedy by Middleton.

13 See for example *The Shoemakers' Holiday, A Woman Killed with Kindness*, or *Thomas Lord Cromwell*.

14 In the introduction to his edition of the play (Lincoln, Nebr. 1966) xvii

15 *'King Lear' in Our Time* (Berkeley 1965) 100

16 This kind of symbolic regrouping occurs frequently in private-theatre drama; in *Amends for Ladies*, for instance, the three ladies whose debate initiated the dramatic action come forward once again at the end, to demonstrate that the process in which they were involved has come full circle. Similarly, parallel speeches by Freevill emphasize fulfilment of the pattern behind Marston's *The Dutch Courtesan*: Freevill's long condemnation of the prostitutes in act 5 stands in revealing contrast to his equally long praise of them in act 1 and rounds off the evolution traced by the play.

17 *This Great Stage* 126
18 See, for instance, Chapman's *Bussy D'Ambois* and *The Widow's Tears*, or Fletcher's *The Faithful Shepherdess*.
19 This cryptic quality is characteristic of emblems; see Rosalie Colie's discussion of Marvell's emblematic technique in *'My Ecchoing Song': Andrew Marvell's Poetry of Criticism* (Princeton 1970) 172–3.
20 *Bussy D'Ambois, The Widow's Tears,* and *Amends for Ladies,* for example
21 *Ram-Alley* ed. Claude E. Jones (Louvain 1952) lines 312–13
22 *Poetics,* tr. S.H. Butcher in *Aristotle: On the Art of Poetry* (New York 1956) 10
23 *Themes and Conventions of Elizabethan Tragedy* (Cambridge 1935) 61
24 See for example Dekker's *Patient Grissil,* Heywood's *The Fair Maid of the West, Part I,* or Jonson's *Volpone.*
25 In the introduction to his edition of *King Lear* (New York 1963) xxi

FOUR

THOMAS F. VAN LAAN acting as action in king lear

THE BRIEF PROLOGUE that opens *King Lear* has for one of its functions the task of instructing us how we are to respond to the crucial scenes in which Lear divests himself of his kingdom and exiles the two people who most wish him well. Kent and Gloucester make it clear that Lear's 'darker purpose' is already known. They are aware of his plan to divide the kingdom, and they have learned enough of the details of the plan to be able to express surprise that the Dukes of Albany and Cornwall are to be allotted equal shares. What we are about to witness, this prologue informs us, is merely a formal ceremony to sanction through public representation a fait accompli.

It is not strange, therefore, that so many of the scene's speeches sound as if they had been written to order and carefully rehearsed. Such is the case, obviously, with the extravagant claims of Goneril and Regan, but the impression also results from the highly artificial rhetoric of Lear's own speeches, especially when he indulges an apparent tendency for formal balance and excessive amplification:

> Of all these bounds, even from this line to this,
> With shadowy forests and with champains rich'd,
> With plenteous rivers and wide-skirted meads,
> We make thee lady.   (1.1.63-6)

Moreover, it is as if all these speeches have been written specifically to Lear's order, for although Goneril and Regan have certainly supplied their own words, they speak in response to formal cues from Lear – 'Goneril, / Our eldest-born, speak first' (53-4); 'What says our second daughter / Our dearest Regan ... ' (67-8) – and his replies, because they ignore the content of what has been said and go directly to the business of pronouncing rewards, define these speeches as having successfully measured up to some preconception of what they ought to have been.

Cordelia's contribution to the ceremony underscores its dominant quality in two ways. The simplicity and directness of her language – both in her asides and in her speeches to Lear – offer a sharp contrast to the high-flown rhetoric being spoken by the other members of her family. And her refusal to say what she knows is expected of her occasions the most forceful indication that what we are witnessing is a kind of play-within-the-play. When Regan has finished and received her reward, the third of Lear's formal cues can be heard:

> Now, our joy,
> Although our last, and least;   (82-3)

> what can you say to draw
> A third more opulent than your sisters? Speak.   (85-6)

The urge to take Lear's repeated requests for speech as formal cues becomes irresistible in the lines that follow. Cordelia has 'Nothing' to say, but Lear insists, 'Nothing will come of nothing: speak again,' and when she still fails to satisfy him, he adds, 'How, how, Cordelia! Mend your speech a little, / Lest you may mar your fortunes' (89-94). Lear means 'a lot,' of course, because the impression he conveys of Cordelia is that of an actress who has forgotten her lines. He is obviously waiting to hear a particular speech, or at least a speech of a particular kind, one that will surpass in its assertions of love even the speeches already recited by Goneril and Regan.

Cordelia's refusal to say what is expected of her changes the entire direction of the scene by initiating a rapid-fire sequence of events which no one onstage could have anticipated. Thus her refusal strikingly highlights the contrived and artificial quality of all that has preceded it. Through her lack of co-operation the beginning of the scene stands fully revealed as a little playlet that its chief actor, director, and virtual author has staged for the sole purpose of glorifying himself in public.

One reason for our responsiveness to the histrionic qualities of Lear's ceremony is our familiarity with Shakespeare's other plays and our realization that his characters generally tend not only to play alien roles – as do, for example, Julia, Portia, Rosalind, and Viola (and, in their quite different way, Richard III and Iago) – but also to improvise little playlets: one thinks immediately of Hal and Falstaff at the Boar's Head Tavern, of Don Pedro and Don John in *Much Ado about Nothing*, and – especially relevant here – of Malvolio in *Twelfth Night*, whose performance on Olivia's garden walk of his misconception of himself as Count Malvolio is a comic version of the same kind of activity that Lear engages in. These characters and their behaviour exemplify Shakespeare's thorough commitment to the Renaissance cliché that 'the world's a stage,' or, as the supposed motto for the Globe Theatre would have it, '*Totus mundus agit histrionem.*'[1] The metaphor appears or is implied constantly throughout Shakespeare's work, and the way it consistently applies to actual behaviour of the plays' characters indicates that Shakespeare, unlike most of his contemporaries, employed it not as a detachable *sententia* but as a fundamental idea in his conception of dramatic man. As Anne Righter has shown, especially in her analysis of Richard II and other 'Player-Kings,' Shakespeare's uses of the metaphor demand careful scrutiny because of the illumination they provide for the actions containing them.[2]

Lear's playlet is no exception. It is itself a complex metaphor charged with several important implications. First, it helps to characterize Lear's own condition, for as the originator of the playlet, he defines himself as inhabiting a world of unreality. This is made especially clear through his failure to penetrate beyond the limits of the play-world he has himself devised. The real world is very much in evidence on Shakespeare's stage, by implication in the true feelings held by Goneril and Regan, more concretely in the asides spoken by Cordelia. But Lear is blind to these hints and glimpses of alternative possibilities; for him they do not exist. Cordelia soon compels him to recognize the existence of some of them, it is true, but his response merely confirms his allegiance to his own world of unreality: instead of altering his vision so that it will conform to the facts before him, he tries to destroy the facts, to make the real world coincide with his own.

Second, Lear's playlet calls to our attention another kind of role-playing with which the role-playing in his playlet interferes. Cordelia refuses to play the role Lear has assigned her because it conflicts with other roles – or 'offices,' as the Elizabethans would have said – which she feels to be more valid. As a daughter, she is obliged through her bond to obey, love, and honour her father – though not to indulge him by practising a 'glib and oily art' (1.1.224) – and as a wife, which she is soon to become, she is obliged to surrender to her husband 'Half my love ... , half my care and duty' (102). This contrast between the social and familial roles imposed by life and the artificial roles called for by the playlet pertains as well to the other actors in the playlet, and it is especially pertinent to Lear. As king, Lear occupies an office that fulfils the notion of 'role' especially well, not only because – like the roles of daughter and wife – it prescribed a fixed pattern of behaviour for its holder, but also because of its highly theatrical attributes: its costume, distinguishing props, ceremonial speech and gesture, and the like. 'It is a true olde saying,' remarked James I in *Basilicon Doron*, 'That a King is as one set on a stage, whose smallest actions and gestures, all the people gazinglie doe beholde.'[3]

In using the role-playing of the playlet to call our attention to the characters' other, permanent roles, Shakespeare is by no means merely indulging the fatal passion for 'quibbles' that disturbed Dr Johnson. He is, instead, establishing a most crucial element in the dramatic design. In a society like Shakespeare's – or Lear's – which feels secure about what constitutes proper behaviour, social and familial roles are basic sources of order, and untroubled adherence to them symbolizes the continued existence of order. From the point of view of society, the obligations imposed by such roles prevent the individual from acting spontaneously and therefore dangerously. From the point of view of the individual, his social and familial roles provide him with a set of bearings which place him in relation to reality and thereby enable him to cope with its otherwise bewildering complexity.

What Shakespeare presents in *Lear*, however, is not untroubled adherence to the roles of this type but, rather, their constant violation or loss, or at least the loss of the external circumstances normally attending them. This emphasis begins with the opening scene and is initiated by Lear's playlet. Lear's plan to partially divest himself of his role as king – that is, to shed its responsibilities and retain only its rights and privileges – clearly involves him in a violation of the demands of his role. Yet, as the playlet indicates, Lear has already violated its demands by becoming a Player-King. Instead of role-playing, he has been play-acting; for the fixed pattern of behaviour belonging to the office of king – 'the wise Kings part' (to quote King James once more)[4] – Lear has substituted an imaginary role, his distorted conception of himself as king. *King Lear* begins, then, with Lear's double violation of the most important social role of them all, and his act simultaneously causes and signifies a complete disruption of order for his kingdom.

Cordelia's breaking off of Lear's playlet establishes a symbolic action by means of which we can more readily perceive the abstract disruption of order, and the events her act sets in motion provide further evidence to confirm the full significance of her father's errors. Once order *per se* has crumbled, its individual constituents rapidly fall as well, and so Shakespeare immediately shows a number of other roles being subjected to violation or nullification. Through his treatment of Cordelia, Lear, as France suggests (213–23), violates his role as father; his ultimate mistreatment of her, of course, is to attempt to deprive her of her role as daughter:

> Here I disclaim all my paternal care,
> Propinquity and property of blood,
> And as a stranger to my heart and me
> Hold thee from this for ever. The barbarous Scythian,
> Or he that makes his generation messes
> To gorge his appetite, shall to my bosom
> Be as well neighbour'd, pitied, and reliev'd,
> As thou my sometime daughter.   (1.1.113–20)

Despite Lear's rejection of her, Cordelia continues to be his daughter and still strives to fulfil the demands of her role to the extent of her ability. But although Lear cannot separate her from her role (in contrast to his ability to un-king himself, or Edmund's ability to separate both his father and his brother from their more socially created and sanctioned roles), he obviously manages to deprive her of both the material circumstances appropriate to her role and the counter-responsiveness from himself necessary for its wholly satisfactory performance.

Kent suffers a similar loss almost at once. His one and only role is that of Lear's loyal follower, a role he emphasizes even as he voices his objections to Lear's behaviour:

> Royal Lear,
> Whom I have ever honour'd as my King,
> Lov'd as my father, as my master follow'd,
> As my great patron thought on in my prayers ...   (1.1.39–42)

Lear symbolically deprives Kent of his role the moment he acts in such a way that he compels Kent to become 'unmannerly'; then, in pronouncing Kent's banishment, Lear converts symbol to reality. Kent's response, 'Freedom lives hence, and banishment is here' (181), is for him the most telling way possible of evoking a topsy-turvy world, and it thus forms a fitting climax to the rapid series of events through which Lear's initial disruption of order is confirmed.

Probably the most important significance of Lear's playlet, however, is the way in which it ensures continued disorder through the precedent it establishes. By introducing play-acting into his world, Lear sanctions a mode of action that can favour only masters of deceit like Goneril, Regan, and Edmund, who, because they lack any sense of the integrity of social and familial roles, are capable, both psychologically and morally, of making what Lear has introduced a truly viable mode of action. Although this result of Lear's playlet is clear enough already in the opening scene, where only Goneril and Regan succeed in fulfilling their ends, it becomes even clearer in the two following scenes, where, as if deliberately going Lear one better, first Edmund and then Goneril create playlets of their own.

Lear's nullification of the roles upon which order depends has created an ideal setting for Edmund. As bastard he is roleless, so that although this condition has previously made him unable to function, he is the one character in the play wholly suited to operate in a context where roles have lost their meaning. Furthermore, because he has no social role, Edmund is also the one character most able to thrive in a context where play-acting has become the primary mode of action; like liquid, which takes its form from its surroundings, Edmund is free to assume whatever role he needs at the moment. This is why he is able to bring off so successfully the complicated sequence of role-playing which begins in 1.2 and concludes in 2.1. In 1.2 he plays for Gloucester's benefit the part of a son so loyal that he is compelled to bring to his father's attention the possible villainy of the brother to whom he is also loyal. Later in the same scene he plays for Edgar's benefit the part of a brother so loyal that he must warn him of the danger threatening him, even though that danger would seem to stem from their father. And in both episodes, he is carefully laying plans for the playlet he will stage in 2.1, the playlet in which the father as spectator shall be made to behold the versions of Edmund and Edgar that Edmund wishes to convey. Like Richard III before him, Edmund is quite consicous of himself as playwright-actor. He sees Edgar in terms of 'the catastrophe of the old comedy' (1.2.141–2); he knows that his own 'cue is villanous melancholy, with a sigh like Tom o' Bedlam' (142–3); and just before he is about to begin the playlet of 2.1, he refers to it as 'one thing, of a queasy question, / Which I must act' (2.1.18–19).

The playlet produced by Goneril – or 'Vanity' the puppet, as Kent will later call her (2.2.36) – is far less complicated than Edmund's sequence, but it admirably fulfils its purpose. Goneril begins not as actor but as playwright-director, working through her agent Oswald. When Lear returns from hunting, she informs Oswald, she will not speak to Lear, and Oswald is to say that she is sick. Moreover, Oswald and his fellow servants are to 'Put on what weary negligence' they please with Lear (1.3.13) and to 'let his knights have colder looks' (23). In this way, she feels, Lear will be taught to accept the new status he has created for himself by giving away his kingdom:

> Idle old man,
> That still would manage those authorities
> That he hath given away! Now, by my life,
> Old fools are babes again, and must be us'd
> With checks as flatteries, when they are seen abus'd. (1.3.17–21)

Goneril's playlet extends into the following scene, where Oswald, playing the role his mistress has coached him in, refuses to 'entertain' Lear with 'that ceremonious affection' (1.4.62) he expects. Lear still considers himself *King* Lear, but Oswald will address him as no more than 'My Lady's father' (84), defining him as no better than Oswald's equal. Goneril's playlet reaches its climax when the lady herself, like a matador confronting the victim his picadors have carefully prepared, enters to administer the *coup de grâce*. Her chastisement of Lear is so thorough, and so unexpected to him, that Lear, in a pair of responses unwittingly underscoring the idea of the playlet and of Goneril's deliberately performing a role in it, first wonders, 'Are you our daughter?' (227) and then concludes she is not: 'Your name, fair gentlewoman?' (244).

In isolation from its context Lear's original folly might seem harmless enough; after all, he has merely sought publicly to glorify himself. But the context cannot be ignored, and it defines Lear's folly as a supreme example of tragic error. For not only has he thereby disrupted order, he has also provided his enemies with the instrument through which they can accomplish their evil purposes. By establishing play-acting as a viable mode of action, Lear has created the 'great stage of fools' he will eventually refer to explicitly (4.6.185). The central importance of this theatrical metaphor is demonstrated by the thoroughness with which it applies to the action. Almost every character engages in play-acting of one kind or another, and his skill or lack of skill in play-acting is a crucial factor in determining the nature of his experience.

Three relevant categories quickly emerge. The first consists of those characters who find play-acting to be a congenial mode and who employ it either (like Goneril) to enhance their social roles, or (like Edmund) to enhance themselves by seizing roles not rightly theirs. The paradigm for this category is the rapid rise of Edmund, whom we see become, in quick succession, Gloucester's favourite son and promised heir (2.1.83–5), Cornwall's trusted follower (2.1.112–16), Earl of Gloucester in his father's place (3.5.17–18), lover of both Goneril and Regan, and virtual leader of the combined English forces: the discarded kingship is but a step away. The second category consists of those characters whose lack of guile costs them their social roles, or at least the possibility of effectively fulfilling them, and who must therefore either temporarily leave the world Lear has created (as Cordelia does), or (like Kent and Edgar) engage in play-acting of their own – Kent so that he can safely fulfil his role at least partially, Edgar as a means of protecting himself and of establishing new, fictional bearings to replace those he has lost. The paradigm for this category is the situation Edgar articulates in his soliloquy of 2.3: he decides to assume the role of a Bedlam beggar both to 'preserve' himself (2.3.6) and because 'Poor Turlygod! Poor Tom! / That's something yet: Edgar I nothing am' (20–1). The plight of Gloucester exemplifies the third category. In 3.7, as Cornwall and Regan abuse him, he reminds them that both as their host and as an old man, he deserves better treatment from them (3.7.30–1, 35–41). But he pleads in vain, since these roles are no longer acknowledged. With the disruption of order *per se*, there can be only temporary, moment-to-moment order, and it is established by those who control the situation. Here it is Cornwall and Regan who have the upper hand, and they have recast their host in the role of 'the traitor Gloucester' (22). Like Kent and Edgar, Gloucester lacks guile and therefore like them he stands at the mercy of those who thrive in Lear's new world. Unlike Kent and Edgar, however, he has no place to hide, and so he becomes one of the new world's chief victims.

Lear also belongs to the category exemplified by Gloucester – but with some significant differences. He has, of course, created the conditions that make possible his suffering, and more important, he collaborates in bringing it about. Lear's problem is that he is unwilling to play the new role his errors have cast him in and that Goneril and Regan are so eager to compel him to fulfil. Instead of playing the 'Idle old man' that Goneril maintains he has become, he persists in speaking and acting as if his roles of king and father had not been nullified. And he expects that others will so respond to him. This quality of Lear's condition is quickly established by Shakespeare in 1.4 through the contrasting receptions Lear accords Kent and Oswald. The disguised Kent offers to serve Lear because, as Kent says, 'you have that in your countenance which I would fain call master'; that is, 'Authority' (1.4.29–32). Kent addresses Lear, in other words, as a king, and therefore he is welcomed, though with proper aloofness: 'Follow me; thou shalt serve me; if I like thee no worse after dinner I will not part from thee yet' (43–5). But when Oswald very deliberately refuses to perceive any vestige of authority in the face of the man he can now call simply 'My Lady's father,' he becomes in Lear's eyes 'my Lord's knave,' a 'whoreson dog,' a 'slave,' and a 'cur' (85–6). He becomes a recreant deserving the blow he receives from the king he has slighted and the kick he receives from the king's new follower, who thus once again defines his master as king and thus once again is rewarded with the king's approval: 'I thank thee, fellow; thou serv'st me, and I'll love thee' (92–3).

Throughout the first two acts of the play, Lear's contribution to the action consists of his steady search for others who will acknowledge his kingship and fatherhood by treating him in the appropriate manner and by feeding him the proper cues. His decision to leave Goneril for Regan is an attempt to find a setting that will correspond to the roles he is still determined to play:

> Yea, is 't come to this?
> Ha! Let it be so: I have another daughter,
> Who, I am sure, is kind and comfortable:
> When she shall hear this of thee, with her nails
> She'll flay thy wolvish visage. Thou shalt find
> That I'll resume the shape which thou dost think
> I have cast off for ever.   (1.4.313–19)

But apart from Kent and, more problematically, the Fool, he can find no one who will respond to him as to a king, and no one at all whose treatment of him defines him as a father. The cues he hears when he finally reaches Regan are obviously not the ones he expects to hear –

> Deny to speak with me! They are sick! They are weary!
> They travell'd all the night! Mere fetches, ay,
> The images of revolt and flying off.
> Fetch me a better answer –   (2.4.88–91)

and so he directs that Regan and Cornwall be reminded who he is:

> The King would speak with Cornwall; the dear father
> Would with his daughter speak, commands, tends service.   (101–2)

Yet even before they enter to confirm that their 'remotion ... / Is practice only' (114–15), Lear's eyes light on inescapable proof that he has not found the setting he sought, for to him Kent's imprisonment in the stocks is 'Death on my state!' (112). As he soon realizes, moreover, the setting he has entered is just as uncongenial to his intention of continuing to play the father. What he discovers when he confronts Regan is not a daughter who is 'kind and comfortable' but a new enemy, one who denies the relationship he assumes she holds toward him by directing him to perform an act for Goneril's benefit which completely negates his conception of fatherhood:

> Ask her forgiveness?
> Do you but mark how this becomes the house:
> 'Dear daughter, I confess that I am old;
> Age is unnecessary: on my knees I beg
> That you'll vouchsafe me raiment, bed, and food.'   (2.4.153–7)

With this lack of co-operation from his fellow players, the only way Lear can continue to speak like a king is to adopt the tone of righteous indignation he has already tried out on Kent in 1.1 and Oswald in 1.4. This is why the formal and florid maledictions he pronounces against Goneril in 1.4 and 2.4 are simultaneously so appropriate and so pathetic. They constitute Lear's last valiant attempt to keep hold of the roles he still feels are rightly his and thus to keep hold of his identity. Yet he cannot sustain even this last vestige of his sense of himself as king and father. The complete loss of self that he will demonstrate in acts 3 and 4 begins as early as 2.4 when, in summoning Regan, he alters 'commands' to 'tends' (2.4.102) and when, a moment later, he interrupts his cursing of Cornwall in order to fabricate possible excuses that will account for Cornwall's neglect (105–12). When Regan turns out to be exactly like her sister, Lear capitulates. He responds not with a new formal curse but with the 'reason not the need' speech (2.4.266–88), a speech that doubly reveals his inability to sustain any longer the fiction of his kingship. In this speech for the first time Lear stops trying to talk like a king; instead, he is now desperately fighting merely to hang on to the material properties that allow him to *look* like a king. In doing so, moreover, he sounds for the first time as if he actually fits the conception of him that Goneril and Regan hold, that of the helpless old man whose lack of status compels him to beg rather than demand.

In 1.4, after mistreatment from Oswald and Goneril, Lear had
asked:

> Does any here know me? This is not Lear:
> Does Lear walk thus? speak thus? Where are his eyes?
> Either his notion weakens, his discernings
> Are lethargied – Ha! waking? 'tis not so.
> Who is it that can tell me who I am?   (1.4.234–8)

These questions were, however, merely rhetorical – Lear's way of
commenting not upon changes in himself but only on changes in
his surroundings. The process carried out in the succeeding scenes
converts these rhetorical questions into substantial ones; it turns
Lear into the 'O without a figure' (200–1) – the 'nothing' (202) –
that the Fool had seen him to be as early as 1.4. For the loss that
Lear experiences in these succeeding scenes is defined not only by
his realization that he can no longer perform his former roles but
also by the further realization that he is losing a role more basic
than either of these: his manhood. As early as 1.4, he feared the
loss of his manhood, but then he was able to resist it:

> Life and death! I am asham'd
> That thou hast power to shake my manhood thus,
> That these hot tears, which break from me perforce,
> Should make thee worth them.   (1.4.305–8)

In 2.4, his plea to Goneril and Regan makes this ultimate loss im-
minent once again, and once again he tries to resist it:

> You see me here, you Gods, a poor old man,
> As full of grief as age; wretched in both!
> If it be you that stirs these daughters' hearts
> Against their father, fool me not so much
> To bear it tamely; touch me with noble anger,
> And let not women's weapons, water-drops,
> Stain my man's cheeks!   (2.4.274–80)

The 'noble anger' would allow him to retain his manhood and at the
same time regain his lost kingliness, and so he tries once more to
adopt the tone of righteous indignation. This time he cannot sustain
it at all. This time, though he insists he will never give way to 'these
hot tears,' the 'noble anger' quickly dissipates into the constant
reiteration of the word 'weep':

> No, you unnatural hags,
> I will have such revenges on you both
> That all the world shall – I will do such things,

What they are, yet I know not, but they shall be
The terrors of the earth. You think I'll weep;
No, I'll not weep:
I have full cause of weeping, but this heart
Shall break into a hundred thousand flaws
Or ere I'll weep.   (2.4.280–8)

'O Fool! I shall go mad' forms the only possible appropriate conclusion to this speech. Unable to play the roles of king and father,
and unwilling to play the 'Idle old man,' Lear already necessarily
experiences the madness that is simultaneously a condition caused
by his plight and a metaphor to represent its exact nature. Without
any valid roles to perform, Lear has lost the bearings that place
him in relation to reality; he no longer possesses an identity. What
he and we call his madness must occur at this point, therefore, because as a concrete dramatic fact his madness is nothing more nor
less than a series of speeches characterized on the one hand by the
presence of assertions that imperfectly correspond to external reality and on the other hand by the absence of an identifiable voice.
Lear's madness is not itself a role, as is Edgar's feigned madness;
it is, instead, the presence of all possible roles simultaneously, and
Shakespeare establishes the absence of an identifiable voice through
the ease, rapidity, and inexplicability with which Lear shifts from
one new role to another. What we hear in the mad scenes of acts 3
and 4 is not a voice we can call 'Lear' but rather a series of voices we
must give separate names, including Lear as 'poor, infirm, weak, and
despis'd old man,' Lear as castigator of vice, Lear as pitier of 'Poor
naked wretches,' Lear as 'unaccommodated man,' Lear as prose-
cutor, Lear as philosopher, Lear as fool, and even, occasionally, Lear
as king. Separately, none of these voices provides an accurate representation of its speaker; in their confused intermingling, however,
they quite accurately represent the nothing he has become.
   Through the care of Cordelia and the Doctor, Lear is finally cured
of his madness. The dressing of Lear in new garments, the calculated use of music, and the Doctor's manipulation of the action –

COR. He wakes; speak to him.
DOCT. Madam, do you; 'tis fittest –   (4.7.42–3)

make the scene of Lear's recovery every bit as stagey as the playlet
in 1.1. Cordelia and the Doctor have, in other words, adopted the
mode of action sanctioned by Lear and practised by Goneril and
Edmund; but in doing so, like Edgar at 'Dover cliff' they have con-
verted it to a benevolent instrument and thus purged it of evil.
   As the change of garments and other indications of rebirth sug-

gest, they have used it to help Lear acquire a new identity. The new identity includes many of the roles he had played during his madness and even some of those he had sought or refused to play during the period of suffering that induced his madness. At the core of the new identity stand both his role as man and his role as father – 'Do not laugh at me; / For, as I am a man, I think this lady / To be my child Cordelia' (4.7.68–70) – but the concern with the feelings and welfare of others is much in evidence, and so also is the strong sense of himself as sinner, fool, and 'Idle old man.' What distinguishes Lear's new condition from his madness, then, is not a total lack of continuity but rather the fact that these miscellaneous roles have coalesced to form a consistent and identifiable voice. And the voice is one we have never heard before. In finding Cordelia, Lear finds what he had sought in vain during the first two acts, for Cordelia's responses to him – 'No cause, no cause' (75); 'Will't please your Highness walk?' (83) – define him as both the king and the honoured father he had originally seen himself to be. But in this respect Cordelia's responses are ironic. The man she addresses now speaks with a voice totally devoid of the role of king as Lear had originally conceived it and thus totally devoid as well of his conception of the father as king within the family. The new voice, in contrast to the old, is characterized by its humility, its simplicity, and its directness, above all by its clear evidence of a desire to communicate rather than rule:

> Pray, do not mock me:
> I am a very foolish fond old man,
> Fourscore and upward, not an hour more or less;
> And, to deal plainly,
> I fear I am not in my perfect mind. (4.7.59–63)

There can be no question that Lear has at last found an identity – a blending of roles – which is wholly congenial to him, and in the following act we hear him experimenting with his new voice, improvising in order to define it even more concretely. Gone now are all traces of the original desire for public self-glorification, of the need for justification through the responses of others. The relation to external reality that Lear has now achieved is one in which nothing beyond Cordelia and his feeling for her matters:

> Have I caught thee?
> He that parts us shall bring a brand from heaven,
> And fire us hence like foxes. Wipe thine eyes;
> The good years shall devour them, flesh and fell,
> Ere they shall make us weep: we'll see 'em starv'd first. (5.3.21–5)

As long as he has Cordelia, the rest of external reality, whatever it may actually be in itself, will in Lear's mind become transformed into an appropriate setting where they can act out their love for each other. Prison is to be welcomed because it provides them a place where they can be alone to 'sing like birds i' th' cage' (5.3.9). Mutability and the threats posed by the ambitions of others no longer need to be feared, for through their love they will be able to 'wear out, / In a wall'd prison, packs and sects of great ones / That ebb and flow by th' moon' (5.3.17–19).

Lear's resumption of an identity, his return to a personal order, coincides with a restoration of order for the entire kingdom as the masters of deceit who had thrived on disorder are serially exposed and destroyed. The turning point in the movement that traces the fortunes of the kingdom occurs as early as 3.7, when through the rebellion of Cornwall's servant the nullification of the bonds that guarantee the stability of social roles finally begins to take its toll even on those who have been capitalizing on it:

> Hold your hand, my Lord.
> I have serv'd you ever since I was a child,
> But better service have I never done you
> Than now to bid you hold.   (3.7.71–4)

From this point until the play's final scene, numerous signs, including the adoption and purgation of play-acting first by Edgar and then by Cordelia, help convey the idea of a return to order, but this idea is most effectively dramatized in the later career of Edgar. His rapid changes, in 4.6 and 5.3, from one role to another – from 'Poor Tom' to the guide of Gloucester whose 'voice is alter'd' and who speaks 'in better phrase and matter' than poor Tom (4.6.7–8), to the 'bold peasant' who kills Oswald (232), and finally to the nameless knight in armour who challenges and destroys Edmund – carry him gradually and smoothly back up the social ladder from his temporary status as social outcast to his final position as restored nobleman – from 'Edgar I nothing am' to:

> I am no less in blood than thou art, Edmund;
> If more, the more th' hast wrong'd me.
> My name is Edgar, and thy father's son.   (5.3.167–9)

Edgar's statement of his restored identity is accompanied by a proper re-identification of all the play's characters: of Goneril and Regan; of 'Kent ... the banish'd Kent; who in disguise / Follow'd his enemy king, and did him service / Improper for a slave' (5.3.219–21); of Edmund, whom Edgar identifies as 'a traitor ... A most toad-spotted traitor' (133, 138); and of Gloucester, whose death is the direct result of his rediscovery of himself as a loved and loving father. Edgar's progress parallels the similar rise of Edmund in the first half of the play, and just as Edmund's rise betokened increasing disorder, Edgar's symbolizes its elimination; as Edmund remarks, 'The wheel is come full circle' (174).

Shakespeare's stage is now set for an ending like that which Tate later substituted. But in defiance of minds like that of Tate, in defiance of all other known versions of the Lear story, and in defiance of the expectations carefully aroused in us, Shakespeare instead provides us with a different kind of 'promis'd end.' There is no logic in Cordelia's death, dramatic or otherwise, no explanation for it any more than Lear can explain the 'cause in nature that make these hard hearts' (3.6.78–9). This is why Dr Johnson found the ending to be too painful to re-read and also, I suppose, why we find it so dramatically right: it is true *because* it is painful. The source of our pain, however, is not Cordelia's death but its effect on Lear. For Lear loses not only Cordelia but with her his new identity, the new relation to reality his rediscovery of her had brought him, and thus he loses himself as well.

Lear's first sound upon entering with Cordelia dead in his arms is 'Howl, howl, howl!' (5.3.257) and what follows merely reiterates in various forms this initial response. The fact of Lear's pain is always present in our consciousness, but not because he carefully articulates it. Unlike Macbeth and Othello at the end of their tragic careers, Lear is unable to articulate a fully elaborated self-conception with its own appropriate language, its own recognizable voice. Macbeth and Othello speak from sure and distinctive perspectives that supply them with a meaningful vocabulary and that allow them to move coherently from one idea or image to another as they place themselves in relation to external reality. In contrast, Lear lacks all coherence. His first two speeches set the pattern for all that is to follow. He begins by telling us that Cordelia is 'gone for ever' and that he knows 'when one is dead, and when one lives' (259–60). But he actually knows nothing of the kind, nor can he really believe that Cordelia is dead – otherwise he would not see the feather stir or hear her voice or expend so much energy to prove that she is still alive. As his speeches addressed to others indicate, he does not even know where he is, for Albany, Edgar, and Kent are not 'murderers, traitors all!' as he calls them (269), nor is Caius (Kent's false identity) 'dead and rotten' (285). Lear has completely lost contact with external reality, and his tendency to leap from thought to thought while speaking of – and to – Cordelia suggests that he has not compensated for this lost contact by discovering (as Othello does) a sure inner reality. Each of the things Lear says while focussing on the only fact in his experience that now matters to him makes sense in itself, but the several utterances do not make a coherent whole. Since, moreover, the utterances related to Cordelia's death coexist with his unresponsive replies to Kent and the others, the impression of incoherence is greatly magnified. The common source of Lear's speeches – the pain he feels – comes through consistently, but the speeches themselves seem no more than noises forced from him, no more than additional 'howls.'

In Lear's final speech (5.3.305–11), the incoherence is even more pronounced: he has moved from disjointed speeches to a speech of disjointed elements. And here, also, his use of words gains a new characteristic, the inability to express unequivocal meaning. The first line of this speech – 'And my poor fool is hang'd' – loses certainty of meaning through the ambiguity of 'fool.' The next few lines are unequivocal enough, but it is the logic of pain rather than the laws of exposition that determines their continuity, and by ending with 'Never, never, never, never, never!' they veer back toward the howl of Lear's entrance. It is impossible to determine the function of 'Pray you, undo this button: thank you, Sir.' Is it a request and the acknowledgment of the request's having been granted? Or is it simply an echo from the stripping scene in the storm? And it is also impossible to determine the significance of Lear's final line and a half. To read 'Do you see this? Look on her, look, her lips, / Look there, look there!' as an indication that Lear dies joyfully, content in his belief that Cordelia still lives is an act of wishful thinking not unlike the act this reading attributes to Lear. These words no more surely indicate that Lear is calling attention to some sign of life than they do that he has discovered some equally convincing testimony of death. These words in themselves do not and cannot make any kind of statement or convey with clarity any definite fact about Cordelia, or Lear himself, or anything else. And this is as it should be, for the words are spoken by a man who, in every sense, has been reduced to a howl.

He is a speaker without language, and he is so because he has no identity, no roles to provide him with language. But he has not returned to his earlier state of madness. Once more we fail to hear a recognizable voice, but this time the failure is owing to the fact that his speeches are only a prolonged cry of pain. Lear's final condition makes us realize that madness, in Edgar's words, is 'something yet,' that it does provide, after all, some kind of relation to external reality. For in this last speech Lear is experiencing an even emptier state of nothingness. He dies (in our sense) when he does because he is already dead. Without roles, without an identity, without the language they provide, he cannot continue to exist.

NOTES

1 The history of the world-as-stage metaphor is traced by E.R. Curtius in *European Literature and the Latin Middle Ages* tr. Willard R. Trask (New York 1963) 138–44. Its various manifestations in Shakespeare and other English Renaissance writers have been thoroughly surveyed by Thomas B. Stroup in *Microcosmos: The Shape of the Elizabethan Play* (Lexington, Ky. 1965).
2 *Shakespeare and the Idea of the Play* (London 1962) especially chap 5
3 ed. James Craigie (London 1944) 163
4 *Basilicon Doron* 101

FIVE

MAURICE CHARNEY

'we put fresh garments on him': nakedness and clothes in KING LEAR

IN THE 1968 SEASON the Royal Shakespeare Company at Stratford decided to shock the audience by nudity rather than violence. Helen, in Marlowe's *Doctor Faustus*, pranced about the stage with all her immortal charms plainly exposed, and in *Troilus and Cressida*, Greeks were distinguished from Trojans by differently coloured jockstraps. Nakedness was most disturbing in *King Lear*, where Eric Porter stripped to his underwear at the climactic lines: 'Off, off, you lendings! Come; unbutton here' (3.4.111–12). I do not think anyone had ever before seen Lear in long johns – an image for which Aristotle's *Poetics* has not prepared us – nor had most of the audience ever imagined any but the tamest sort of unbuttoning. Lear is a grotesque figure at this point. In recognizing his own 'sophistication' and in casting his lot with poor Tom, the naked Bedlam beggar, he abandons the system of restraints and social deference represented by clothes. His stripping marks a new identification with those 'Poor naked wretches, whereso'er you are, / That bide the pelting of this pitiless storm' (3.4.28–9). How different is this knobby-kneed old man making imprecations against the cosmos in his underwear from the royal Lear of the opening scene.

Lear's speeches on the theme of nakedness[1] assume that clothes represent a corrupt social order based on the false appearances money can buy. While the tempest rages on the heath, he runs about 'bare-headed' (3.2.60) – 'unbonneted,' as a Gentleman calls it earlier (3.1.14). All thought of personal comfort or even decency has been replaced by a monomaniac sense of outrage:

> When the mind's free
> The body's delicate; this tempest in my mind
> Doth from my senses take all feeling else
> Save what beats there – filial ingratitude!   (3.4.11–14)

Lear is impervious to the outer weather; he cannot be broken by mere physical torment.

The king's prayer in the midst of the storm shows a new awareness of his role as the agent of divine justice:

> Poor naked wretches, whereso'er you are,
> That bide the pelting of this pitiless storm,
> How shall your houseless heads and unfed sides,
> Your loop'd and window'd raggedness, defend you
> From seasons such as these? O! I have ta'en
> Too little care of this. Take physic, Pomp;
> Expose thyself to feel what wretches feel,
> That thou mayst shake the superflux to them,
> And show the Heavens more just.   (3.4.28–36)

Pomp is the external display of majesty, but pomp must now 'Take physic,' or cure its own superfluity, in order to set a mean between itself and the 'loop'd and window'd raggedness' from which 'Poor naked wretches' suffer. This moral formulation parallels Gloucester's wish that 'distribution should undo excess, / And each man have enough' (4.1.70–1). Nakedness symbolizes the claims of 'unaccommodated man' (3.4.109), of whom Lear has 'ta'en / Too little care.' In one sense, act 3, scene 4 develops more radically the theme of the education of a sovereign that Shakespeare sketched in *Measure for Measure*.

Lear's encounter with Edgar disguised as poor Tom brings the argument about nakedness to its climax in the stage action. There is an urgency here that goes beyond what can be expressed in words:

> Thou wert better in a grave than to answer with thy uncover'd body
> this extremity of the skies. Is man no more than this? Consider him
> well. Thou ow'st the worm no silk, the beast no hide, the sheep no wool,
> the cat no perfume. Ha! here's three on's are sophisticated; thou art the

thing itself; unaccommodated man is no more but such a poor, bare, forked animal as thou art. Off, off, you lendings! Come; unbutton here.   (3.4.103–12)

Although exposed to the weather, poor Tom is a free man who owes nature no debt for the superfluities of civilized life: the fine cloth spun by the silkworm, the perfume from the civet cat's genitals, or even the cow's leather or the sheep's wool. He is a noble savage, independent and true to the integrity of his own being. Compared with the Bedlam beggar, Lear, Kent, and the Fool are all 'sophisticated,' or adulterated, but in this context of civilization and its discontents, 'sophisticated' also connotes false urbanity, a veneer of worldly wisdom, next to which poor Tom is the representative natural man, 'the thing itself.' If man in a state of nature is 'a poor, bare, forked animal,' clothes are mere 'lendings' that offer no defence against the tempest. Only a naked man can survive on the heath.

In his madness Lear accommodates himself to life on the heath as if he were a native wild man or gymnosophist.[2] Cordelia describes her father in his faun-like, if not bacchic, progress through the fields:

> singing aloud;
> Crown'd with rank fumiter and furrow-weeds,
> With hardocks, hemlock, nettles, cuckoo-flowers,
> Darnel, and all the idle weeds that grow
> In our sustaining corn.   (4.4.2–6)

The garlands of common weeds and wildflowers associate Lear with the mad Ophelia, and both have that mysterious communion with nature denied to those in their right wits. When Lear enters in act 4, scene 6 for his encounter with the blind Gloucester, he is presumably 'fantastically dressed with wild flowers' (80 sd), as Capell interprets the Quarto I direction: 'Enter Lear mad.' In this frenzied scene Lear is preoccupied with the themes of sex and justice, and he speaks with the imaginative energy and lyric free-association that characterize the Elizabethan 'mad' style.

Everywhere ceremonial usages and the robes and titles of one's function conceal the naked truth. Lear's imperatives conjure up scenes of violent duplicity:

> Thou rascal beadle, hold thy bloody hand!
> Why dost thou lash that whore? Strip thine own back;
> Thou hotly lusts to use her in that kind
> For which thou whipp'st her. The usurer hangs the cozener.
> Thorough tatter'd clothes small vices do appear;
> Robes and furr'd gowns hide all.   (4.6.162–7)

'Robes and furr'd gowns' suggest the costume of the 'robed man of justice' (3.6.37), as poor Tom was earlier represented. In the clothes-morality on which fashionable society is based, nakedness makes one vulnerable, because 'small vices do appear' through ragged tatters, whereas 'Robes and furr'd gowns' can mask inner rottenness. The sadistic beadle sins against the law of love, for which he must atone in kind: 'Strip thine own back' and be whipped for lustful thoughts. The intensity of Lear's indignation is measured by his own previous indifference to the ways of the world: 'O! I have ta'en / Too little care of this' (3.4.32–3). Lear's speech to Gloucester ends with another attempt to strip off the last remnants of his civilized 'lendings': 'Pull off my boots; harder, harder; so' (4.6.175).

The old king's return from madness is expressed by costume. In the care of Cordelia, he is no longer the naked madman crowned with wildflowers of the previous scenes. He enters *in a chair carried by Servants* (4.7.20 sd), and we notice immediately what the anonymous Gentleman tells us: 'in the heaviness of sleep / We put fresh garments on him' (21–2). Stage tradition gives Lear a loosely flowing white robe at this point, something like the *candidatus*, or gown of humility, in which both Coriolanus and Titus Andronicus solicit the votes of the people. Lear's 'fresh garments' are part of his cure, and he needs to recognize what they are before he can re-establish his identity: 'all the skill I have / Remembers not these garments' (66–7).

But the cure is never complete, and Lear can never take up his former status. He has gone too far in the pursuit of the naked truth to return to the royal robes and crown of the opening scene. At the very end of the play, he is still thinking of the constriction of his clothes: 'Pray you, undo this button: thank you, Sir' (5.3.309). As in the scenes on the heath, Lear remains 'unaccommodated,' and his death seems the only possible fulfilment for him. His prophecy in an early scene cannot be realized:

> Thou shalt find
> That I'll resume the shape which thou dost think
> I have cast off for ever. (1.4.317–19)

'Shape' is a theatrical term, meaning the whole make-up and appearance demanded by a specific role, but Lear has indeed cast off his shape for ever. In the corrupt society of the play, he can return neither as ruler nor as subject.

Renaissance symbolism makes nakedness the most important symbolic attribute of truth.[3] *Nuda Veritas*, the naked goddess, is without pretence, disguise, or duplicity. 'As naked as Truth' is a proverbial simile,[4] and it appears often in Shakespeare as a moral formula. In *1 Henry vi*, Richard Plantagenet declares:

> The truth appears so naked on my side
> That any purblind eye may find it out. (2.4.20–1)[5]

This is like the exchange in *Timon of Athens*, where the glozing Poet protests that he 'cannot cover / The monstrous bulk of this ingratitude / With any size of words' (5.1.62–4), but Timon asserts the moral commonplace that honesty needs no outward display: 'Let it go naked: men may see't the better' (65). In *Love's Labour's Lost*, Don Armado puns on 'naked' in a literal and figurative sense: 'The naked truth of it is: I have no shirt' (5.2.697–8). This sort of wordplay has ironic overtones in Hamlet's letter to the king: 'High and Mighty. You shall know I am set naked on your kingdom' (4.7.42–3). 'Naked' means unclothed and unprovided, but it also suggests an innocent defencelessness that may be set against Claudius' treachery. Truth is also the daughter and handmaiden of Time,[6] and, as Cordelia puts the emblematic maxim: 'Time shall unfold what plighted cunning hides' (1.1.280). For 'plighted' Quarto 1 reads 'pleated,' which fits even better into the costume symbolism: truth strips away the draped and pleated robe that cunning wears.

The nakedness-clothes theme is a moral polarity, in which the truth of nakedness is contrasted with the false appearances created by clothes. At the very beginning of the play, Lear conveys in a clothes image his 'darker purpose' (1.1.36) to abdicate the throne, as if it were a way of undoing the coronation ceremony: 'now we will divest us both of rule, / Interest of territory, cares of state' (49–50). Lear will 'divest' himself in order to 'invest' Goneril and Regan and their husbands

> jointly with my power,
> Pre-eminence, and all the large effects
> That troop with majesty. (1.1.130–2)

The power of the kingdom can be conferred by its external tokens, so that the old father-king may 'Unburthen'd crawl toward death' (41). Later in the scene, France demands to know how Cordelia

> should in this trice of time
> Commit a thing so monstrous, to dismantle
> So many folds of favour. (1.1.216–18)

The imagery is still in the courtly mode, but 'folds of favour' suggests the deception and fickleness of royal patronage that we have just witnessed. Cordelia's exit speech in this scene makes the essential moral comment on the clothes imagery:

> Time shall unfold what plighted cunning hides;
> Who covers faults, at last with shame derides.   (1.1.280–1)

The pairing of 'divest' and 'invest,' 'folds' and 'unfold' stresses the moral symmetries that are at issue in the first scene. In this most typical image, clothes represent illusion triumphing over reality, false appearances deceiving our common sense.

The simple dualism of the nakedness-clothes imagery can be brought home to the audience by costume. Shakespeare constantly deprecates overdressed persons, or at least those guilty of 'bravery,' an excessive concern with outward show. In *Henry V*, we know that the gallantly dressed French are doomed to defeat, and in *The Tempest*, Caliban and his drunken crew are caught with the bait of *'glistering apparel'* (4.1.193 sd). The satirical associations of dressing up are not emphasized in *King Lear*, yet there are some strong implications. Lear's passionate 'reason not the need' speech, for example, contains an incidental portrait of Regan, chicly but scantily clad at the very moment when the *'Storm and Tempest'* are about to begin:

> Thou art a lady;
> If only to go warm were gorgeous,
> Why, nature needs not what thou gorgeous wear'st,
> Which scarcely keeps thee warm.   (2.4.269–72)

Regan proves she is a lady of fashion by not choosing clothes for warmth (or not, presumably, for their durability); gorgeousness 'Which scarcely keeps thee warm' is distinctly in the micro-miniskirt tradition. In his search for the meaning of 'true need' (272), Lear will finally be forced to abandon even this socially defined sense of the word. Man's minimal need turns out to be something much closer to the life of the beasts.

The treachery of Oswald, Goneril's steward, is also expressed in clothes imagery. He is Goneril's creature, and the scene with Kent puts a strong emphasis on his fastidiousness both in words and appearance. 'A tailor made thee' (2.2.55), says Kent in a proverbial phrase, and as the action has shown, Oswald 'wears a sword' – as if it were an article of apparel rather than defence. Through Kent's satirical diatribe runs a special concern with Oswald's unassailable self-love: he is a 'glass-gazing, super-serviceable, finical rogue' (16–

17) and a 'whoreson cullionly barber-monger' (33), or haunter of barbershops. For all the difference in social class, the steward is a fop like Osric in *Hamlet* (they are also associated by the phonetic resemblance of their names).

Curiously enough, Edgar in his disguise as poor Tom plays the role of a discarded servingman in a style that imitates Oswald. In answer to Lear's question, 'What hast thou been?' (3.4.84), Edgar relates his imaginary history: 'A servingman, proud in heart and mind; that curl'd my hair, wore gloves in my cap, serv'd the lust of my mistress' heart, and did the act of darkness with her' (85–8). Poor Tom concludes with a set of moral precepts drawn from clothing: 'Let not the creaking of shoes nor the rustling of silks betray thy poor heart to woman: keep thy foot out of brothels, thy hand out of plackets, thy pen from lenders' books, and defy the foul fiend' (95–9). There is irony in this precautionary tale of high life delivered by the naked Tom, but clothes have come to represent false enticements and glossy deceits. The mad Lear is probably still thinking of this imagery when he tells Edgar, 'You, sir, I entertain for one of my hundred; only I do not like the fashion of your garments: you will say they are Persian; but let them be chang'd' (3.6.80–3). Persian attire suggests the rare and costly fabrics of the East, an opulence beyond the capacity of even the most fashionable servant. The mad Lear sees poor Tom in a courtly perspective, but splendid or even ceremonial attire has now lost all its former meaning. On the heath, all the false appearances on which social life is predicated have been stripped away.

Besides the naked truth, nakedness has at least two other related symbols in *King Lear*: the naked babe and naked nature. The 'naked new-born babe' of *Macbeth* (1.7.21) is a familiar image of innocence and defencelessness, in which clothes serve as armour to shield one from the world. In the proverbial simile, 'As naked as they were born,'[7] naked may connote vulnerability. This imagery raises a teasing ambiguity about Lear's abdication. Does he resign his powers to his daughters and their husbands in order to become a child again, so that he may 'Unburthen'd crawl toward death' (1.1.41)? Or does he do it because he has actually entered the second childhood of dotage? At the end of the first scene, Goneril and Regan agree that their father is becoming senile. 'You see how full of changes his age is' (1.1.288), says Goneril, and she complains of his 'unruly waywardness' (298) – a specifically childish quality. Regan mentions his 'unconstant starts' (300), and the sisters act in collusion to treat their father with the tyrannical authority of parents over children. As Goneril tells Oswald, setting him on to punish her father,

> Old fools are babes again, and must be us'd
> With checks as flatteries, when they are seen abus'd.   (1.3.20–1)

Thus Lear becomes, almost from the beginning, a 'child-changed father' (4.7.17), which might mean a father who has been transformed into a child as well as a father whose children have become 'changelings' – switched or metamorphosed through the black arts of gypsies. Gloucester laments these moral reversals in his account of evil portents:

> Love cools, friendship falls off, brothers divide: in cities, mutinies; in countries, discord; in palaces, treason; and the bond crack'd 'twixt son and father. This villain of mine comes under the prediction; there's son against father: the King falls from bias of nature; there's father against child.   (1.2.110–17)

The reversal of traditional roles between parents and children is carried through in almost exactly matched plot parallels. One of the pernicious doctrines that Edmund attributes to his brother Edgar is: 'sons at perfect age, and fathers declin'd, the father should be as ward to the son, and the son manage his revenue' (1.2.72–4) – a sentiment that Goneril and Regan have already announced as their guiding principle.

The effect of these reversals is powerfully felt in the stage action when Lear kneels to Regan and ironically requests from her the minimum that might be due to a child:

> Dear daughter, I confess that I am old;
> Age is unnecessary: on my knees I beg
> That you'll vouchsafe me raiment, bed, and food.   (2.4.155–7)

We think of Lear's later kneeling to Cordelia, who is shamed by his guilty penitence:

> O! look upon me, Sir,
> And hold your hand in benediction o'er me.
> No, Sir, you must not kneel.   (4.7.57–9)

She will devote all her loving efforts to restore Lear to his rightful role of father. There are some interesting echoes of these kneelings in *Coriolanus*, where the intransigent son is temperamentally incapable of accepting his mother's kneeling to him:

> What's this?
> Your knees to me, to your corrected son?
> Then let the pebbles on the hungry beach
> Fillip the stars ...   (5.3.56–9)

Coriolanus's shock is a measure of the moral outrage of Lear's sub-
servience to Goneril and Regan.

As critics have noted, the Fool sustains the role of Cordelia while
she is absent from the stage, and he elicits from Lear a fatherly
tenderness and concern: 'Come on, my boy. How dost, my boy?
Art cold?' (3.2.68); 'In, boy; go first' (3.4.26). In many ways, poor
Tom also offers Lear the possibility of loving the son he has never
had. But the Fool insists on his prerogatives as a satirical, malcontent
railer. He is 'A bitter Fool' (1.4.142), who constantly twits Lear on
his irresponsible return to childhood, and who will not let him forget
that he deliberately chose to do so. Lear

> mad'st thy daughters thy mothers; for when thou gav'st them the rod
> and putt'st down thine own breeches,
> *Then they for sudden joy did weep,*
>   *And I for sorrow sung,*
> *That such a king should play bo-peep,*
>   *And go the fools among.* (1.4.179–85)

The gross image of Lear exposing his bare bottom to be whipped by
Goneril and Regan continues the humiliation of his fatherly role.
Like the naked babe, Lear's only birthright now is as a fool:

LEAR   Dost thou call me fool, boy?
FOOL   All thy other titles thou has given away; that thou wast born with.
    (1.4.154–6)

And the babe's intuitive wisdom understands the corruption of this
world: 'When we are born, we cry that we are come / To this great
stage of fools' (4.6.184–5).

Our third nakedness theme – naked nature – is radically different
from the optimistic assumptions of the naked truth and the naked
babe, since it derives from the ruined paradise created by man's fall.
After the fall, nature has become wild, illicit, chaotic, and caprici-
ously destructive, which prevents it from being so neatly dichoto-
mized as Danby would have us believe.[8] There are striking similarities between Edmund's 'Nature' and that of Lear; in both the appeal
is to powers beyond human comprehension or control, powers that
are associated with the lawless gratification of the will, especially
sexual licence. There is an exact verbal parallel between Edmund's
apostrophe: 'Thou, Nature, art my goddess' (1.2.1) and Lear's:
'Hear, Nature, hear! dear Goddess, hear!' (1.4.284). Lear goes on to
invoke against Goneril the powers of sterility and monstrous birth:

> Dry up in her the organs of increase,
> And from her derogate body never spring

> A babe to honour her! If she must teem,
> Create her child of spleen, that it may live
> And be a thwart disnatur'd torment to her! (1.4.288–92)

This is a baleful, 'disnatur'd' nature, in whose dynamism Lear participates by the very occasion of his curse. On the heath, Lear calls up the annihilating forces of primal nature to destroy not only human institutions, but also the seeds of all being:

> Blow, winds, and crack your cheeks! rage! blow!
> You cataracts and hurricanoes, spout
> Till you have drench'd our steeples, drown'd the cocks! (3.2.1–3)

>   And thou, all-shaking thunder,
> Strike flat the thick rotundity o' th' world!
> Crack Nature's moulds, all germens spill at once
> That makes ingrateful man! (3.2.6–9)

Whatever we may think about the magnitude of Lear's provocation, he is still invoking a vision of chaos that allies him with Edmund, Iago, Macbeth, and other Shakespearean villains.

We feel this link most strongly in the naturalism of sex, where man is a naked, lustful animal outside the workings of natural law. *King Lear* begins with Gloucester's libertinism, which is meant to account for both Gloucester and Edmund's fate. For the benefit of his repentant brother, Edgar works out the morality of his father's blinding:

> The Gods are just, and of our pleasant vices
> Make instruments to plague us;
> The dark and vicious place where thee he got
> Cost him his eyes. (5.3.170–3)

As the wheel of the plot comes 'full circle' (174), Shakespeare has to rely on the most simplified moral conventions, and he is also in a hurry to rehabilitate the villain Edmund. His role as bastard – the natural, independent, untrammelled man, like Philip Faulconbridge in *King John* – is crowned by the discovery of his own irresistible fascination: 'Yet Edmund was belov'd' (5.3.239). He makes this remarkable discovery right after the bodies of Goneril and Regan are brought in, whose deaths Edmund can only interpret as a tribute to his overpowering sex appeal: 'The one the other poison'd for my sake, / And after slew herself' (240–1).

In Lear's part, his sexual fantasy is unlocked by madness (as it is for Ophelia), and he now sees nature deprived of all protective restraints. Lust has become the law of nature:

> The wren goes to 't, and the small gilded fly
> Does lecher in my sight.
> Let copulation thrive; for Gloucester's bastard son
> Was kinder to his father than my daughters
> Got 'tween the lawful sheets. To 't, Luxury, pell-mell!   (4.6.115–19)

Animal instinct is the model for human impulse, which is no longer governed by reason, the image of God in man. When 'yond simp'ring dame' is stripped, 'The fitchew nor the soiled horse goes to't / With a more riotous appetite' (125–6). Respectability is only an outward show, and for Lear, the rampant sexuality that surrounds him is an image of man's bestial, diabolic urges:

> Down from the waist they are Centaurs,
> Though women all above:
> But to the girdle do the Gods inherit,
> Beneath is all the fiend's: there's hell, there's darkness,
> There is the sulphurous pit – burning, scalding,
> Stench, consumption; fie, fie, fie! pah, pah!   (4.6.126–31)

It is notable how closely the mad Lear recapitulates the role of poor Tom, including his preoccupation with the foul fiend. Lear is overwhelmed by the sulphurous stink of women in heat, which evokes a primary image of hell. This is the ultimate concealment of 'Robes and furr'd gowns' (167).

In Maynard Mack's recent appeal for a broader interpretation of the sources of *King Lear*, he cites various versions of the abasement of the proud king motif. 'In one common form of this archetype, the king comes from swimming or his bath to find his clothes and retainers gone. His role has been usurped by an angel sent from heaven to teach him, in the words of the Magnificat, that God humbles the proud and exalts the humble. In his nakedness, he finds that the evidence of his kingliness, indeed his whole identity, is gone.'[9] The king then sets about to find his clothes, which is the only way he can recover his kingship. This quest for one's proper clothes is not unlike Macbeth's symbolic search for clothes that will fit him, because his newly acquired royal garments are 'like a giant's robe / Upon a dwarfish thief' (5.2.21–2).[10]

In all of Shakespeare, and especially in *King Lear*, clothes represent the values of society, of the status quo, of an external, socially conceived morality, whereas nakedness is the traditional image of unadorned truth; of innocent and vulnerable babes, fools, and madmen; and also of a wild and bestial nature, untempered by law, kindness, or justice. There is an element of dream-like terror in nakedness, because one's clothes are familiar, warm, and protecting. To be naked is immediately to be in peril, to be adrift in the world of an unknown id. Symbolically, clothes represent one's identity, and it is only by first becoming naked that one can be reclothed and achieve a new identity. Tragic recognition always involves a stripping away of pretences, so that one may emerge from his agony, like Lear, with 'fresh garments.'

NOTES

1 See Robert Heilman *This Great Stage: Image and Structure in 'King Lear'* (Baton Rouge 1948) especially chap 3. See also Thelma Nelson Greenfiield, 'The Clothing Motif in *King Lear*,' *Shakespeare Quarterly* V (1954) 281–6; and Dean Frye, 'The Context of Lear's Unbuttoning,' *English Literary History* XXXII (1965) 17–31. Emily W. Leider's fascinating essay, 'Plainness of Style in *King Lear*,' *Shakespeare Quarterly* XXI (1970) 45–53, draws many of the same conclusions as I do about the play, but in relation to a 'naked' style.

2 See Richard Bernheimer *Wild Men in the Middle Ages* (Cambridge, Mass. 1952).

3 See Erwin Panofsky *Studies in Iconology* (New York 1962) 150–60, and Russell A. Fraser *Shakespeare's Poetics in Relation to 'King Lear'* (Nashville, Tenn. 1966) 110–12.

4 See Morris Palmer Tilley *A Dictionary of the Proverbs in England in the Sixteenth and Seventeenth Centuries* (Ann Arbor 1950) T561. See also T589: 'The Truth shows best being naked.'

5 Works of Shakespeare other than *King Lear* are quoted from the Tudor edition, ed. Peter Alexander (London 1951).

6 See Fritz Saxl, '*Veritas Filia Temporis*' in *Philosophy and History: Essays Presented to Ernst Cassirer* ed. Raymond Klibansky and H.J. Paton (London 1936) 197–222. See also Samuel C. Chew *The Virtues Reconciled* (Toronto 1947) chap 3.

7 See Tilley *Dictionary of the Proverbs* B137.

8 See John F. Danby *Shakespeare's Doctrine of Nature: A Study of 'King Lear'* (London 1961) especially Part I: 'The Two Natures.' G. Wilson Knight's chapter on 'The *Lear* Universe' in *The Wheel of Fire* (Cleveland, Ohio 1957) puts salutary emphasis on the 'primitive, animal power' and 'pagan ferocity in *Lear*' (183).

9 '*King Lear' in Our Time* (Berkeley 1965) 49

10 See Cleanth Brooks *The Well Wrought Urn* (New York 1947) chap 2.

the artist exploring the primitive King Lear

F.D. HOENIGER

THERE MAY ONCE HAVE BEEN a King Lear in ancient Britain after whom the city of Leicester was named, and perhaps he had three daughters. But the story about him which Shakespeare retells, both in the form in which he found it and the form into which he cast it, is highly unreal, utterly remote from any familiar history. King Lear lived, according to Tudor historians, at some vague time during the era of the Kings of Judea. Of the mocking prophecy which the Fool recites at the end of 3.2, he says that it will be made by Merlin, 'for I live before his time.' The events of the play are as unreal as its chronology: no king within reliably recorded history, we may be sure, ever performed as Lear does in the opening scene. Nor do we believe that any young sixteenth-century nobleman, cast out by his father, ever disguised himself as Tom of Bedlam – and it is difficult to think of Edgar's encounters with the mad king and his own blinded father as anything that could 'really' happen. And what of Gloucester's jump, on the level stage, from what he has been persuaded are the cliffs of Dover, that most improbable episode in any of Shakespeare's tragedies? By comparison with the world and action of *King Lear*, those of *Hamlet* and *Othello* seem very real. All the same, Shakespeare's *Lear* comes intensely home to us. This we know, as many before us have known it the world over. The utterly unreal becomes profoundly real.

I still remember how when I saw *King Lear* for the first time on the stage, I was intensely absorbed by it though I certainly did not understand what it was all about. I was fourteen. I had tried to read the play before the production but found it too difficult a task, yet I went to see it because it was, after all, by the great Shakespeare. I remember how overcome I was by an acute sense of strangeness and unreality mixed with awe, the latter no doubt encouraged by the majesty of Lear, by his white beard, and by the astonishing energy of the old man; and I remember feeling keenly that all this was important, that it had bearing on life, on my life, though I could hardly fathom why. To use another term, which I will come back to later, the play seemed to reach down to the very sources of the primitive, and at the same time hold some, however obscure, wisdom for the audience and me in the twentieth century. This sense of the primitive and profound reached its climax in the mad scenes of the third act, with Lear, the Fool, and Edgar, where the strangeness itself was awesome. It must, I think, have been an extraordinarily good production though I remember no details of it, no name of producer or actors. Lear's folly is not balanced by his majesty in every production: he should be 'royal Lear' in the first scene and royal still when he casts off his garments. Now, over thirty years later, my need to grapple with the strangeness and primitiveness of the play is as acute as ever. Like all great art, *King Lear* has a mysterious core beyond explanation which we yet strive to approach and to apprehend more closely. But with *King Lear* this urge is particularly strong in our time, perhaps because modern man has experienced with a new intensity both the lure and the terror of the primitive. Can it be that the play has become even more vitally relevant to us than it was to previous generations?

In the opening paragraphs I have used the terms 'unreal' and 'primitive,' and the reader may well wonder in what sense or senses I use the term 'primitive.' It is part of this essay's strategy to leave the word's connotations and reverberations to the reader himself; at the moment he may want to involve even moral connotations, though my concluding section clearly points in a different direction. So far, I have suggested that the term fits not only the story of Lear as Shakespeare found it in his sources but also, in far wider connotations, the immense play which Shakespeare developed from it.

As we read the story of King Lear or Leir, apparently first written by Geoffrey of Monmouth in 1136, whence it reached the authors of *A Mirror for Magistrates*, Spenser, Holinshed, and the anonymous third-rate dramatist of *The Chronicle History of King Leir*, we realize that we are not reading history in the modern sense at all, but versions of the same simple story. Whether Holinshed believed his account of Lear to be factually true does not much matter. What is important is that Shakespeare in *King Lear* is not in the least concerned with history, but with his redramatization and reinterpretation of an old story. In his history plays we know that Shakespeare sometimes took great liberties with historical facts, for instance by making Hal and Hotspur of roughly the same age. Yet essentially *1 Henry* IV is a history play, while *King Lear* is not what the Quarto title suggests, a chronicle-history, but the dramatization of what Ben Jonson called, referring to *Pericles*, 'a mouldy tale.' Some critics have questioned the Shakespearean authorship of the Fool's prophecy in *King Lear* at the end of 3.2, regarding it as a later actor's interpolation; but while it may make its point with a bluntness that does not suit the subtlety of the Fool's characterization in the rest of the play, his joke about the prophecy that 'Merlin shall make' amounts to Shakespeare winking at his audience: 'we all know by now, don't we, that whatever this play is, it is not a chronicle history.'

Further, it is by no means certain that Shakespeare first became acquainted with the Lear tale through his reading. We cannot be certain that he first heard it told over a winter's fire by his mother or a grandam, by a friend or schoolmaster, but this seems to me highly probable, once we associate the following facts and considerations: Geoffrey of Monmouth surely did not invent all or even most of his chronicle history of ancient Britain, but wrote down what had been passed on from mouth to mouth; a ballad based on the Lear story from the seventeenth or eighteenth century has survived; folk tales of the story of a king and his three daughters, in many versions, have been told in many parts of the world for centuries, and are still told today in some parts of Sicily and Latin America; no English folk tale of the Lear story from any age has survived, but if none from the Middle Ages passed down to Elizabethan England, then it is highly probable that the very story so often repeated in chronicles and poems of the time gave rise to oral or folk versions. Is it unreasonable to conjecture that almost every Englishman of Shakespeare's time, whether he read widely or could not read at all, knew the tale of Lear and his three daughters? And if that is granted, then the likelihood is strong that Shakespeare became acquainted with the story early in his life, long before he came to read Holinshed. The first version of the story that Shakespeare heard, it seems probable, was either a folk tale that had been passed from mouth to mouth for generations, or a more recent tale derived from literary sources. In either case, the version would have been a simple, unsophisticated, pure story. If I am right about this, then the significance does not depend on the precise version that Shakespeare may have heard; that may have been quite close to the version in the *Mirror for Magistrates* or in Holinshed, or it may have taken the moralizing form, directed to children, familiar in many parts of Europe: Cordelia answers her father's question with 'I love you as much as salt.' Some time after Lear has been cast out by his elder daughters, he is discovered by Cordelia's soldiers wandering about in rags, is dressed again in royal garments, and is invited to a banquet where magnificent dishes are served, but without salt. And so Lear, and through him the children listening to the story, learn the simple moral. What matters is not whether Shakespeare became first acquainted with that version or one closer to Holinshed's chronicle, but that he thought of the story as an old tale of the folk about primitive Britain.

As his imagination dwelt on it for his play, it penetrated, as I will argue later, into the very origins of the story of the deep past. At present I wish to enlarge on the point previously made: that it is not just the kind of story which Shakespeare chose to dramatize, with its obscure setting in pre-Roman, pre-Christian Britain, that accounts for those elements in the play that seem so 'primitive' to us. Shakespeare reinforced those elements in several ways, one of which was by bringing the major characters very close to nature. Take Lear himself: in his most intimate scenes in the first half of the play, Lear is in the company of his natural, his Fool. Near the end of the scene in act 2 with Goneril and Regan, when the propriety of his keeping even a single retainer is questioned, he explains:

> Allow not nature more than nature needs,
> Man's life is cheap as beast's. (2.4.268–9)

We are aware, though, that Lear has not yet learned from nature, that he does not yet know what his own 'nature' needs most. We begin to sense the complex intermingling of the meanings of the word 'nature,' as Lear rushes out into nature at its most inhospitable, into the storm on the heath. There he meets Edgar, the 'natural philosopher,' of whom he asks, among other things, 'the cause of thunder.' In these gaunt surroundings, Lear learns slowly and fitfully. It is not the storm in nature that drives him mad, but the storm in his mind, produced by his sense (so frequently commented on by the Fool) that the world has been turned upside-down, and by his awareness of his own folly, of ingratitude and injustice, of the daughters' cruel exercise of power against their own kin. His exposure and suffering teach him his kinship to 'Poor naked wretches' and to Edgar-Tom, although his own self-concern makes him believe that only Tom's *daughters*, never his father, could have brought him to such a pass. Lear learns about 'unaccommodated man' whose 'life is cheap as beast's.' He learns that he is not ague-proof. When he is later awakened from his madness in Cordelia's presence, his experience has prepared him for this encounter, so that he knows at last that his real need is for love, not for power.

In the play, Lear begins by taking it for granted that his power is absolute – which means not merely that he can do anything he wishes in his state, but that he can control even love and nature. I need not comment here on his illusion that love is subject to power, but only on his illusion, which persists until the middle of the play, that he has power over nature. When thwarted in his plan by Cordelia in act 1, he swears:

> For, by the sacred radiance of the sun,
> The mysteries of Hecate and the night,
> By all the operation of the orbs
> From whom we do exist and cease to be,
> Here I disclaim – (1.1.109–13)

all sorts of things, including propinquity and property of blood, with the ironic conclusion that 'The barbarous Scythian, / Or he that makes his generation messes / To gorge his appetite' (1.1.116–18) shall be as close to him as his 'sometime daughter.' It is not its cannibalism alone, but the sheer, crude assertion of power, that makes this speech so fundamentally primitive. One might object that the speech is merely naïve, that very soon we will see Lear powerless and beginning to face his folly, and that blind assertions of power are not confined to primitive men. But we must perceive that one of the basic causes of Lear's blindness is that as king he assumes that he is also a magician: that not only his subjects but also the sun and the orbs, 'The mysteries of Hecate and the night,' will follow his bidding.

Later in act 1, after his experience with Goneril, Lear invokes the goddess Nature:

> Suspend thy purpose, if thou didst intend
> To make this creature fruitful!
> Into her womb convey sterility! (1.4.285–7)

Nowadays when a man tries to exercise such power, he does not invoke 'Goddess Nature,' he applies it directly – the difference, really, between an age of black magic and an age of black science. In 3.2, on the heath, Lear still believes that he can command the thunder, even to 'Crack Nature's moulds.' But as Lear is brought closer to nature itself, this attitude gradually disappears. The primitivism of his mind has started a series of reactions, culminating in Lear's reduction to a totally primitive state of body and mind, where he must learn painfully what nature and human nature are really like.

For this aspect of the theme of nature, Shakespeare found hardly a hint in his sources, and it is pertinent that this view of nature informs the subplot of Gloucester, Edmund, and Edgar as much as it does the main plot. It is often said that the subplot, with its parallel action to the main plot, helps us accept the Lear plot because its characters are closer to average experience; that Lear and his daughters belong in ancient Britain, while Gloucester and his sons are somehow Elizabethan. This may be so, up to a point, but, as I stressed at the very opening of this essay, improbabilities dictate the action of the subplot characters quite as much as those of the main plot. Moreover what I have called 'the primitive' involves them deeply, too. Gloucester has a primitive's superstition, as is clear from his speech on 'These late eclipses,' as well as from his ready acceptance of Edgar's contrived miracle at Dover – that a fiend lured him to commit suicide but that 'the clearest Gods' (note the plural) preserved him. Edmund is, like Lear, a worshipper of power; significantly enough, he too is given a speech on goddess Nature:

> Thou, Nature, art my goddess; to thy law
> My services are bound.   (1.2.1–2)

What is that law? It is a law that frees him from what he calls 'the plague of custom' and 'The curiosity of nations,' by which others are bound. 'Custom' amounts to the laws of human society. 'Curiosity of nations' Kittredge has glossed as 'The nice distinctions which the laws of nations make in defiance of nature and common sense' – by which he meant Edmund's interpretation of nature and Edmund's view of common sense. He himself was created, Edmund says, 'in the lusty stealth of nature,' and he asks the gods (for Nature is only one of the gods in his world, as in Lear's) to 'stand up for bastards.' More, he asks 'the gods' to allow him to triumph by his wits and his strength. In other words, Edmund's goddess Nature presides over the jungle where only the strong and crafty can survive. Edmund will apply the laws of the lion and the fox, exercising thereby absolute power for himself alone. What this amounts to is a variation on Lear's blind worship of power, one equally primitive but, paradoxically, also more obviously modern. I say 'more obviously modern,' since Edmund is a representative of the new man in the Jacobean age whose descendants flourish among us, but we have also seen men in our century whose blind trust in their absolute power reminds us more of Lear. In our age of power acquired with the help of machines devised by science, magic has made itself felt by entering through the back door. Drugs have magic attributes by which they can even transform human nature.

But Shakespeare's most interesting treatment of nature and the primitive in the subplot involves Edmund's first victim, his brother Edgar. With Gloucester's help, Edmund's actions reduce Edgar to a primitive condition; and as if this were of itself not enough, Edgar grotesquely selects his shape and place in society as a disguised outcast from that society in such a way as to make his condition seem even *more* primitive than it objectively is. The disguise he chooses for himself is that of Bedlam beggar, that is to say, he presents himself not only as self-deprived of all human possessions, but also as a natural, a man not in thorough control of his wits but innocent enough, like the Fool, to be allowed his freedom. Here is a response to injustice and tyranny that is remarkably unfamiliar in this present-day world, in the West at least, whatever the Edgar-like garments donned by youngsters of rich families on our main streets. The place to which Edgar retires as Tom is barren nature, the heath. There, as he says in his monologue, he will

> take the basest and most poorest shape
> That ever penury, in contempt of man,
> Brought near to beast. (2.3.7–9)

This 'baseness' that Edgar assumes is in counterpoint to Edmund's reaction to the 'baseness' of his bastardy, and it prefigures as well the condition to which Lear is brought. As Edgar says, he will 'with presented nakedness outface / The winds and persecutions of the sky' (2.3.11–12), and will strike in his 'numb'd and mortified bare arms / Pins, wooden pricks, nails, sprigs of rosemary' (15–16). Later, in a terrifying emblem of these words, Lear will seek for re-assurance that the world to which he awakes in Cordelia's presence is real: 'let's see; / I feel this pin prick' (4.7.55–6).

Important as all this is to interlink the various disparate parts of the play, it is not all there is to Edgar's adopted role. On the heath, he pretends to believe that the foul fiend follows and possesses him, and he performs his possession-act so convincingly that the Fool runs from him, shouting 'here's a spirit. / Help me! help me!' (3.4.39–40). Nor is the Fool the only one in the play to believe in fiends: when Edgar changes his role after Gloucester's imagined fall at Dover, he persuades him that 'poor Tom' was none other than a fiend.

> As I stood here below methought his eyes
> Were two full moons; he had a thousand noses,
> Horns whelk'd and wav'd like the enridged sea:
> It was some fiend.   (4.6.69–72)

But this is all an act: we know very well, just as Edgar does, who are the real fiends in this play.

In giving Edgar the role of enforced primitive and natural, Shakespeare made him react in an extreme but entirely logical way to the blows he must endure from the differently primitive world about him. It is only one step from Gloucester's gods and from Lear's and Edmund's goddess Nature, both linked to the exercise of bare unmitigated power, to the belief that a man can be possessed by fiends. Driven into a barren nature, Lear too becomes a natural, a madman. Edgar, the other outcast, goes of his own will into the same inhospitable nature, there to take on the role of a natural haunted by fiends. It is a measure of Lear's growing insight that he sees through that mime of possession, and turns to Edgar for counsel as his 'natural philosopher,' for Edgar's insights into both man and nature have by then begun to make him indeed the play's 'philosopher.'

I have said that in seeking refuge as a victim of power, Edgar's instinct makes him assume a role and a place which anticipate Lear's role and place after he flees from his daughters, that is, a madman's, exposed to barren nature and its fierce storm. Judging by the naïveté with which he falls into Edmund's trap early in the play, Edgar like Lear has much to learn about the world he inhabits. His experience during his stay in primitive nature is, in at least three ways, different from Lear's. First, though he is like Lear in being one of power's victims, he is a young man who has never exercised power, as Lear has. Second, Edgar only acts the role of natural or madman, though in doing so he shows an extraordinary understanding of the madman's mind, while in direct touch with the Fool and with Lear himself, then going mad. Third, far more acutely than Lear, Edgar is distracted from his personal suffering by experiencing the havoc which suffering has played with others – and knows these others to be no ordinary men, but his king and his

father. Edgar recognizes the plight of others; it is an important
part of Lear's experience, too, that he becomes aware of the suffering, first of his Fool, then of poor naked wretches like the Tom he
meets on the heath, then of what 'his daughters' have done to Tom-
Edgar, and, later, of what blindness, lust, and the brutality of others
have done to Gloucester. Since his mind is far too preoccupied with
himself, Lear's outgoing sympathy toward them comes only in
brief snatches. Sleep, medicine, music, and Cordelia's love are
needed to rescue Lear from his descent into the primitive world of
chaos which we recognize as both his own disordered mind and his
recognition of the disorder about him. Edgar, on the other hand,
first learns how to endure 'worse,' then the worst – by which he is
roused to action. He rescues his father from despair; he casts off
his role of poor Tom, the natural; he slays the villainous Oswald:
but all these deeds he does still in disguise. Only after successfully
asserting the integrity of his name in his challenge to Edmund does
he reveal himself.

Now, as Edgar is shown to undergo these stages of development
and to realize himself through action, we in the audience experience
a like uplift, for we are more and more drawn to identify ourselves
with Edgar. Not with Edgar only, of course, for we have come to
identify with Lear as well, as he endures and changes, in the process
never entirely losing his royal integrity. How important a part of
Lear's need that integrity is, Cordelia well knows. In the scene of
their reunion she enquires: 'How does my *royal* Lord? How fares
your Majesty?' (4.7.44). Shortly before his end, with Cordelia dead
in his arms, Lear still exclaims:

> A plague upon you, murderers, traitors all!
> I might have sav'd her ...
> I kill'd the slave that was a-hanging thee.   (5.3.269–70, 274)

Upon acknowledgment by the officer, he says,

> Did I not, fellow?
> I have seen the day, with my good biting falchion
> I would have made them skip.   (5.3.275–7)

With Edgar, we endure the worst that the world of *King Lear* has
in store. We rise with Edgar from the descent into nature and the
primitive, and we reach with him, as we do with Lear, a new sense
and assertion of integrity. The ending of the play departs sharply
from that of the folk tale; the world at the end of the play is no
longer primitive. After Lear departs, Edgar (at least in the more
reliable Folio text) is fittingly given the last speech.

Basically what I have so far tried to show is first that the story which reached Shakespeare was not only primitive in its setting but also primitive in origin; second, that in transforming the simple story into a complex and powerful drama, he explored the primitive in all its depths and terror, as the story in the form it reached him certainly did not, but leaves us in the end (again quite unlike the story) with Edgar, Kent, and Albany as the civilized witnesses to the conclusion of a stark tragedy. The heath in the storm with its hovel; Lear, the Fool, and Edgar as outcasts enduring it by probing the deepest recesses of their minds, even to madness; interrupted by scenes of crazy power leading up to the episode of the gouging out of Gloucester's eyes by Cornwall: that is a primitive world entirely of Shakespeare's creation.

Creation certainly, but, amazingly enough, also recreation. So at least I will argue in the concluding section of this essay. The sense of story rather than history in the play seldom leaves us, as I said earlier, and the hypothesis that will now be developed is reconcilable with Maynard Mack's interesting suggestion that the play has many archetypal elements of a folktale – the play as it is, not merely its source.[1]

About forty years ago, the Italian ethnologist Giuseppe Cocchiara collected versions of the Lear folktale from many different countries; in his book[2] (which hardly any Shakespeare scholar seems to have looked at), after narrating many versions, Cocchiara developed a thesis of the primitive origins and meanings of the tale. He argues that the Lear story is related to other stories of fathers and banished children, sometimes daughters, sometimes sons, and that these stories all have their ultimate origin in tribal initiation rites. The book is written in Italian, and copies of it are hard to find; I came upon one by accident in the Widener Library at Harvard. Cocchiara was no Shakespearean scholar and only barely mentions the existence of the play, and his subject, initiation rites, is calculated to make most Shakespeareans say, 'oh, that nonsense again.' But as a student of Shakespeare reads his book, he cannot help noticing features in some of Cocchiara's retellings common to those folk tales and King Lear; even when the parallels are not precise, they suggest things in the play which are not found in any of Shakespeare's known literary sources.

The first striking point is that Cocchiara insists upon a close family resemblance between versions of the Lear story and folk tales that deal with fathers and their good and evil sons;[3] for Shakespeare chose to combine two such stories in King Lear. The kinship between these two kinds of folk tales is supported by the

existence of occasional versions of the Lear tale with both daughters and a son, as Cocchiara points out. The majority of the Lear-
type tales collected in this volume include the moral point about
the value of salt, mentioned earlier. But what are we to make of
the version from Corsica which Cocchiara narrates as follows?

> The demand the father makes of his daughters to know how much
> they love him is changed. And so the heroine replies: 'Only as much
> as a devoted daughter can and should love her father.' Banished from
> the house, taking with her only her embroidered clothes, the heroine
> encounters on the road a dead ass whose skin she takes, and thus
> disguised, she is employed in the home of a nobleman. One day,
> nostalgia for her own home overtakes her; she guides her flock into
> a secluded place and dresses herself in her old garments. Suddenly
> she is discovered by the king's son, but she flees, leaving behind a shoe
> that fits only her. [On being caught,] she is asked to marry [the
> prince] but will not consent without first seeing her father again.
> Messengers sent to the other kingdoms find that his remaining chil-
> dren have imprisoned him in an underground cell, into which no one
> can penetrate and where he is almost mad. His throne regained and
> the other children, a male and a female, banished, the king takes part
> in the marriage of the heroine, whose care restores him to his reason.[4]

For the Shakespearean, the most remarkable aspect of this tale is
that it dwells on the king's madness and that the heroine's care
'gives him back his reason.' A second element, which the story
shares only with Shakespeare's play and not with his acknowledged
sources, is the motif of disguise assumed by the banished person,
although Shakespeare of course applies it to Kent and Edgar, not to
Cordelia. Much less, I think, should be made of the fact that the
heroine's disguise in the tale is an ass's skin, although this detail
suggests folly and the Fool, and animal and garment imagery plays
such an important part in *King Lear*. The themes of madness and
disguise are encountered in the Corsican tale and in Shakespeare,
but in no literary version that Shakespeare knew, unless Mack is
right in hinting that Shakespeare knew a version of the story of
King Robert of Sicily. As he points out, this story includes the
theme of madness and 'in the finest of all the retellings of this archetype, the repudiated king is not driven out but made the court Fool
and compelled to take his food with the palace dogs.'[5]

No other Lear-type story retold by Cocchiara is of quite the same
interest at this one, but two other versions deserve mention. In one,
from Cosenza, about a king of Turkey and his three daughters, the
king is abandoned by the elder daughters and left to wander about

without companions, 'blind, nothing remaining of him'. We note the parallel to the story of the Paphlagonian king in Sidney's *Arcadia*, the source of Shakespeare's subplot, where the king is similarly treated by his bastard son; but also how in Shakespeare's play the two elder daughters are directly implicated in Gloucester's blinding; it is Goneril who first suggests it – 'Pluck out his eyes' (3.7.5); and ironically, Gloucester, when forced to explain to Regan why he sent Lear to Dover, answers: 'Because I would not see thy cruel nails / Pluck out his poor old eyes.' (3.7.55–6). In the other tale, from Calabria, the abandoned king is thus described: 'the poor king, torn, with bleeding feet, his skin scratched by thorns, is reduced to sleeping in haystacks or in stalls with animals, or in shepherds' hovels made with branches.' Even though it is the motifs rather than their exact relation that strike us, we cannot help recalling Edgar's lines:

> Strike in their numb'd and mortified bare arms
> Pins, wooden pricks, nails, sprigs of rosemary;
> And with this horrible object, from low farms,
> Poor pelting villages, sheep-cotes, and mills ... (2.3.15–18)

as well as Lear in 4.6, '*fantastically dressed with wild flowers*,' his speech on the 'Poor naked wretches,' the hovel and the heath, and the beast imagery of the mad scenes.

So far we seem to be on fairly safe ground, but Cocchiara takes a further step in his seventh chapter, where a mere literary critic untrained in ethnology fears to tread with him. Having found in many versions of this tale of an old king or father whose youngest daughter or son is banished the common theme of apparent death and rediscovery or revival, Cocchiara traces them back to initiation ritual among primitive tribes, specifically a ritual of puberty. In some of these initiation rites, boys are made to believe that they will either be swallowed up or otherwise killed by a phantom or demonic spirit, and afterward brought back to life. In others (for example from the west of Ceram), the ceremony itself takes place around a hovel in the depth of the forest. When the boys to be initiated have gathered in front of the hovel, the chief priest calls loudly to all the demons, and immediately a terrible uproar is heard from inside the hovel, made by men with bamboo trumpets who have secretly entered from behind. The women and children believe that demons are present, and are full of terror. The priest then enters the hovel, followed by each boy in turn; as soon as a boy has disappeared into the enclosure, a frightful cry is heard and a lance, dripping with blood, is thrown across the roof of the hovel. This causes the onlookers to believe that the boy's head, which the demon wants to carry into the subterranean world and transform, has been cut off. Can we help recalling Edgar in the hovel, haunted by the fiend, and the Fool's calling him 'a spirit,' when he finds Edgar inside?

To invoke initiation rites of primitive tribes in an essay on *King Lear* may seem preposterous, but let us look at Edgar's lines at the very end of the third scene on the heath:

> *Child Rowland to the dark tower came,*
> His word was still: *Fie, foh, and fum,*
> *I smell the blood of a British man.* (3.4.186–8)

In the Arden edition, Kenneth Muir warns us not to associate Rowland, who comes from a well-known ballad about Charlemagne's nephew, with the giant who cries 'fee, fie, foh, fum' in the story of Jack the Giant-Killer, for the giant's words are intentionally incongruous with the heroic Childe Rowland. Incongruous they are, of course; still, Harry Levin points to a more profound link between them: 'As the pair enters the hovel, Edgar's snatches of balladry and fairy-tale transform it into a legendary dark tower, where a young squire is undergoing a ritual of knightly initiation while nameless giants objurgate: "Fie, foh, and fum." '[6] There is a great distance between Levin's ritual of knightly initiation and Cocchiara's primitive rites, but both rites fundamentally involve initiation, and the one is clearly the origin of the other; furthermore, Edgar *does* become a knight. The squire is in a dark tower, the primitive boy at puberty in a hovel in a dark forest, and by his words, Edgar associates the two, metaphorically transforming the hovel into a dark tower.

The critical reader will find much to question in this material. But even if he rejects parts, the data point to some amazing correspondence between Shakespeare's play and folk tales and the rituals from which they may derive, correspondences which could hardly have been known to Shakespeare, even if he heard a version of this tale in his youth.[7] We have noted the parallels to the hovel in the wilderness and to fiends and giants, the hints in some versions of madness and blindness, the allusion to garments and animals, the use of disguise by a banished person, and the links between stories about fathers and a banished young man and those with a banished daughter. Because several of these motifs are very common, a single such correspondence might be dismissed as accidental; indeed hovels, madness, beasts, disguise, are all met in several other folk tales which may have influenced local versions of the Lear tale. Cumulatively, though, they suggest nothing less than that Shakespeare's imagination, dwelling on the significance of the Lear story and reshaping it into a play of profound dramatic impact, recaptured elements from the primitive past that at some time were a fundamental part of its shape and meaning.[8] Of course he not only recaptured, he transformed as well, to make of primitive horror and brutality the highest kind of art. To us in an age fearful that primitive forces might utterly overwhelm us, *King Lear* should be a work of very special meaning and some comfort.

NOTES

1 *'King Lear' in Our Time* (Berkeley 1965) 49–51
2 *La Leggenda di re Lear* (Studi di etnologia e folklore 1) (Torino 1932).
   I wish to acknowledge assistance from Miss Peggy Bridgland for reading a microfilm of Cocchiara and translating passages from Italian.
3 But Maynard Mack refers to a story of a king and his two brothers who, when the king travels to them seeking assistance, fail to recognize him (49,n4).
4 Translated from Cocchiara, who found the tale in J.B. Ortoli *Les contes populaires de l'ile de Corse* (Paris 1883)
5 See note 1, above.
6 In his lecture on 'The Heights and the Depth: A Scene from *King Lear*' in *More Talking of Shakespeare* ed. John Garrett (New York 1959) 87–103
7 Though, again, see Maynard Mack.
8 I think we can safely say this even though we have no evidence that a folk tale of *Lear* as such existed long before Shakespeare's time.

SEVEN

W.F. BLISSETT recognition in KING LEAR

'WHAT ART THOU?' Lear asks, and the disguised Kent answers,
'A very honest-hearted fellow, and as poor as the King.' 'If thou
be'st as poor for a subject as he is for a King, thou are poor enough'
(1.4.19–23). We are still in the first act of the play; only about
one-seventh of the playing time of *King Lear* has elapsed, and already the protagonist is experiencing 'recognition' and the audience
is perceiving 'reversal of situation.' It is this fact (most unusual in
dramatic literature) and its bearing on the structure of the play and
on the phases of our response to it that I propose to discuss.

Everyone approaches this play with fear and trembling – actors
and producers, critics and teachers, readers and audiences. It is
hard enough to find some new way to humble oneself in the face
of it, let alone something new to say about it. However, a play
simply does not exist uncriticized or uninterpreted. And so I will
attempt a definite, limited thing: to consider 'recognition' in an
Aristotelian sense and its applicability to Shakespeare and particular bearing on *King Lear*; to look at the pace and process of
recognition in the play; to consider the difference in this respect

between the main plot and the subplot; and finally to contrast *King Lear* with another tragedy, *Othello*, in this one respect.

Aristotle defined tragedy not as an imitation of life in general or of one great person's life in particular but as an imitation of an action. His basic point, which is as elusive as it is obvious, is the primacy of action over character. It is clarified by the analogy suggested by Professor Elder Olson in a useful and lively book, *Tragedy and the Theory of Drama*: 'When an executive has a position to fill, the job is the first consideration, and the man to hire is second. If a given kind of work is to be done properly, he must have a man qualified to do it. Similarly, if certain actions are to happen in the plot, and to produce a given effect, a character must be invented or found who can perform them.'[1]

Being an imitation of an action, not of the persons doing the action, tragedy is under no obligation to account for 'empty time.' All the time on the tragic stage is filled by the action. This action comprises an initial error or erroneous self-commitment, that Aristotle calls *hamartia*; and the double consequence of this *hamartia* – the reversal of situation (or *peripeteia*) as experienced by the audience and the act of recognition (or *anagnorisis*) on the part of one or more of the actors, with its usually concomitant scene of suffering – completes the whole pattern of change of the play. Though Aristotle himself does not use the term except in the clarification of mistaken identity, it would seem that its meaning can be extended to apply to the realization of any relevant truth, most especially the realization by the protagonist of the erroneous basis of his conduct. If *hamartia* is freely rendered (somewhat barbarously, I regret) as a 'state of unrecognition,' it will be clear that *anagnorisis*, the 'act of recognition,' is its necessary consequence and complement. And at least we have avoided 'tragic flaw,' with all its penumbra of tedious moralization about how characters in tragedy should have conducted themselves so as, presumably, to have lived harmlessly and forever.

Recognition also mitigates suffering. Learning always has something of pleasure about it, and so, no matter how painful the realization, how destructive its outcome, there is thus an element of gain and growth, of less impeded function, present in it. Actor and audience move into a state of insight closed to them in common experience – an imaginative comprehension of suffering, loss, and death. Most theorizing about tragedy (including this) gives the impression of being heartless, since it cannot accomplish, only describe, what tragedy does. At worst, it echoes the words of Regan after Lear rushes out into the storm:

> O! Sir, to wilful men,
> The injuries that they themselves procure
> Must be their schoolmasters. Shut up your doors ... (2.4.304–6)

At its least obnoxious, 'in its flattest form,' the idea is present, says William Empson, 'if you think "it is very sad, but after all I am not really sorry it happened, because it teaches us so much." And the scapegoat who has collected all this wisdom for us is viewed at the end with a sort of hushed envy, not I think really because he has become wise but because the generally human desire for experience has been so glutted in him; he has been through everything and "we that are young / Shall never see so much, nor live so long." ' (5.3.325–6)[2] And so with these final words of Edgar's, we are back to *King Lear*.

I can think of no explosion of *hamartia* to equal that of its first scene. Gloucester's remarks about his bastard son are uncalled for and dangerously unperceptive enough, but from his first entrance Lear's errors are as much greater than Gloucester's as the king is more considerable than the earl in position and power, in presence and language. The division of the kingdom, the rejection of Cordelia, the banishment of Kent – what might have filled the opening third of a play – are despatched in a single scene. Lear may have waited until extreme old age to make these decisions, but he makes them here with such force as to obliterate all anterior action. The entire remainder of the play, as it concerns Lear, is discovery, recognition of what he has done and, beyond that, of who he is.

I must hasten to make two qualifications. Lear in the succeeding action proceeds to the place of understanding not by direct march but by an errant course, much as the play itself wanders across the kingdom. Often he repeats his initial error – dispensing spurious justice, raging and cursing as if he had power to punish or uncreate; but these subsequent errors are all contained within the initial one and are no more new actions than Macbeth's subsequent murders are separate from the murder of Duncan. The really new action for Lear is the long, protracted, magnificent unlearning of a lifetime of self-conceit and delusion.

The second qualification. The Gloucester plot, as Bradley well observed, is what keeps the play moving, and its shape, though roughly parallel to that of the Lear plot, is much more in line with usual dramatic practice. Recognition begins for Gloucester at the centre of the play: he learns of Edmund's treachery when his eyes are put out, and the fourth and fifth acts bring with them a descent into despair and an achievement of hope and reconciliation. It is mainly in terms of this plot that the time-honoured image of orderly reversal, the slow inexorable turning of the wheel, is used. The dying Edmund says, 'The wheel is come full circle; I am here' (5.3.174). Edgar, to whom he speaks, has concurrently risen to a share in the government of the island.

How different is this sentence of Lear's, also one of recognition:

Thou art a soul in bliss; but I am bound
Upon a wheel of fire, that mine own tears
Do scald like molten lead.   (4.7.46–8)

This is another kind of wheel – more painful as being an instrument of torture, yet strangely radiant as being luminous and seen by eyes having vision. It is not a rolling or a turning wheel but a stretching wheel: with pain it stretches Lear to the measure of a man.

I have anticipated most of what I plan to say, but a continued prowling round about the question may imitate what the play itself does. We are in a position now to consider the phases, or moments, or flashes of recognition in Lear during the play and to relate them to the action as it comes to be comprehended by the audience – that is, to treat them in terms of dramatic irony.

To lay down the burden of office in old age is not in itself a tragic error, nor is the division of property among one's children, if strict justice is observed as we are told is the case here. When that property is a kingdom, one may have misgivings, certainly if that kingdom is England; and yet it is hard to think of something else for an old king without male heir to do. Even the demand for a public profession of love is not altogether irrational in Lear or unbelievable to us: as Professor Olson says, 'if Lear is giving up his authority and still wants security and dignity, he can only trust to their love; and his insistence upon their public profession of it is an attempt to have it warranted and witnessed as a formal part of the compact of the delivery of property and power.'[3] However, in this last matter Lear himself betrays a sense of danger or fatality in referring to it as 'our darker purpose,' and with an irony that cannot be lost on his auditors on the stage or in the theatre he expresses his most over-reaching unrecognition in the language of recognition – 'while we / Unburthen'd crawl toward death' (1.1.40–1). This must be received with an embarrassed titter of deprecation by the other characters. We realize at once that it is no more a genuine renunciation of the world than a potlatch is genuine charity; Lear reaches toward death, but on his own terms, not the terms of death. This unregenerate royal priest will find that he cannot compose his soul by royal fiat. Divest or invest as he may, Lear holds fast to the will to power, and it roars

forth as soon as his purposes are crossed, in the rejection of Cordelia
and the banishment of Kent. In dividing the kingdom and making
demand upon his daughters' love Lear mistakes for renunciation the
self-glorifying aspect of suicide, and in the rejection of Cordelia and
of Kent he exhibits its malicious and punishing aspect. All further
'purposes' must really be dark, and Lear has nothing left to do but
'crawl toward death.' There can be no doubt of the destination of
the action when Cordelia says of the sisters, 'Time shall unfold what
plighted cunning hides' (1.1.280).

We are so used to hearing it stated, paradoxically, that the Fool
brings wisdom and insight, that it may come with paradoxical force
to state that the king from the beginning shows the greater wit and
penetration. Even before the Fool enters, Lear says to Kent, 'If thou
be'st as poor for a subject as he is for a King, thou art poor enough'
(1.4.22–3), and (describing what he is to do for the rest of his life) 'I
will look further into't' (1.4.74). When it is remarked that the Fool
has pined away since Cordelia's going to France, 'No more of that,'
he says: 'I have noted it well' (1.4.79). The Fool, when he appears,
talks of rents and fees, of power and rule, the things he never possessed, always as if they were supremely good, and yet proves his
folly by attaching himself to Lear, who has begun the process of
divestment of wordly goods. But it is Lear who is stung to understanding by such a barb as 'thou hast pared thy wit o' both sides, and
left nothing i'th'middle' (1.4.194–5). It is Lear and the audience, not
the Fool, who feel the ironic force of 'nothing' here. The king's
earlier reply, 'nothing can be made out of nothing' (138–9) – the
echo of his irate words to Cordelia, 'Nothing will come of nothing:
speak again,' – combines with the worldly man's sense of terror at
really losing the world he falsely believes he has renounced.

> Does any here know me? This is not Lear:
> Does Lear walk thus? speak thus? Where are his eyes?
> Either his notion weakens, his discernings
> Are lethargied – Ha! waking? 'tis not so.
> Who is it that can tell me who I am? (1.4.234–8)

The passage begins with an old man's display of irritation: it ends
with the crucial question of the play. The Fool's answer, 'Lear's
shadow,' is wiser than the initial question, Lear being in fact the
shadow of royal greatness. That insight makes the Fool an ironic
commentator; but surely the audience already, and Lear soon, will
far outstrip that insight; and the answer in full context can mean that
only Lear's shadow, only Lear as unaccommodated man, can tell
Lear who he is.

Unrecognition returns with a ferocity greater even than in the opening scene, now in the clash with Goneril. 'Are you our daughter?' (1.4.227) is an ignorant question since the asker does not properly know himself; 'Woe, that too late repents' (1.4.266) is as ignorant a comment – it is the message of the Fool without his wit, and it vulgarly mistakes regret for repentance. It is not repentance but culpable blindness at its most splendid and vicious that issues in the curse of Goneril, and here the audience outstrips Lear in understanding, for we have full ironic awareness of the anticlimax of the succeeding words and tears. 'Take the Fool with thee,' nuncle. But this great spirit moves nearer the repentance he missed when he says (surely) of Cordelia, 'I did her wrong' (1.5.24). The act ends with the Fool saying, 'Thou should'st not have been old till thou hadst been wise,' but it is Lear who can see with terror what wisdom will mean for him, for his answering line is, 'O! let me not be mad' (1.5.45–7). What is a hint at the end of the first act is explicit by the end of the second, when Lear storms out and

> Strives in his little world of man to out-storm
> The to-and-fro-conflicting wind and rain. (3.1.10–11)

The movement of the outward plot and the inner movement of Lear's mind are 'to-and-fro,' directionless except in the direction of greater intensity. Recognition came and continues to come in flashes between claps of thunder and torrents of rain. *Storm still.* But the original act of unrecognition is also repeated and intensified. Lear summons all the regal authority of which he has divested himself to command the elements to return to anarchy. The shouted words, their magnificent and defiant tone, ironically belie the apparent recognition in

> here I stand, your slave,
> A poor, infirm, weak, and despis'd old man. (3.2.19–20)

Thoughts of resignation attend him, but he turns them to covert *hubris*:

> No, I will be the pattern of all patience;
> I will say nothing – (3.2.37–8)

and to the exact opposite and negation of repentance:

> I am a man
> More sinn'd against than sinning. (3.2.59–60)

But the immediately following speech recovers what was lost and places Lear closer than he has yet come to the state of divestment and

mere humanity that he had chosen without full imaginative fore-
knowledge and foresuffering:

> My wits begin to turn.
> Come on, my boy. How dost, my boy? Art cold?
> I am cold myself. Where is this straw, my fellow?
> The art of our necessities is strange,
> And can make vile things precious. Come, your hovel.
> Poor Fool and knave, I have one part in my heart
> That's sorry yet for thee.   (3.2.67–73)

Necessity transmutes vile things into precious, but we are witnessing
a heavenlier alchemy in Lear's charitable concern for the Fool as
fellow creature.

The same circling of the storm is evident in the second scene on
the heath. To recognize 'this tempest in my mind' (3.4.12) is to
transcend it. 'I will punish home' (16), is a relapse, 'I will endure'
(18), a recovery; 'I'll pray, and then I'll sleep' (27), brings for a
moment the end in sight. In his mind Lear makes an act of charity
toward 'Poor naked wretches' and adds to it a specific confession
that he had been grievously at fault:

> I have ta'en
> Too little care of this.   (3.4.32–3)

Immediately poor Tom appears, and Lear sees as never before the
implications of his relinquishment of power and goods: 'unaccommodated man is no more but such a poor, bare, forked animal as
thou art' (3.4.109–10).

The last storm scene, with its arraignment of the sisters, takes us
to the eye of the hurricane: advance and regression, reason and madness, recognition and renewed acts of unrecognition, all unite to
produce an impasse expressed in Lear's answer to the Fool's question
– 'Prithee, Nuncle, tell me whether a madman be a gentleman or a
yeoman?' 'A King, a King!' (3.6.9–11). The knowledge that he is
mad sets Lear free; but at the same time he remains captive to the
regality that he has forfeited.

The dramatist's problem at this point is how to prevent the play
from dying when the storm blows itself out. Only a possible reconciliation with Cordelia and a certain death remain to Lear, both of
them reversals of situation too happy to contain without diminution
and anticlimax the expectations of the storm scenes. What is needed
is a strong and still-rising plot-interest and a revived dramatic irony
of the more usual kind, and both of these needs are supplied by the
Gloucester plot.

> Our flesh and blood, my lord, is grown so vile,
> That it doth hate what gets it.   (3.4.149–50)

To this easy generalization of the kindly Gloucester to Lear in the hovel, Edgar disguised as Tom o' Bedlam murmurs, 'Poor Tom's a-cold.' The carnal-minded man at this point is totally impercipient: he has everything to learn, and many things must simply happen before he can even begin. It has long been noted that the sufferings of Gloucester, for reasons of dramatic variety, must be of a different quality from those of Lear. Lear in the storm is magnificent: he and the audience would not miss a minute of it, and the Fool is a fool to try to moderate him. The blinding of Gloucester is in contrast as close to pure outrage and agony as the theatre can come. It occurs, we may observe, at much the same point in this play as the killing of Polonius in *Hamlet*. The contrast is instructive. Every spectator laughs from a sense of release when Hamlet shouts 'a rat? Dead, for a ducat,' and will chuckle gleefully when he says, 'I'll lug the guts into the neighbour room.' The remainder of the play travels the huge distance, for audience no less than for protagonist, between this state of mind and a readiness for a good death. In *King Lear*, Gloucester (an acting part not unlike Polonius) undergoes such pain that our nerve ends wince to recall it. There is a limit to pain, and we have crossed that threshold. In the prayer scene, the killing of Polonius, and the closet scene, Hamlet and his audience reach a total denial of fellow feeling, a full entry into the spirit of accusation; here, in most extreme contrast, when the vile jellies are dashed to the floor and stamped on, complete identification in sympathy is reached, without the slightest distancing. The steel-bright insensitivity of the satirist, which we enjoy in *Hamlet,* is seen here to be monstrous as Regan says, 'Go thrust him out at gates, and let him smell / His way to Dover' (3.7.92–3). In a line of strongest dramatic irony, Gloucester's first moment of blindness is his last – 'All dark and comfortless. Where's my son Edmund?' (84). Such a thing cannot be borne for long. See what happens before the scene is done:

> O my follies! Then Edgar was abus'd.
> Kind Gods, forgive me that, and prosper him!   (3.7.90–1)

Gloucester thus begins to learn the art of dying, and with recognition comes mitigation of pain. A servant says, 'I'll fetch some flax and whites of eggs / To apply to his bleeding face' (3.7.105–6) – a line that must never be cut, for it expresses simply what is done to the sensibilities of the audience in the rest of the play.

This terrible scene makes possible the whole remainder of the action. The encounter and reconciliation of Gloucester and Edgar become obligatory, so too the working out of the plot of the sisters and Edmund and the combat of the brothers; but more inwardly, it permits a further development of recognition in Lear, which had been held at an impasse in the storm scenes; and most important of all, it makes bearable the death of Cordelia and gives the distance of numbness to the final anguish of Lear.

We have observed that the Gloucester family thinks in terms of the wheel – the natural course of events, the cycle of nature, the wheel of fortune. Edmund, on stepping into his father's rights and title, says 'The younger rises when the old doth fall' (3.3.27). Edgar sees not worldly fortune but happiness and misery in the same image:

> The lamentable change is from the best;
> The worst returns to laughter,   (4.1.5–6)

and again,

>   O world!
> But that thy strange mutations make us hate thee,
> Life would not yield to age.   (4.1.10–12)

This last speech (in keeping with a recurrent device that we have been observing in the play) seems like recognition but proves ironic because the speaker has incompletely realized or incompletely felt what he is saying; for when, a moment later, his blinded father appears before him, Edgar exclaims:

>   the worst is not
> So long as we can say 'This is the worst.'   (4.1.27–8)

The wheel is greater than he had thought and in its revolution has deeper yet to go. Gloucester himself perhaps thinks of himself as falling from the wheel of fortune in that grotesque act of despair in the very presence of grace, in which he blesses Edgar as if he were absent, and finds out in the most physical way on Dover cliff that he has nowhere to fall to or fall from but his son's care. 'Thy life's a miracle,' Edgar says, on two levels of meaning, and Gloucester resolves:

>   henceforth I'll bear
> Affliction till it do cry out itself
> 'Enough, enough,' and die.   (4.6.75–7)

From that point affliction ends for him; for him are Edgar's words spoken of a providential cycle:

> Men must endure
> Their going hence, even as their coming hither:
> Ripeness is all.   (5.2.9–11)

Meanwhile reason rages in madness. The burden of simple pain being borne by Gloucester, whose bandages remind as they heal, Lear continues the rapid oscillation between renewed unrecognition and deeper recognition that has been observed in the storm scenes. No sooner has he realized that he is not ague-proof than he asserts himself to be 'every inch a king' (4.6.110), and from there he moves to the observation that 'A dog's obey'd in office' (161). 'I will die bravely,' he promises, but to forestall any ironic comment coming to our mind he adds with mad humorous delight, 'Like a smug bridegroom' (4.6.199–200).

A new phase of Lear's recognition occurs at the end of the fourth act. Here he achieves such an emptying of self, so perfect a reconciliation with Cordelia, here by the subtlest of quiet transitions consolation succeeds desolation, that one would think him ready for death and the audience ready to share in it imaginatively:

> You do me wrong to take me out o' th' grave;
> Thou art a soul in bliss; but I am bound
> Upon a wheel of fire, that mine own tears
> Do scald like molten lead.   (4.7.45–8)

The dramatist must keep this scene of pure recognition from so blazing up as to consume the remaining stuff of the play. Lear's strongest speech is the one just quoted. As he advances, he gropes, is illogical, inconsequential:

> I am a very foolish fond old man,
> Fourscore and upward, not an hour more or less;
> And, to deal plainly,
> I fear I am not in my perfect mind.   (4.7.60–3)

Recognition in drama typically comes to focus in the discovery of a person's identity; but what a tiny bright quiet focus this is:

> Do not laugh at me;
> For, as I am a man, I think this lady
> To be my child Cordelia.   (4.7.68–70)

And the end of royal self-delusion is likewise quiet:

> LEAR   Am I in France?
> KENT   In your own kingdom, Sir.
> LEAR   Do not abuse me.   (4.7.76–7)

At which the doctor comments, 'the great rage, / You see, is kill'd in him' (78–9).

But Lear is the sort of person who must make every possible mistake, and one enormous one remains to be made, the commission and expiation of which will enable the old, dying, defeated man to dominate the end of the play in the midst of battles and combats and resolutions of action. He and Cordelia are captured, and he says:

> Come, let's away to prison;
> We two alone will sing like birds i' th' cage:
> When thou dost ask me blessing, I'll kneel down,
> And ask of thee forgiveness: so we'll live,
> And pray, and sing, and tell old tales, and laugh
> At gilded butterflies, and hear poor rogues
> Talk of court news; and we'll talk with them too,
> Who loses and who wins; who's in, who's out;
> And take upon's the mystery of things,
> As if we were Gods' spies: and we'll wear out,
> In a wall'd prison, packs and sects of great ones
> That ebb and flow by th' moon.   (5.3.8–19)

The vision here of a resigned and contented existence is so beautiful and of so spiritual a beauty – Lear at last reconciled with Cordelia because at last worthy of her – that it seems graceless to find anything amiss; and yet the fact that the play could not conceivably end on this note makes closer examination necessary. Lear has one last, hidden, attachment to life: it is detachment, contentment of mind. He has not resigned the joys of resignation. Earlier he said, 'they told me I was every thing; 'tis a lie, I am not ague-proof' (4.6.106–8). Now he persuades himself that he and Cordelia in the world of Edmund and the sisters can take upon themselves the mystery of things and live retired. And that is not so: he has yet to suffer her death and his own.

'Nothing almost sees miracles, / But misery,' Kent said at the beginning of the troubles (2.2.165–6). Gloucester blind meeting Lear mad exclaimed:

> O ruin'd piece of Nature! This great world
> Shall so wear out to naught.   (4.6.136–7)

No mildness, no contentment, nothing short of the day of wrath can end the course of action Lear chose for himself: even as a bird in a cage he would smell of mortality. When Lear is at the point of death, Kent looks back over the initial intention and subsequent course of the action and asks, 'Is this the promis'd end?' And Edgar, more perceptive, thinks of the last day – 'Or image of that horror?' (5.3.263–4). And so I believe Lear's final 'Look there, look there!' is addressed to himself and to the audience and means, primarily, 'look upon death.' Kent's comment supports this reading:

> Vex not his ghost: O! let him pass; he hates him
> That would upon the rack of this tough world
> Stretch him out longer.   (5.3.313–15)

And it is significant that Edgar's final couplet assigns to Lear a supreme distinction among men in terms of recognition:

> we that are young
> Shall never see so much, nor live so long.   (5.3.325–6)

King Lear and *Othello* are adjacent plays of opposite structure and represent the two poles of tragic effect, at least in terms of the working out of dramatic irony in the audience and recognition in the protagonist. In *King Lear*, as we have observed, recognition begins almost at once and is spread over the widest possible dramatic field; so perfect is it at the end that it is not the protagonist but the spectators, in so far as they continue to cling to the life of the self, who are in ignorance of their true condition. In *Othello* recognition for the protagonist is postponed until (perhaps beyond) the latest possible moment, and everything said and done thereuntil is ironic. Spendthrift of passion though Othello becomes at the end, he cannot reach calm of mind: he has hardly begun to learn. If I were to choose two passages as keys to the final room of each play, I would take for *Lear*:

> O ruin'd piece of Nature! This great world
> Shall so wear out to naught,   (4.6.136–7)

and for *Othello*:

> Excellent wretch! Perdition catch my soul
> But I do love thee! and when I love thee not,
> Chaos is come again.   (3.3.90–2)

In both passages what is intended as a metaphor has a more reverberative meaning for the audience than for the speaker and so is ironic; but Gloucester comes close to realizing what he is saying, whereas Othello stands altogether in his own light.

Othello is always a separate, an alien person out there, not seeing anything that we see, and at the end he dies unhealed, in remorse. The irony becomes ever more sharp; the action takes place on stage, its pace dictated by Iago's plot. Lear for all his age and royalty and folly, which might be expected to distance him, is much more a piece with our inner experience, perhaps because there is not a blessed thing that he can do (like the audience), whereas Othello (unlike the audience) could reverse the plot at any moment. Lear comes to see *what* we see, and we come to see *as* he sees; at the end he dies healed and contrite, and we experience what a good death might be, though without any of its imaginable consolations. The irony is suffused, now the audience, now the protagonist penetrating it further. The action takes place in a theatre of the mind – Lear's, the spectator's – and its pace and rhythm are not determined by the intrigue.

Dramatic irony (which is recognition on the part of the audience) is inherently pleasurable, combining the pleasures of learning with the pleasures of superiority; and *Othello* until its dénouement raises rather than depresses the spirits. The last scene, however, removing the pleasures of ironic overview and offering so brief and partial a recognition on the part of the protagonist, I find cruelly painful and profoundly depressing. The end of *King Lear* – but here a tardy diffidence seizes me and I fall back upon a wise paragraph in which Charles Lamb protested against the happy ending that had been obtruded into performances of the play:

> A happy ending! – as if the living martyrdom that Lear had gone
> through, – the flaying of his feelings alive, did not make a fair dismissal
> from the stage of life the only decorous thing for him. If he is to live
> and be happy after, if he is to sustain the world's burden after, why all
> this pudder and preparation, – why torment us with all this unnecessary
> sympathy? As if the childish pleasure of getting his gilt robes and
> sceptre again could tempt him to act over again his misused station, –
> as if at his years and with his experience, any thing was left but to die.[4]

To this I add, echoing Sigmund Freud,[5] that the death of Cordelia should not shock us since in her silence and steadfastness she embodies that 'good death' that Lear imperfectly chose and wilfully repudiated in the first scene. Only with her dead in his arms can he 'renounce love, choose death and make friends with the necessity of dying.'

NOTES

This is a revised version of a paper which originally appeared in *English Exchange* (Spring 1973).

1 (Detroit 1961) 79
2 'Fool in *Lear*' in *The Structure of Complex Words* (London 1952) 157
3 *Tragedy* 201
4 'On the Tragedies of Shakespeare' in *Shakespeare Criticism* ed. D. Nichol Smith (London 1946) 206
5 'The Theme of the Three Caskets' in *Complete Psychological Works* (London 1958) XII 291–301

the energies of endurance: biblical echo in KING LEAR

ROSALIE L. COLIE

ALTHOUGH MANY STANDARD moral, social, and literary paradoxes have been brought to life in *King Lear*, reanimating the difficulties of moral living in a particularly absorbing and involving way,[1] these paradoxes do not, as they might, utterly confuse the audience's own set of values: from beginning to end in this play, we know whose side we are on; we know, at least relatively, the right from the wrong, virtue from vice. Shakespeare's dramaturgy is partly responsible for this – Edmund tells us his intentions before we see him putting his schemes into action; Regan and Goneril draw off some of the natural repugnance to Lear's violent rage by their cool exchange at the end of the first scene; Goneril and Oswald are seen trumping up their ostensibly rational criticism of Lear and his knights. The playwright has put to work other devices as well, however, to provide us with some sense of security, in spite of the terribly unbalancing actions of the play. One such device is implicit in paradoxy itself: although a paradox is usually formulated so as to confound the mind, at least for a moment, paradoxes often make very simple statements. In his *Paradoxa Stoicorum*, for instance,

Cicero criticized the run-down morality of his time by flatly re-
stating the 'official' moral saws so glaringly counter-illustrated in
the social practice around him. His unparadoxed statements of stoic
morality were designed to remind quixotic Romans of the falsity of
the life they had chosen to lead. In *King Lear* something like this
happens, too: the play shows how, in extreme situations, paradox
is unparadoxed, or 'unfigured,' to become normative, actual, 'true,'
ultimately to assert rather than to question moral and ethical
standards. Paradox becomes (paradoxically!) a description of a
normal condition, rather than a prescription stated in terms of
abnormality.

Primarily, of course, the paradoxes in this play make up a set of
schemata for topsy-turvydom, but, though they question 'received
opinion' (as in the play's opening interlude), they also return to
affirm some forms of the received opinion they seem at first to
question. Edmund may speak correctly, after all, about the condition
of bastards: why should they be accorded such social disadvantages?
But Edmund proves to be thoroughly illicit and lawless, scornful of
law, natural, moral, or manmade. In the simple pejorative sense, he
is a bastard – and 'his' paradox serves to reinforce conventional
views of moral behaviour. Again, why should not an old king give
up his kingdom? Stoics would applaud him, and in some Christian
moral tales such rulers became saints. If his daughters are to be
believed (which is, after all, doubtful), King Lear showed wisdom
in abdicating when he did, before falling into senility. That is, the
paradoxy of the play makes us aware at once of how problematic
all customary formulations are, how unreliable generalization can
be in any particular case. If we too simply fall into the received
opinion that order must be maintained at all costs, as many critics
do, then we must remember that it is Gloucester at his most
Polonius-like who utters the familiar clichés about an hieratic social
order.[2]

Another way of saying this is that *King Lear*, among so much that
it does, demonstrates how men defend themselves, how rationaliza-
tions are constructed for living, for acting, for feeling – and for
protecting one's self against living, acting, and feeling. We see at
the same time the limitations of such defences: we see how people
do *not* defend themselves, or how little they can defend themselves,
either by falling back upon received morality or by venturing into
wild, daring, and irrational schemes of behaviour. The irrational
and the unexpected are given literary support by the use of paradoxy, by which the playwright can rob us of our normal holdfasts
upon situations such as those presented in the play. We do not know

for sure, any more than the characters in the play know (or we know in our lives), from what direction or in what form disaster will strike. Nor do we know, really, what to make of specific disasters. Gloucester's blinding is a fearful thing, as the death of the First Servant confirms; but his blindness and extrusion from society bring Gloucester to such insight as he achieves and, in the end, to reconciliation with the son he has wronged. Cordelia's death is an unmitigated waste, the result of unpardonable policy and careless-ness: it is, as many critics have observed, intolerable. Conversely, for all its unnerving intensity and ambiguity, Lear's death offers relief, however unwelcome may be the means to that relief. Kent is in fact right:

> O! let him pass; he hates him
> That would upon the rack of this tough world
> Stretch him out longer. (5.3.312–15)

Amongst the deaths of her moral superiors, Goneril's suicide seems an easy escape. Life, on the other hand, is suddenly under-stood to be less an unquestionable 'good' than a burden of re-sponsibility and realization almost too heavy to bear. One cannot, for instance, envy Albany and Edgar their task of reconstituting the state:

> The oldest hath borne most: we that are young
> Shall never see so much, nor live so long. (5.3.325–6)

Another way of saying all this is that, in the handy-dandy world of men, formal paradoxy offers a literary mode of decorum. It ques-tions received opinion, and it questions its own questioning of re-ceived opinion; its forensic purpose is to present problems – not necessarily to solve them, but to make problems imaginatively real. Although it *may* offer ultimate holdfasts upon truth, the primary purpose of paradox is to keep the audience off balance, to remind men of the frightening extent of their unknowing.

And yet, within the boundaries of this play, some simple things *are* always known, always taken for granted. We know, through all the bruising horror of the action, where the right lies, if not what the right is. This play teaches that virtue is hardly its own reward, but it provides us with no substitute reward, nor hope for other reward; the play makes perfectly plain that lives lived without virtue are not worth living.

In its odd way, with all its emphasis on violence, cruelty, wanton-ness, and destruction, *King Lear* is a play about life in all its excrucia-tions. It holds out no promises of reward after death: death simply *is*, an end put to alternative attempts at self-preservation, self-improvement, or self-abasement. Precisely by its unyielding stress on death and dying, *King Lear* points to the fact that our life is all we have, and that in our life, the only thing that counts is to try to live well – since anyone can die like a dog. Intellectual values are almost absent from this play: the self-knowledge that is so clear a value in *Hamlet* makes no guarantees in *King Lear*, where those who come to know themselves at the play's end meet their fates as stripped and as defenceless as those who do not or who make no effort to know themselves. Nonetheless, as Maynard Mack put it in his eloquent peroration, we know that in spite of everything, 'it is better to have been Cordelia than to have been her sisters, ... it is a greater thing to suffer than to lack the feelings and virtues that make it possible to suffer.'[3]

By what technical means does the playwright provide us with a moral measuring rod to bring us so inevitably to this conviction? Very early in the play, we feel that we know what the 'better' course of action is, without having to wonder about it; our knowledge of that 'better' is what makes the terrible last act bearable at all. In spite of the regular assertion by critics that *King Lear* is a Christian play, there is little evidence of that in the text itself: it seems more reasonable to say that it is a play that, like Shakespeare's other plays and those of most Elizabethan dramatists, rests upon generally assumed Christian principles of morality. Against the views of Chambers, Ribner, and Siegel, Roland Frye's caveats provide a common-sense bulwark for our reading.[4] More recently, William Elton's study of 'the gods'[5] urges a fourfold category of paganism against the Christian arguments for the play, with the additional suggestion that a contemporary crisis in Christian belief is masked by the schemata of paganism presented in the play. One need not reach so far, either stretching the *figurae* of Christianity to see in Cordelia a Pauline charity or in the weed-crowned Lear a type of Christ; or concluding, simply because the play is not overtly a Christian tragedy (and which of Shakespeare's tragedies *is*?), that it is an esoteric exercise of the sort Elton urges. First of all, the question of Christian tragedy needs some examination, however brief. Of course Lear, like his youngest daughter, is a *pharmakos*, bearing more than his fair share of the world's pain and giving his life in payment for that pain. But how is it possible to write a tragedy in which the suffering of the hero is *not* incommensurate with the act or acts that brought it all upon him? Hamlet is as 'innocent' as Cordelia, at least at the beginning of his play; we do not need to take him as a type of Christ, even before we are forced to note that, in contradistinction to Christ, his errors in judgment bring many others to their ruin, not to their salvation. No more than Ophelia and Cordelia has Desdemona given cause for the treatment to which she is subjected, but we do not therefore turn her into a Christian martyr for love's sake – indeed, the strict Christian argument is sometimes adduced to consign her to hell because of the charitable lie of her last breath. Really, is it not rather that the literary tradition impressed the notion of a *pharmakos* upon Christ than that Christ has superseded earlier traditions to become archetypal for all *pharmakoi* since?

Of course, to deny *King Lear* its figural Christian interpretation is by no means to deny its reliance upon Christian imagery or its argument for conventional morality. One of the most paradoxical things about this play is that when all the complexities and confusions have been experienced, we come to accept the fact that traditional morality, however hackneyed its customary rhetoric, affords some guidelines in a world in which values are questioned and tested at every move. This essay deals with one literary device of security, with the ground bass of echoing meaning derived from Scripture itself. In many of his plays, Shakespeare draws upon biblical language to remind us both of man's predicament and of the options he has within that predicament. In *King Lear* he exploits that language softly, uninsistently, to remind us of one particular kind of human resource displayed, even stressed, in scriptural example.

Echoes of scriptural language, and religious language generally, have been noted and traced throughout Shakespeare's plays; the Bishops' Bible, the Geneva Bible, and the Authorized Version have been ransacked for phrases he may have used. The Psalms, usually in the Prayer Book version, and the great Homilies have been cited as sources for Shakespeare's phraseology. The likelihood of his having used such sources need not be argued here; the different English translations were heard in the various services of the Elizabethan Church, and Shakespeare could readily have heard – the most careful student of his biblical borrowings thinks, *must* have heard[6] – the Bible cited in several different English versions. Again and again, the phrases ring out to support the theme of his plays – *The Merchant of Venice* and *Measure for Measure* provide ready examples; Hamlet, both at his most mischievous and at his steadiest, quoted Scripture and paraphrased the Catechism. To Shakespeare's audience of parishioners, we may assume, phrases from such sources called forth their natural referents even more readily than, say, Shakespearean borrowings from Seneca, Ovid, or Plutarch, or from the national chronicles we are urged to believe were read by every literate Englishman of the Renaissance. For the Elizabethan audience, biblical phrase, like proverbial and sententious expression[7] (with which it overlapped, of course), spoke at once to the ear and to the mind, reinforcing with particular sanction that body of belief and commonsensical truth by which men of different views, stations, and interest, could affirm their community.[8]

Thematically, biblical texts are particularly relevant to *Lear*. Ecclesiasticus 33:18–22 is an apt one, since it so unqualifiedly recites the doctrine of generations:

> Give not thy sonne and wife, thy brother and thy friend, power over thee while thou livest, and give not away substance to another, lest it repent thee, and thou intreat for the same againe.
>
> As long as thou livest and hast breath, give not thy self over to anie personne.
>
> For better it is that thy children shulde pray unto thee, then that thou shuldest looke up to the hands of thy children.
>
> In all thy workes be excellent, that thine honour be never stained.
>
> At the time when thou shalt ende thy dayes and finish thy life, distribute thine inheritance.[9]

In the play, biblical echoes recur, largely to Old Testament and apocryphal moral books: to the patience of Job, the endurance enjoined in Ecclesiastes and Psalter, to the experienced consideration of Ecclesiasticus and the Book of Wisdom, as well as to such New Testament themes as the charity of the Gospels and of Paul, exemplified chiefly in Cordelia's language. In Cordelia's case, Shakespeare probably drew deliberate attention to the scriptural reference, but in most cases the 'quotation' is slanting rather than direct. In Proverbs 27, for instance, so many of the *Lear* themes are touched on that it is difficult to believe its language did not echo for the playwright and his audience:

> A stone is heavie, and the sand weightie: but a fooles wrath is heavier then them both.
>
> Angre is cruell, and wrath is raging: but who can stand before envie?
>
> Open rebuke is better than secret love.
>
> The woundes of a lover are faithful, and the kisses of an enemie are pleasant [King James Version: deceitful].   (Prov. 27:3–6)

Upon the political parts of *King Lear*, Proverbs offers an almost constant gloss; similarly, many verses from Job,[10] Ecclesiastes, and Wisdom speak to the private moral and psychological problems of Lear and his friends, deepened now and again by echoes from Mark and the Epistles.

From the very beginning, these echoes sound, as motifs or re-
frains counterbalancing the vigorous language of cursing and of
action. Lear speaks of his Cordelia as 'our last, and least,' in terms
that make clear how much, for him, the last is first. She can expect
to draw, he says, 'A third more opulent than [her] sisters.' Cordelia,
however, is not one to exchange what she truly knows for a lie, even
for a gracious or kindly lie: her 'Unhappy that I am, I cannot heave /
My heart into my mouth' (1.1.91–2) not only recalls the phrasing
of Ecclesiasticus 21:26, 'The heart of fooles is in the mouth; but the
mouth of the wise men is in their heart,' but also reminds us of
the meaning of her name, borne out in her heart-directed, cordial
behaviour. One of the characters in the play who, in Mack's acute
phrase, operates on a gamut from naturalism to morality, Cordelia
behaves in a way ever more emblematic of her name. Of her many
virtues, unquestionably the greatest is charity, the love lodged in the
heart; across the play, she gradually turns into her singular virtue.[11]

Cordelia's emphasis on love slants through the language of her
first exchange with her father, for in her answer to him she paraphrases the marriage service:[12] 'I ... Obey you, love you, and most
honour you' (1.1.96,98), reminding us of the difference between
filial and marital devotion by asking,

> Why have my sisters husbands, if they say
> They love you all?   (1.1.99–100)

As critics keep saying, in this play is involved the meaning of social
relations, the traditional structure of rank, and the significance of a
deference society;[13] another way of looking at the play is to see that
it deals with the problems of love, including lust, possessing, and
possessions. It seems to assume that love is subject to weighing and
measuring, until the plot teaches everyone differently.[14] One critic
has characterized *King Lear* by its 'root sexuality';[15] certainly there
is a great deal about lust in the play. Gloucester's lust eventuated in
Edmund, in turn capable of arousing singular passions in the breasts
of both Lear's elder daughters. Lear's heavy demands on his
daughters' devotion, weighing particularly upon Cordelia, and
Cordelia's own complicated response to his demand, all point to a
love not fundamentally charitable.[16] Lear's cursing of sexuality,
later, may indeed provide one clinical signal for his 'madness,' an
obsessional preoccupation all too common in those struck down by
psychic blows; his curses also mark the degree of his own disbelief
that *his* loins could have produced such incredibly hard-hearted
children. It is Cordelia's conventional directness and clarity about
the proprieties and proportions of love, though, that enrage her
father most at the beginning of the play, although her remarks be-

speak her own good sense and social orthodoxy. Half her love, she says, must go with the husband she is about to receive.

The marriage theme, involved with the paternal-filial theme and the bastardy theme, is lightly but regularly touched on, one of the many social links scrutinized in this play. The strength of France's love for Cordelia, the faith with which he honoured his marriage bond, even to subordinating his own interests to those of justice and his wife's father, serve to underscore the falsity of Goneril and Regan to their husbands, whose interests they manipulate for themselves. In effect, shortly after her husband's murder, Regan published the banns for her marriage to Edmund; when Goneril, for her own reasons, objects to her sister's plan, Goneril's husband says to his wife, 'The let-alone lies not in your good-will' (5.3.80) – a double meaning couched against her right to object to the arrangement or to impede it. The husband, however, *does* 'know cause, or just impediment' why Regan and Edmund should not be joined in matrimony: his speech reveals the machinations of the three wicked children and preaches the moral topsy-turvydom in which they live:

> For your claim, fair sister,
> I bar it in the interest of my wife;
> 'Tis she is sub-contracted to this lord,
> And I, her husband, contradict your banes.
> If you will marry, make your loves to me,
> My lady is bespoke.   (5.3.85–90)

The language of the marriage service, intertwined with the language of commercial transaction (which is, of course, precisely what many noble marriages were), serves Albany's ironic purpose. As so often in this play, received morality is turned seamy side out.

Many marriages, of course, have their seamy side: an unpleasant variation of the marriage theme is Edmund's speech just before the battle, in which he thinks of ways to get rid of Albany:

> Now then, we'll use
> His countenance for the battle; which being done,
> Let her who would be rid of him devise
> His speedy taking off.   (5.1.62–5)

One cannot fail to remember the inconvenience of Uriah the Hittite to David, and the successful arrangements for *his* taking off (2 Sam. 11:15–24). After Albany's early espousal of his wife's policy, he came to reject her and to choose 'right' – though only after his wife's perfidy had been made absolutely plain to him. Like her father, he feels her serpent tooth and tongue (cf. Ps. 140:3; 1.4.297–8;

2.4.161–2), and speaks to her, in images of dust and withering; 'the text is foolish' is her rejoinder. The word 'text' sends us to the multiple sources of Albany's language – the first and other psalms; Hebrews 6:8. Goneril answers him by implicitly rejecting a major New Testament tenet as she cries,

> Milk-liver'd man!
> That bear'st a cheek for blows ... (4.2.50–1)

The injunction to turn the other cheek comes from Matthew 5:38; from that chapter come passages on adultery and the lust of the heart (verses 27–8), plucking out of eyes (verse 29), and speech by yea and nay (verse 37), all with reverberations in this play. As the Goneril-Albany marriage is spiritually dissolved, in this scene, the fundamental cruelty of the woman and the ultimate kindness of the man are given scriptural authority.

France's words in accepting the rejected Cordelia ring with quite another note, the paradoxy of Christian ethics:

> Fairest Cordelia, that art most rich, being poor;
> Most choice, forsaken; and most lov'd, despis'd – (1.1.250–1)

and are by many editors associated with 2 Corinthians 6:10:

> As sorrowing, and yet always rejoycing; as poore, and yet make manie riche: as having nothing, and yet possessing all things.

For those who remembered this Pauline passage, there was double gain in the all-nothing play, so bitterly acted out between Cordelia and her father a few lines before France's speech (which also picks up the 'for richer, for poorer' of the marriage service, to demonstrate France's orthodox, secure sense of values). 'Service'[17] is another bond examined in the play; we find overlapping languages of marriage and of service. Kent says to his master, reversing the order of the words Cordelia used in her speech to her father:

> Royal Lear,
> Whom I have ever honour'd as my King,
> Lov'd as my father, as my master follow'd ... (1.1.139–41)

his 'follow'd' being, in terms of fealty, the equivalent of the wifely 'obey.'

Throughout *King Lear*, as throughout *Hamlet*, the relation of word to deed is explored, questioned, commented upon, so that the connection of speech to action is more than a thematic element of the play. Kent's farewell to Regan and Goneril plays on the inevitable differentiation between word and deed,

> And your large speeches may your deeds approve,
> That good effects may spring from words of love ...,   (1.1.184–5)

though his speech makes plain that he expects little from those two daughters. The First Epistle of John (3:18) sets the text for the whole linguistic behaviour of Cordelia and Kent, whose plainness of speech is so significant throughout the play:

> My little children, let us not love in worde, neither in tongue onely, but in dede and in trueth.

Obviously, the moral message, such as it is, in *King Lear* asserts the superiority of deed over word. The Senecan style of the disguised Kent, as much as Cordelia's 'pride, which she calls plainness,' speak directly from the essential truth of their natures, as they match their speech both to their feelings and, when they can, to decorum. As Cordelia says,

> If for I want that glib and oily art
> To speak and purpose not, since what I well intend,
> I'll do 't before I speak ...   (1.1.224–6)

The dangers in words, the dangers of mere affirmation – of faith without works – as opposed to the 'word' a true man gives,[18] is of course a recurrent theme, beginning with Cordelia's

> Time shall unfold what plighted cunning hides;
> Who covers faults, at last with shame derides.   (1.1.280–1)

The high point of the words-deeds theme comes with Lear's 'To say "ay" and "no" to every thing that I said! "Ay" and "no" too was no good divinity' (4.6.100–1). He means that men must not lie, and must not equivocate either, but rather must affirm their intention and perform what they affirm. '[L]et your yea, be yea, and your naye, naye, lest yee fall into condemnation' (James 5:12); 'But let your communication be, Yea, yea; Nay, nay. For whatsoever is more than these, commeth of the evil' (Matthew 5:37); 'Yea, God is faithful, that our worde toward you, was not Yea, and Nay' (2 Cor. 1:18). Since the paradoxy of the play insists upon equivocation, Edmund illustrating both the skill and the wickedness of the equivocator, the contrapuntal insistence upon corresponding word to deed faces off the two moralities against each other. From Lear's remark, 'To say "ay" and "no" to every thing that I said!' we read his unwisdom still, for, as the opening scene demonstrates, he had brooked no gainsaying, had forced his daughters and his courtiers into falsehood and flattery.

The exchanges between Kent and Lear, when Kent challenges his angry master, illustrate the two styles. In another exchange between the two, this time with Kent disguised, Scripture corroborates the moral virtues exemplified in the Senecan rhetoric. When Lear asks Kent who has stocked him, 'ay' and 'no' become crucial. Lear cannot accept the truth of 'Your son and daughter':

LEAR No.
KENT Yes.
LEAR No, I say.
KENT I say, yea.
LEAR No, no; they would not.
KENT Yes, they have.
LEAR By Jupiter, I swear, no.
KENT By Juno, I swear, ay. (2.4.15–22)

Kent's answer is 'yea,' and it is true. The plainness of this speech is the moral key to Kent's character. His rhetoric is not at all times plain, however, and it would be a mistake to cast him simply (like Coriolanus, say) as a Senecan 'honest' man and plain speaker: as Kent loses his temper with Oswald, to berate him almost hysterically, he quite loses control over role and speech. Here again, though, something of the Senecan pattern is consistent: Kent's high emotion is rendered in his wild language. Across the play, Kent displays a wide mastery of styles, from Ciceronian balance and courtly conceit at one extreme through moral axiom and exhortation to rage at the other. He is capable of witty exploitation of styles from within the difficulties of his personal situation as well – his exchanges with Cornwall provide one instance of this; his solution to being stocked – 'Some time I shall sleep out, the rest I'll whistle' (2.2.156) – provides another. In the very first scene, as he tries to turn Lear from his disastrous course, Kent speaks formally, beginning with 'Royal Lear' and going on to a fine Ciceronian triad, only to be jarred by the king's angry interruption into the plain speech of human truth:

> be Kent unmannerly,
> When Lear is mad. What would'st thou do, old man?
> Think'st thou that duty shall have dread to speak
> When power to flattery bows? To plainness honour's bound
> When majesty falls to folly. (1.1.145–9)

Much later, in the guise of Caius, Kent works his rhetoric the other way, from plainness to conceit, satirizing the false manners of false courtiers. In answer to Cornwall's challenge to his genuineness, Kent says of those standing about the stage – that is, the mighty in the kingdom –

> I have seen better faces in my time
> Than stands on any shoulder that I see
> Before me at this instant;   (2.2.94–5)

though when characterized by Cornwall as a compulsive plain-speaker, or railer, he easily shifts his style. Suddenly he says,

> Sir, in good faith, in sincere verity,
> Under th'allowance of your great aspect,
> Whose influence, like the wreath of radiant fire
> On flick'ring Phoebus' front ...,   (2.2.106–9)

to Cornwall's astonishment, going 'out of [his] dialect.'

For the implications of this rhetorial flexibility, among other things, Kent is stocked. His Senecan rhetoric is of an order more complicated than simply the selection of style to match conditions. His language works often doubly, not only because he is, after all, in disguise for the better part of the play, but also because he speaks to the common-sense humanity of his auditors, within and without the play.[19] His shifting styles draw attention to the hypocrisies he perceives in those around him; his own stoicism, in his person as Kent and his person as Caius, comes through in his stern acceptance of his duty and its responsibilities. He speaks roughly to his master in the first scene and stoically about being stocked; his last speech, with its strange ambiguities, brings his stoical role to its proper close.

Stocked, Kent says, 'A good man's fortune may grow out at heels' (2.2.157). The feet-heels-soles-kibes images cluster to conjoin with the stocks, perhaps to echo Job 13:27: 'Thou puttest my fete also in the stockes, and lokest narrowly unto all my paths, and makest the printe thereof in the heeles of my fete.' The stoicism of Job has often been remarked, and Job's patience has been coupled with Lear's endurance. The *Lear* echoes pick up the biblical literature of endurance to marry it to the Senecan rhetoric of emotional truth. Job, Ecclesiastes, Proverbs, the Psalms, Ecclesiasticus, the Book of Wisdom, all have their echoes in the play, deepening the pagan moral precepts by references to the extraordinary biblical record of experience in pain sturdily borne. Very early the echoes from Job begin, as Lear says to Cordelia:

> Better thou
> Hadst not been born than not t' have pleased me better.   (1.1.233–4)

Job 3:3 runs: 'Let the daye perish, wherein I was borne, and the night when it was said, There is a manchilde conceived.' The man-worm comparison, so powerful in Job, occurs in *Lear* as well: much later, when Gloucester reiterates his belief in a fatality he is at last learning to endure, he likens the figure of his disguised son to a worm:

I' th' last night's storm I such a fellow saw,
Which made me think a man a worm.   (4.1.32–3)

So spoke Bildad the Shuhite (Job 25:6): 'Howe muche more man, a worme, even the sonne of man, which is but a worme?' And so spoke Job himself: 'I shal say to corruption, Thou art my father, and to the worme, Thou art my mother and my sister' (Job 17:14). Most beautifully, and most appropriately to Edgar's condition, so also the Psalmist in the Prayer Book version: 'But as for me, I am a worme, and no man: a very scorne of men, and the outcast of the people' (Ps. 22:6).

Lear's great speech on clothing (3.4.103–12) begins with the worm, this time the silkworm from which 'gorgeous' ladies dress themselves, and echoes the scriptural phrase used in many contexts throughout the Bible: 'What is man, that thou shuldest be mindeful of him! Or the sonne of man that thou wuldest consider him!' (Heb. 2:6). Lear's 'Is man no more than this? Consider him well' is a purely earthbound question: there is no reference here to deity, not even to 'th' Gods' endorsed by Gloucester's simplistic fatalism. Lear considers the nature of man abstracted, a naked and unarmed man powerless against the forces arrayed (to his astonishment) against him, forces natural, political, and personal: so too Job and the Psalmist considered man, out of the depths of their own misery and the disgrace and dejection of Israel (Job 7:17; Ps. 8:4). Finally, it is 'the thing itself,' man alone and stripped, that must be existentially examined, man without 'lendings,' without conventional social and moral protections and disguises.[20] Comparing the considerations of naked man made by Lear to those made by Job and the Psalmist, however, we can see the contrast plainly – for Lear, there were no comforts of suprarational faith in divinity on which Job and the Psalmist could rely.[21]

From Job comes the suggestion that the storm scene in Lear owes something to scriptural hyperbole. Certainly in the play, 'th' Gods' keep a dreadful pudder o'er men's heads: natural catastrophe is reckoned as quite beyond human control, and the puniness of man's strength set against tempests can be measured in Lear himself, trying to outshout the storm. The scene is, as Mack has suggested,[22] an extraordinarily daring antipastoral – nature reflects man's inward state, as it habitually does in pastoral settings, but the state it reflects is not peaceful, creatural, contented, but violent, broken, and breaking. This storm overmasters the singular strengths of particular men; through its power over great and weak, great men discover their weakness. It is apocalyptic indeed: this storm is so great that indeed 'the Kings of the earth, and the great men, and the riche men, and the chief captaines, and the mightie men, and everie bondman, and everie fre man, hid themselves in dennes, and among the rockes of the mountaines' (Rev. 6:15 and cf. Luke 21:25–26). With this storm, as in the great tempest of the Apocalypse, comes the judgment too, invoked by Lear and later acted out in the arraignment scene. In that spiritual judgment in which he and his curious benchfellows take part, judgment is forced on the king and his ministers, a final moral statement in which they too have their share of the sentence they give.[23]

The storm indicates the correspondence between a disturbed natural world and a disturbed social world – the night is mad, as Lear is mad. Human will is 'like' that storm, but cannot stand against the storm's force. With his customary mastery of the ambiguities of human experience, Shakespeare works through the storm scene to present the simultaneous weakness of unaccommodated man and his indomitable self-assertion against impossible odds. Further, in spite of the sharp and severe reduction of man to himself alone, unaccommodated for anything, it is from the storm that Lear emerges at last to some understanding of himself and of the society of which he should have been head. As in the Book of Job, where the great storm was the medium of God's pedagogy as well as the symbol of His incomprehensible power, the storm in Lear teaches the protagonist what it is to be human. Lear's storm is so wild that

> the cub-drawn bear would couch,
> The lion and the belly-pinched wolf
> Keep their fur dry, (3.1.12–14)

just as, in Job's storm, 'the beasts go into the denne, and remaine in their places' (Job 37:8). Job and his God speak in dialogue, God rebuking his most notable servant for *hubris*:

> Canst thou lift up thy voyce to the cloudes, that the abundance of water may cover thee?
> Canst thou send the lightnings that they may walke, and say unto thee, Loe, here we are?
> Who can nomber cloudes by wisdome? or who can cause to cease the bottels of heaven,
> When the earth groweth into hardnes, and the clottes are fast together? (Job 38: 34–5, 37–8)

Almost as if in answer to those questions, Lear attempts exactly this prideful, impossible task:

> Blow, winds, and crack your cheeks! rage! blow!
> You cataracts and hurricanoes, spout
> Till you have drench'd our steeples, drown'd the cocks!
> You sulph'rous and thought-executing fires,
> Vaunt-couriers of oak-cleaving thunderbolts,
> Singe my white head! And thou, all-shaking thunder,
> Strike flat the thick rotundity o' th' world!   (3.2.1–7)

His bravado is grand, as he seems to direct and lead the storm that helps drive him beyond himself, to greater pain and greater understanding; although the storm seems somehow to have instilled in him an awareness of other people and of social bond, at the very moment in which he challenges the wild weather Lear is totally isolated. He is 'comrade with the wolf and owl' (2.4.212) indeed – as Job was 'brother to dragons, and a companion to owls' (Job 30:29, Authorized Version; Geneva: 'companion to ostriches'). What Job's disposition was like before his afflictions took him, we are not told; but Lear had evidently shown some signs of irascibility before the play began. So much the more remarkable, then, that Lear acquires a kind of patience: to such a man, as he, accustomed to authority and wilful in its exercise, patience is the most difficult of virtues. 'I can be patient,' he says (2.4.232). 'You Heavens, give me that patience, patience I need' (2.4.273). Like Kent and Gloucester, he must tame his fierce spirit to endurance, even in the 'open night' 'too rough / For nature to endure' (3.4.2–3). He can say, in the end, to the storm, 'Pour on; I will endure' (3.4.18). The lessons of stoicism fuse with the scriptural lesson of Job to deepen the accomplishment of the old madman on the heath.

The apocalyptic chiaroscuro of thunder and lightning in the storm scene is the most dramatic of the play's many alternations between light and dark, between sight and blindness. The contrast of sight and blindness runs from the factual brutality of Gloucester's blinding[24] to the figurative language expressing Lear's spiritual darkness, raising echoes from scriptural phrasing, too, where the doctrines of insight are classically expressed in the language of vision. Gloucester's 'I stumbled when I saw' recalls 'The seeing see not,' of Matthew 13:13, as well as the verse from Isaiah (59:10):

> We grope for the wall like the blinde, and we grope as if one without eyes: we stomble at noone day as in the twilight: we are in solitaire places, as dead men.

The passage from Job is nearer yet – 'They mete with darknes in the day time, and grope at noone day, as in the night' (5:14); it contains both the sight-blindness theme and the topsy-turvy scheme of Lear's last exchange with his Fool:

LEAR   We'll go to supper i' th' morning.
FOOL And I'll go to bed at noon.   (3.6.86–8)

By the time this exchange takes place, Lear is evidently mad, and the Fool about to disappear from the play. Two mad ones, then, may be expected to keep a disorderly daily schedule – but withal, there may also be a reference to Ecclesiastes 10:16 – 'Woe to thee, O land, when thy King is a childe, and thy princes eat in the morning.' Certainly during the struggle with Goneril, the Fool reminds Lear of his second childhood; and the king then shows the greed and impatience of a very small child. But these disorders are trivial compared to the deeper disorder, in Lear's personality and in the kingdom; the king's folly early in the play is very different from his madness later. The quality of the Fool's fooling changes too. Early on, he attempts to bring Lear face to face with his real plight, and presses the old man cruelly by reminding him of his mistakes in judgment. Goneril and Regan complain of their father as if he were merely the naughty child the Fool calls him – the proper text for this is Ecclesiastes 4:13, 'Better is a poore and wise childe, then an old and foolish King, which wil no more be admonished.' Throughout Proverbs, 'fools' and 'foolishness' are, I think, usually treated in their simplest meaning of 'unwisdom'; the book chastises that kind of folly. But it also advocates folly as a therapeutic device: one text for the Fool's insistent harping on Lear's folly is Proverbs 26:5: 'Answere a foole according to his foolishnes, least he be wise in his owne conceite.' The more irrationally the king behaves, the more realistic seems the Fool's treatment of him – 'Seest thou a man wise in his owne conceite? more hope is of a foole then of him' (Prov. 26:12). In most of Proverbs, folly is treated satirically and morally, as one cause of the world's disorder. In such a world, values come loose from their customary moorings, riding so askew in the world that at times even the possibility of fixed value seems meaningless. We see before us Gloucester's time-serving, his late decision to act for the king; we see Lear's irresponsibility about privilege and, more important, about love; we see Goneril's pursuit of lust and power, and Regan's sly ways with her father and everyone else. Edmund dissimulates almost unconcealed – certainly values must have collapsed in a society in which these great people do such things. From Gloucester's 'late eclipses' speech we may read the playwright's

deliberate choice of a pre-Christian setting. The churchgoer, however, could hardly fail to catch the echo of Matthew 10:21:

> And the brother shall betray the brother to death, and the father the
> sonne, and the children shall rise against their parents, and shall cause
> them to die.   (Cf. Luke 21:16)

Their life crises do not cause the evil ones to question themselves
or their actions, but the 'good' members of society are forced back
upon the most basic question in human ethics: 'Is man no more than
this? Consider him well.' The moral egalitarianism at which Lear
arrives reduces all men to 'Poor naked wretches,' all of them reduced
ultimately to 'the thing itself.' Two biblical echoes sound here, one
of Job, also reduced to the bottom limit of humanity, the other of
the Prodigal Son,[25] like Edgar sunk to the bottom of society, and
like Lear, fain

> To hovel [him] with swine and rogues forlorn,
> In short and musty straw ...   (4.7.39–40)

But like Job and the Prodigal Son, the prodigal father Lear finds his
way back to some realization of worth and truth; Edgar too, comes
out of his disguise to lead *his* prodigal father back to a peculiar but
poignant happiness.

What the play seems to assert is that all men – all of them, poor
naked wretches – may expect misfortune as their portion. In the
face of disaster, deserved or undeserved, expected or unexpected,
men can only endure. When his stoical suicide-attempt fails by
Edgar's kindness, Gloucester adopts his son's stoicism, determining
to endure whatever his life will bring him:

> henceforth I'll bear
> Affliction till it do cry out itself
> 'Enough, enough,' and die.   (4.6.75–7)

Having realized the almost unendurable truth that

> the worst is not
> So long as we can say 'This is the worst,'   (4.1.27–8)

Edgar comes through to 'Bear free and patient thoughts,' until he
can say, finally, to his father (and mean it), 'Ripeness is all.'[26] Para-
phrasing the great passage in Wisdom 7,

> And when I was borne, I received the commune aire, and fel upon the
> earth, which is like nature, crying and weping at the first as all other
> doe.

For there is no King that had anie other beginning of birth.
All men then have one entrance unto life, and a like going out,
(Wisdom 7: 3, 5–6)

the mad Lear tells the blinded Gloucester the extent of his new learning:

Thou must be patient; we came crying hither:
Thou know'st the first time that we smell the air
We wawl and cry ...
When we are born, we cry that we are come
To this great stage of fools.   (4.6.180–2, 184–5)

Connected with this passage too, is Ecclesiastes 5:14: 'As he came forthe of his mothers belly, he shal returne naked to go as he came, and shal beare away nothing of his labour, *which he hathe caused to passe by his hand*' (my italics).

In the very ecstasy of madness, Lear found some reason, both to accept his plight and his responsibility for that plight, and to accept the harsh justice of men's lives. Edgar's speech to his father makes Lear's wisdom manageable in aphorism, and carries some of the weight of the 39th Psalm, the one used in the burial service: 'O spare me a little, that I may recover my strength, before I go hence, and be no more seen.' Quite simply, Edgar states the stoical formulation to which Lear had come independently:

Men must endure
Their going hence, even as their coming hither:
Ripeness is all.   (5.2.9–11)

All men must ultimately go to their long home, and cannot alter the date of their going thither. Gloucester lives to die upon the revelation of reconciliation, while Lear, secured by his madness, lives to experience Edgar's terrifying truth, that there is always something worse than what at any given moment seems 'the worst.' He lives, then, to die upon the half-realized recognition that his selfless daughter has been gratuitously slain. Birth and death coincide: as Gloucester was careless in begetting Edmund, Edmund was careless in Cordelia's dispatching. 'Coming hither' is always involved in 'going hence.' As we see them in this play, goings hence are as ambiguous, as undignified, as unfair, as chancy as it is possible for them to be.

For nether doeth man knowe his time, but as the fishes, which are taken in an evil net, and as the birdes that are caught in the snare: so are the children of men snared in the evil time when it falleth upon them suddenly. (Eccles. 9:12)

Those who try to die in their own time – Lear and Gloucester – are taken suddenly, at crucial moments between joy and grief; those who take others' lives – Cornwall, Regan, Goneril, Edmund – are caught in their own snares. The old die with the dignity of having borne most; such a death is, in the play's system of rewards, an honourable one. Their deaths become them, because they have learnt such hard endurance in their lives.

Throughout this play, the notion of a transcendent deity is not invoked. There is none of the overt reference, even by conventional accident, to God and His Son, such as is found in *Macbeth* or *Hamlet*. When 'the gods' are invoked, they are questioned and even jeered at; nor are stars admitted as a supernatural force. Again and again, the audience is brought to realize the extremity of 'the thing itself,' or, to realize that man is totally unaccommodated, can count on nothing, has no governance over his own fate. All he can do is be patient, endure, try to ripen: the most he can do for others is to realize that in their plight his own is involved. 'Ripeness' is self-realization, realization of responsibility for one's self and for others – the realization as well that such realization carries absolutely no guarantee of happiness. As Kent's life shows, or Cordelia's, the proper exercise of responsibility is just that – and no more than that. In this play, all that is certain is that irresponsibility breeds destruction. As Edgar says to Edmund, in the tones of Deuteronomy, Wisdom 11:13, and Wisdom 12:23, of their father's responsibility in his, and their, fate,

> The Gods are just, and of our pleasant vices
> Make instruments to plague us;
> The dark and vicious place where thee he got
> Cost him his eyes. (5.3.170–3)[27]

But, we note, 'The dark and vicious place' was not the direct cause of disaster to Gloucester and his family alone; it could also be said to have cost Cordelia *her* life – and she was entirely unconnected with Gloucester's pleasant vices. Edgar speaks in the *sententiae* of justice with an echo, perhaps, of Matthew 5:28–29 and 6:23, and though we can say, with him, that Gloucester's fate is related to his vice, we cannot apply such generalization absolutely, either to Gloucester or to the other characters woven with Gloucester into the web of the play's disasters. Ruin overtakes the good as inexorably as it does the wicked: Cordelia's tongue-tied truthfulness and Kent's sturdy honesty are by no stretch of the imagination just causes for their suffering. Indeed, Cordelia is most nearly the morality figure in the play,[28] as she literally turns into the charity of which she speaks:

No blown ambition doth our arms incite,
But love, dear love ... (4.4.27–8)

Her godliness was unmistakably proclaimed a line or so earlier:

O dear father!
It is thy business that I go about ... (4.4.23–4)

But all this virtue, all this courage, generosity, innocence, and charity, cannot save Cordelia: she is involved, like all the rest, in the inexplicable vicissitudes of human life and lot, insisted on throughout the length of the play. For that is the point of *King Lear*, surely: that, as the Psalmist proclaims, man is inexorably and inextricably bound in with other men, brought to trial whether or not he deserves it. Man has no choice but to endure his life with such strengths as he can muster, and in his endurance lies his value as a man. Each man makes his choice between moral dignity and moral dishonour: those who choose dignity (Kent, the Fool, Cordelia, Cornwall's servant, Albany, Edgar) relinquish safety and advantage to become more admirable than those who seek their own without regard to others' needs. And that is all one can say. The rewards of the good are simply their comfortless virtues.

Because in its mode life itself is depicted as so inexplicable, so unrelated to distributive or retributive justice, paradoxy is singularly appropriate to this play. Life is neither simple nor single; a man cannot live, no matter how he may try, to himself alone. He is bound to others whom he may love or hate, like or dislike, regard or disregard, by all sorts of recognized or unrecognized ties and bonds. In this play, there are many other bonds besides the feudal ties and ties of social hierarchy celebrated by Richard Hooker and others. When these other ties break, as even Gloucester notes, men come to learn how profoundly important conventional connections are in human society and survival, even though the ameliorations of such connections may be temporarily lost. Service turned false is utterly destructive; family connections make it all too easy to cause personal ruin to others. In this play, individuals bear, not just their own pain, but the burden of others' misdeeds and pains as well. Punishments may be undue and unreasonable; death may be unfair; life may be disproportionately cruel, but *King Lear* does not preach the vulgar lesson of moral absurdity. For everything that happens, there is some cause, that cause fundamental to the personality and the fate of the sufferer.

Human personality and moral life are rarely simple. Moral situations are qualified because of their complexity; even in literature they resist interpretation. It is easy to say that moral measurements cannot be taken in a world upside-down or askew – but since the world is always that, to say such a thing denies the possibility of moral judgment altogether. Shakespeare was, evidently, not one to entertain that view, easy though it is; there are always difficult, as well as extremely simple, moral lessons to be read from his plays. From *King Lear* we learn that to be true to one's self can be as dangerous as to be untrue: nonetheless, that to be untrue is certainly fatal. From *King Lear* we learn that men must do what little they can in a world in which human nature – one's own character, other people's characters – is as variable and as inexplicable as natural vicissitude. In the uncertain world into which he must come, no rules warrant a man's security, though some guidelines for behaviour may be hazarded. In the scene on the heath, ambiguities give way to direct moral precept. Quoting the devil quoting Scripture, Edgar-Tom paraphrases the moral commandments upon which all Christians are raised from childhood:

> Take heed o' the foul fiend. Obey thy parents; keep thy word's justice; swear not; commit not with man's sworn spouse; set not thy sweet heart on proud array. (3.4.80–3)

The last injunction may be a Pauline paraphrase, and certainly relates to the clothing theme running through the play, but it is irrelevant to the other injunctions Tom utters. Those are, as we see, the second and moral part of the Decalogue, what the Calvinists called 'the second table,' the moral and ethical commandments laid upon scrupulous men. In short, these are the simplest, most basic rules of human conduct offered to western civilization. Shakespeare does not offer us conventional morality as a cure for the trials of experience: we are brought back to accept conventional morality's simplistic rules only after recognizing the inadequacy of their simplicity to the confusions and ambivalences of social life. 'Take heed o' th' foul fiend': to avoid the devil, within or without one's self, common commandments must be accepted, since not to do so is to play into the devil's hands. So the devil, as a mimic madman says, frightens man into good morality – and then, how can such morality be 'good' when it springs from such a source?

Since such morality is limited, it may be said at least that it is appropriate to the limitations of being human. Certainly it is no talisman against the interrelated troubles of human living – all that can be said for it is that it is a great deal better than no morality whatsoever. In the play, adultery is made to seem an extraordinarily dark sin, with consequences far beyond its natural veniality.

Gloucester's is 'an old lecher's heart'; he is a 'walking fire,' in the Fool's unconscious characterization (3.4.115–17); Lear's preoccupation with sexuality emerges in his cursing of his elder daughters and in his concern with the objects of 'justice' in 'The great image of Authority' speech and in the 'every inch a king' speech, where though he releases adulterers from the punishments described in Leviticus, he shows his own horror of the sexual act by using the imagery of hell to describe it. Certainly, in this play sexuality is 'dark,' as in so many of Shakespeare's late plays – 'The dark and vicious place where thee he got'; 'Beneath is all the fiend's: there's hell, there's darkness, / There is the sulphurous pit' (4.6.129–30). Misunderstood sexuality corrupts most of the major personal relationships within the play; Gloucester's blinding is one of the punishments for adultery described in the homilies, and has the literary merit, as punishment, of linking the sexual theme to the blindness theme. Dark calls to dark; deeds done in darkness bring other kinds of darkness in their train. Certainly adultery was one obvious disruption of the correct social organization, but that the consequences of so natural, even so innocent, a sin should be made to reach as far as they do in this play reminds us of the extreme simplicity of human understanding. Adultery particularly stresses how in ordinary life deeds are done, almost unconsciously, which henceforward change and force human relationship.

With all this gloom, the play asserts something else about any man's behaviour, even at its most calculated and rational: that it is mad, that it drives other men mad as well, puts them beside themselves with rage and violence, or beyond themselves to revelations of truth. The paradoxy works classically within this particular cluster of ideas, since the wise fool and the possessed poet, from Socrates on, have been regarded as men particularly privileged in insight. The play, like its protagonist, displays 'Reason in madness' – for all its stress on grotesquerie, violence, and irrationality, the play displays many forms of reason beneath and through its disordered surface. First, as analyses of the play's language show, there is an extraordinary rationality underlying the disorder of the mad speeches of Lear and Edgar. Lear's press-money speech follows a natural set of associations; the organization of 'every inch a king' and 'Reason not the need' follows the most rigid Ciceronian structural, if not syntactical, demands.[29] Second, the accuracy of madmen real and feigned in assessing psychological truth is made clear over and over again. The Fool understands the reality of the Lear family. Lear discovers his own fault and remembers to rethink the 'most small fault' that had seemed to him so ugly in Cordelia.

Edgar's naturalistic associative reference to Pillicock and Pillicock hill, evidently called up by Lear's phrase, 'pelican daughters,' reiterates the fundamental sexual problem in his family and, by extension, in the world. Further, the madness of calculation is displayed again and again – the measurements Lear established for 'love,' the economical reordering of Lear's retinue by his daughters, the retributive language used during the blinding of Gloucester, all demonstrate that, to the calculator, other people's lives are far less significant than the calculator's private desires or ambitions, whatever they might be. Calculation for one's self involves, in this play anyway, prodigal carelessness of other people's rights and needs – such exercise of reason is, if not moral insanity, at least moral imbecility.

Though the play condemns the folly proscribed in Proverbs, it praises the folly prescribed by Paul (1 Cor. 1). Folly does not bring rewards on earth, but it can, somehow, bring spiritual comfort. The Fool, Cordelia, and Kent are all foolish in the world's ways; Lear becomes a self-proclaimed fool and an outcast in the kingdom he has ruled.

> There is no health in my flesh, because of thy displeasure; neither is there any rest in my bones, by reason of my sin ...
>   My wounds stink and are corrupt: through my foolishness.
> (Ps. 38: 3, 5)

Lear's hand, like all human bodies, smells of mortality. Recognition of his folly and corruption permits the king to pass through mere folly and corruption, mere selfishness and mere madness, into a condition with claims upon greatness. The play is about the inevitable qualifications of the ideal which follow from having to live. Growing old is by itself a major hazard. Job's comforters speak in the retributive language of the world, 'calculating' Job's punishment according to his (to them) 'necessary' unrighteousness. Against them and in the face of a God who treats His best servant as wanton boys treat flies, Job's affirmation of his own integrity somehow overrides the wantonness of divine fate and the worldliness of his persecutors. Even if God had *not* rewarded Job at the book's end, Job's courage and faith would have proved exemplary, in particular his resistance to his false friends, who offer him a comfort harsher even than the physical pains he had to bear. Much as in the Book of Job, in spite of the horrors of *King Lear*, life itself emerges as a value in spite of its pain – as a value, really, because of its pain. Lear speaks in the *vox humana* of the Psalmist, of Solomon, of the Preacher, to proclaim that lives are given dignity by the sufferings endured in them. All men come to the same end: what distinguishes them is how they come to it:

> All things come alike to all: and the same condition is to the juste and to the wicked, to the good and to the pure, and to the polluted, and to him that sacrificeth, and to him that sacrificeth not: as is the good; so is the sinner ...
>
> There is evil among all that is done under the sunne, that there is one condition to all, and also the heart of the sonnes of men is full of evil, and madnes is in their hearts whiles they live, and after that, they go to the dead.
>
> Surely whosoever is joyned to all the living, there is hope: for it is better to be a living dog, than to be a dead lyon.
>
> For the living knowe that they shal dye, but the dead knowe nothing at all; nether have they anie more a rewarde: for their remembrance is forgotten. (Eccles. 9:2–5)

The literary problem, like the moral problem, is to present so stark a view of human life – in which men and women meet their bitter fates by reason of their irresponsibility and in spite of their efforts at responsibility; in which disaster may be, and often is, total – that there seems no hope for humanity, and, at the same time, to make such a life seem worth the living of it, to make it seem better, somehow, to be a living dog than a dead lion. *King Lear* forces the question to extremes, beyond hope, so that Lear's death, for instance, comes as a relief from the continued horror of having to live. Somehow or other, the shining values of Cordelia's truth and charity, Kent's fidelity, Lear's self-discovery, must be seen to stand out against the cruelty of experienced disaster and evil. The deep undercurrent of scriptural language running through the play, its reference largely to the stoical books of the Old Testament, provides some holdfast upon the idea, at least, of moral order, to remind us, through all the shifting of fortune and point of view, that moral order is an ideal that society cannot afford to let go. The play does not refer us to transcendent morality at all – rather, it produces a rockbed morality, fundamental if comfortless and un-yielding, a minimum prescription for social survival. The use of biblical echo to suggest a morality past ordinary hopes, allows us to work through the complicated paradoxes of the play to accept the essential, inevitable, unalterable limitations of human life. The injustice of experience forces – once more, by paradox – a reasser-tion of the values of life, with all its limitations, even in the teeth of adverse experience. Justice, on which the characters harp, par-ticularly Lear and Edgar (the dispossessed ruler and the future king), is understood finally as another form of calculation, the idiom of Job's comforters, too simple and materialistic a moral notion to serve as a clue in situations so extreme as those of this play. Justice 'reasons' need and punishment – and, as Lear and the play finally uncover, these things cannot be reasoned. Just as the words of Job's comforters, secure in their innocent belief in justice and in effects-from-causes, thin out into platitude and meaninglessness, so do the notions of justice and calculation evaporate as standards for the play, to leave us as Job was left, with no more than the conviction that life, if it is to have meaning at all, must observe the moral choices of men doomed to coming hither and to going hence:

> Man that is borne of woman, is of short continuance, and ful of trouble.
> He shooteth forthe as a flowre, and is cut downe: he vanisheth also as a shadow, and continueth not. (Job 14: 1–2)

In the face of the harshness of living and of dying in a universe indiscriminate in its effects, the holdfast is simple enough. Edgar is right: 'Obey thy parents; keep thy word's justice; swear not; commit not with man's sworn spouse.' The morality is simple not because life is uncomplicated, but because it is not; because only a morality forged to maximum economy upon the anvil of cruel experience – the experience of Job, of captive Israel, of the Preacher, of Lear – is appropriate to the incalculable hazards between birth and death. In the plainness of these moral precepts lies their power, which insists upon self-direction in awareness of the inevitable disproportions of pain, pain justly borne for sins and foolishness, pain arbitrarily laid on, by no fair measure. Man is born to trouble as the sparks fly upward; inevitably, he must learn the suffering from his own and from others' misdoing, must bear the consequences not only of his own faults, but of others' faults as well. From the language of paradox, beloved of the rigorous stoics, fused with that resonant language celebrating human endurance, the proud magnificence of oppressed Israel, *Lear* draws much of its strength. The two languages teach the same hard lesson, that by endurance men test and make their own values. Ripeness is all: the only thing to be achieved is to reach the limit of human achievement. The playwright could, had he wished, simply have paraphrased stoical axioms on this theme from Seneca to Cicero, or from modern stoical writers, as Chapman, for example, did. His choice of a scriptural reference forces on his audience and his readers the charged memory of human pain, the weight of experience that had to be borne before human beings could voice the consciousness of their pain and thus express – literally, 'express' – the extremity of their human achievement. Job and the Psalmist protest before their pain, call their universe to account before they accept and endure it. Like them, Lear arraigns his universe, physical and moral, before he allows himself to open under its rigours and to accept its inevitable power over his life. One measure of human greatness, in all these test-cases, was that these men maintained, discovered, and recovered their humanity in the teeth of their torture: another measure was the capacity to create a vocabulary celebrating humanity in the grip of irremediable suffering.

NOTES

1 See my *Paradoxia Epidemica* (Princeton 1966) chap 15.
2 Gloucester's failure to understand the relations within the order on which he so relied is one indication of his limitation as a character; however, the rigidity of the 'doctrine of order,' so persuasively argued by E.M.W. Tillyard in many of his books, notably *The Elizabethan World Picture* (London 1943) and *Shakespeare's History Plays* (London 1945), and taken for granted in E.W. Talbert *The Problem of Order* (Chapel Hill 1962), is now open to serious question. For a balanced view of the matter, see Julian Markels *The Pillar of the World* (Columbus, Ohio 1968) especially p. 96. I have made some mild comments on the doctrine in 'Literature and History,' in *Relations of Literary Study* ed. James Thorpe (New York 1967) 17–19; and see below, 'Reason and Need,' notes 1 and 2.
3 *'King Lear' in Our Time* (Berkeley 1965) 117. As he does with so many subjects handled in more detail in this book, Mack touches brilliantly upon biblical echo in the play. Some of his references, for instance to Nebuchadnezzar (50–1) and to Paul and Silas (56), are not followed up in this essay.
4 R.W. Chambers *King Lear* (Glasgow 1940); G. Wilson Knight *The Wheel of Fire* (London 1930); Irving Ribner *Patterns in Shakespearean Tragedy* (London 1960); Paul N. Siegel *Shakespearean Tragedy and the Elizabethan Compromise* (New York 1957) and *Shakespeare in His Time and Ours* (South Bend, Ind. 1968) chap 4; also Roy Battenhouse, 'Shakespeare's Moral Vision,' in *Stratford Papers* (1964); 'Shakespearean Tragedy: A Christian Approach,' in *The Tragic Vision and Christian Faith* ed. Nathan A Scott (New York 1957); and *Shakespearean Tragedy: Its Art and Christian Premises* (Bloomington, Ind. 1969), reviewed by Harry Levin, *Journal of the History of Ideas* xxxii (1971) 306–10. Roland M. Frye's *Shakespeare and Christian Doctrine* (Princeton 1963) is an effort to place Shakespeare's conventional, unintense Christianity in the contexts of orthodoxy and of play-writing. Kenneth Myrick's 'Christian Pessimism in *King Lear*' in *Shakespeare 1564–1964* ed. Edward A. Bloom (Providence, RI 1964) 56–70,

locates the play's pessimism squarely within contemporary Christianity. Sylvan Barnet's essay, 'Some Limitations of a Christian Approach to Shakespeare,' reprinted in *Approaches to Shakespeare* ed. Norman Rabkin (New York 1964) 217–29, is a serious commensensical criticism of the Christian reading of Shakespeare.

5 'King Lear' and the Gods (San Marino 1966)

6 Richmond Noble *Shakespeare's Biblical Knowledge and Use of the Book of Common Prayer* (London 1935); Mack 'King Lear' in Our Time 56–7

7 See Martha Andresen, below.

8 As Ethel Seaton's article, '*Antony and Cleopatra* and the Book of Revelation,' *Review of English Studies* xx (1946) 219–24, demonstrates with extraordinary tact, biblical language is apt to 'echo' rather than be quoted or even paraphrased in Shakespeare's usage; her article seems to me a model for this kind of study.

9 Quotations, unless otherwise noted, are from the facsimile of the 1650 Geneva Bible, ed. Lloyd E. Berry (Madison, Wis. 1969); I have in each case checked the *wording* against sixteenth-century editions, but have kept to this post-Shakespearean edition (because I own it) for consistent *spelling*, which varies tremendously from edition to edition.

10 John Holloway, in *The Story of the Night* (Lincoln, Neb. 1961) 85–9, offers some very interesting comments on the relation of the play to the Book of Job.

11 Sears Jayne, 'Charity in *King Lear*,' in *Shakespeare 400* ed. J. McManaway (New York 1964)

12 For comment on this, see Danby *Shakespeare's Doctrine of Nature* 130–1.

13 For the 'deference society,' see Lawrence Stone *The Crisis of the Aristocracy, 1558–1641* (Oxford 1965) 21 and passim; and 'Reason and Need,' below.

14 See Terence Hawkes *Shakespeare and the Reason* (London 1964) chap 6.

15 Sheldon P. Zitner in an unpublished paper, 'Shakespeare's Secret Language'

16 See John Donnelly, 'Incest, Ingratitude, and Insanity: Aspects of the Psychopathology of King Lear,' *Psychoanalytic Review* xl (1953) 149–55.

17 Jonas A. Barish and Marshall Waingrow, 'Service in *King Lear*,' *Shakespeare Quarterly* ix (1958) 347–55

18 Sigurd Burckhardt *Shakespearean Meanings* (Princeton 1968) 239–40

19 Zitner, 'Shakespeare's Secret Language'

20 See Prov. 28:13: 'He that hideth his sinnes shal not prosper,' as well as the references cited in Fritz Saxl, '*Veritas Filia Temporis*,' in *Essays in Philosophy and History Presented to Ernst Cassirer* ed. Raymond Klibansky (New York 1963); and Charney, above.

21 See John E. Hawkins, '*Lear* and the Psalmist,' *Modern Language Notes* lxi (1946) 88ff.

22 Mack 'King Lear' in Our Time 63–6

23 Cf. Rev. 11:18–19

24 The standard comment on Gloucester's blinding is by Robert B. Heilman *This Great Stage* (Baton Rouge, La. 1943) chap 2; the interpretation has been challenged by Paul J. Alpers, 'King Lear and the Theory of the "Sight Pattern",' in *In Defense of Reading* ed. Reuben A. Brower and Richard Poirier (New York 1963) 133–52; see my *Paradoxia*; Bridget Gellert Lyons, above, pp. 28–9; and Nancy R. Lindheim, below, pp. 179–80.

25 See Susan Snyder, 'King Lear and the Prodigal Son,' *Shakespeare Quarterly* XVII (1966) 361–9.

26 See J.V. Cunningham, 'Ripeness is All,' in *Woe or Wonder* (Denver 1951); and Andresen, below.

27 Cf. Wisdom 3:16: 'But the children of adulterers shal not be partakers of the holy things, and the seede of the wicked bed shal be rooted out'; Wisdom 4:6: 'For al the children that are borne of the wicked bed, shal be witnes of the wickednes against their parents when they be asked.' Perhaps more important is the passage from the homily 'Agaynst Whoredome and Adulterie,' *Certaine Sermons* (London 1595): 'Among the Locrensians, the adulterers have both theire eyes thrust out.' Matthew 6:23 has relevance here; surely the blindness-falling pattern of the Dover cliff scene owes something to Luke 14:39.

28 Cf. Jayne, 'Charity in *King Lear*'

29 Edmund Blunden, 'Shakespeare's Significances,' in *Shakespeare Criticism, 1919–1935* (Oxford 1936) ed. Anne Ridler; and Zitner, 'The Language of *King Lear*,' above, and his 'Shakespeare's Secret Language'

NINE

MARTHA ANDRESEN 'ripeness is all': sententiæ and commonplaces in KING LEAR

A CRITICAL COMMONPLACE about *King Lear* is that it is a play full of commonplaces: a recent study has even demonstrated that nearly every utterance in the play has its analogue in favourite Renaissance literary and philosophical sources.[1] In this essay, I am less concerned with identifying these inherited formulations than with considering the thematic and dramatic functions of commonplaces, aphorisms, and sentences in *King Lear*. So closely woven are commonplaces in the fabric of the play that any one of them links with many others in complex patterns of meaning and effect; one example of an aphorism catching up multiple threads is that famous commonplace and crux, 'Ripeness is all.' Obviously, one function of the brief scene in which it occurs is, simply, exposition of the plot. Only two characters speak, and the whole action in the scene is the reporting of an offstage action that in fact determines the outcome of the play.

> [*A Field between the two Camps.*]
> *Alarum within. Enter, with drum and colours,* LEAR, CORDELIA, *and their Forces; and exeunt.*

Enter EDGAR *and* GLOUCESTER.

EDG. Here, father, take the shadow of this tree
For your good host; pray that the right may thrive.
If ever I return to you again.
I'll bring you comfort.

GLOU.   Grace go with you, sir!

[*Exit* EDGAR.

Alarum; afterwards a retreat. Re-enter EDGAR.

EDG. Away, old man! Give me thy hand: away!
King Lear hath lost, he and his daughter ta'en.
Give me thy hand; come on.

GLOU. No further, sir; a man may rot even here.

EDG. What! in ill thoughts again? Men must endure
Their going hence, even as their coming hither:
Ripeness is all. Come on.

GLOU.   And that's true too.

[*Exeunt.* (5.2)

Lear's fortunes have taken their final downward turn; after his re-union with Cordelia, after the alignment on the battlefield of the forces of good and evil in the play, Edgar and Gloucester, whose fortunes in so many ways parallel Lear's, are here briefly seen as outside the main action. The stage directions emphasize that distancing, as Edgar leaves his blind father, joins the battle offstage, then returns to report Lear's defeat.

Gloucester reacts to this news by despairing, just as earlier, in the fields near Dover, he had reacted to his blindness with despair. Now, as before, he renounces the world and seeks death; now, as before, Edgar comforts him. At Dover Edgar had tricked his father into hope, had convinced Gloucester that he had fallen from the cliff but had been saved, and then counselled him to 'Bear free and patient thoughts' (4.6.79). Here, true to his promise, Edgar brings comfort again, but uses a different trick – not sensory illusionism this time, but stoic consolation reinforcing the moral of his earlier counsel.

The auditor's response to Edgar's words, 'Men must endure / Their going hence, even as their coming hither: / Ripeness is all,' might silently echo Gloucester's reply, 'And that's true too.' For Edgar's words *sound* true – there is nothing peculiar about them, nor, for an Elizabethan, was there anything original about them. Familiar, appropriate, commonsensical, what Edgar says has the proverbial ring of those great truths tested by experience and transmitted in simplest form from generation to generation. Here they mark a 'common place,' a recognizable territory in the vast and painful psychological terrain over which we range in *King Lear*.

The form of Edgar's utterance is also arresting: his words stand apart, insular, self-contained, emerging from the dialogue that frames them. They have density, brevity, pithiness: 'going hence' balances 'coming hither,' 'Ripeness' balances 'all.' Such cogency and balance create an oracular absoluteness that shames by comparison any cumbersome paraphrase. The artifice of this apparently artless locution sets it into relief against its artful, but relatively more naturalistic, verbal background.

Edgar's aphorism creates in the audience two different but complementary responses. The familiar content of commonplace truth draws us in: by force of recognition it encourages our sympathetic involvement in the particular dilemma of Edgar and Gloucester. At the same time, the deliberately artificial form works in the other direction to create an aesthetic and psychological distance that permits our momentary detachment from and reflectiveness about the crowded, confusing situation.

The scene's dramaturgy reinforces this second principle. When Edgar is offstage, we have the illusion that he is involved in the experience of Lear's defeat, but when he returns to report to his father, he seems to move entirely away from that unseen arena of action. Such physical remove and distancing suggest the perspective that allows Edgar's generalized reflections: his aphorism in turn takes the audience a step farther, away from Lear's defeat, away from Gloucester's despair, away even from Edgar's stoicism, to a viewpoint from which all this is seen, and more. Even Edgar's vocabulary works to this end: he says to his father, not *you* nor *we*, but '*Men* must endure.' The grammatical setting gradually shifts from personal and specific to general and abstract – Edgar first addresses Gloucester as 'father,' and uses personal pronouns: 'I'll bring *you* comfort.' When he returns, he calls him 'old man.' Gloucester replies with a term even more general – '*a man* may rot.' And Edgar's reply is yet more general: '*Men* must endure.' Shifting from 'I' to 'you' to 'old man' to 'a man' to 'Men,' the increasingly inclusive referents invite an ever wider vision.

Our vision of this scene is thereby rendered multiple and complex. We see Edgar and Gloucester in a field between two camps; a young man and an old man momentarily poised between the forces of good and evil; two men like all men struggling to interpret their experience – which we may understand at several different levels. The dramatic effect of Edgar's aphorism, then – to arrest attention and to encourage reflection – enables the audience to comprehend more fully the thematic significances of the play so far.

This momentarily frozen scene of two representative figures in a representative setting, upon which Edgar's aphorism provides the commentary, is in the dramatic medium structurally like an emblem from Whitney's *A Choice of Emblemes* (Figure 1).[2] There, an old man and a young boy are in a field, away from other people and actions, and (just as in the scene from *King Lear*) the old man stands under a tree. The Latin motto above is translated as 'Precocious things do not last.' The sententious, moralized verses below interpret the picture. Edgar's metaphor is of a piece with Whitney's. The process of ripeness and decay in nature is compared to man's life. In Whitney's context, the topic is intellectualized; knowledge too quickly come is quickly wasted. The apt mind, like ripe fruit, is vulnerable and quickly rotten. The ripe mind, by implication, is slow to develop but sure; it will not, even in the body's decay, fall into rottenness. The modern archaism, 'a ripe old age,' preserves a sense of this commonplace, which Renaissance writers used in many versions – 'time and experience make one wise,' 'age and experience teacheth wisdom,'[3] for instance. The old man in Whitney's picture is the type of ripe old age. His long white beard is a common biblical and classical symbol of wisdom and reverence, even as his robes signify the garb of maturity and knowledge.[4] Thus clothed and protected, he stands firmly on the ground, serene and imperturbable. In contrast to him, the figure of the youth is precariously balanced on a limb of the fruit-laden tree, gathered like the fruit into the natural cycle of growth and decay. He is naked, thus unprotected; ripe in body but not in mind. In their fleeting physical perfection, the blooming flower to the left of the old man, the ripe fruit, and the naked youth, are equally vulnerable; but the wise old man, garbed in wisdom, will weather vicissitude and seasonality, while the youth, like flower and fruit, will be blasted and must rot.

The scene in *King Lear* reverses these types of youth and age, relying on different commonplaces associated with them. Gloucester, the old man, is by no means the wise man impervious to the vicissitudes of fortune. On the contrary, he explicitly connects his age and state of mind to 'rottenness' – 'a man may rot even here.' Edgar, the young man, is the wiser; ripe in wisdom despite his youth, he personifies his own aphorism, that ripeness is all. His knowledge is precocious, that is, early and quickly won, and yet he endures. What Gloucester has learned (and expresses aphoristically in act 4) has

THE fruicte that fooneſt ripes, doth fooneſt fade awaie.
  And that which ſlowlie hath his time, will not ſo ſoone decaie.
Our writing in the duſte, can not indure a blaſte:
But that, which is in marble wroughte, from age, to age, doth laſte.
Euen ſo it is of wittes, ſome quicke, to put in vre:
Some dull to learne, but oftentimes the ſlowe are ſounde, and ſure.
And thoughe the apte, and prompte: ſoone learne, and ſoone forget.
Yet ofte the dull doe beare in minde, what firſt therein was ſet.
Hereof the prouerbe comes: *Soone ripe, ſoone rotten turnes* :
And greeneſt wood, though kindlinge longe, yet whotteſt moſt it
  burnes.

O formoſe puer, nimium ne crede colori.
Alba liguſtra cadunt, vaccinia nigra leguntur.

Figure 1, courtesy of The Huntington Library, San Marino, California also come quickly to him, perhaps too quickly, since finally he cannot encompass all that he knows. "'Twixt two extremes of passion, joy and grief,' Edgar later tells Edmund, '[his heart] Burst smilingly' (5.3.198–9). In the paradoxical world of *King Lear*, Gloucester is the type of vulnerable child, Edgar of ripe old man. The paradoxes linking ignorance and old age, youth and wisdom, are also Renaissance commonplaces. Like his king, Gloucester typifies the proverb, 'Old men are twice children';[5] and Edgar is a type of *puer senex*, familiar in classical literature, Christian hagiography, and myths of East and West.[6] In the archetypal figure of *puer senex*, the ideals of ripening body and ripened mind are joined together.

Edgar's words about 'going hence' and 'coming hither,' as well as the staging of this emblematic scene, recall another traditional commonplace that Shakespeare made use of again and again – the notion of life as a stage, the world as a theatre.[7] Even the conventional gestures of drama can be used emblematically, to call attention to the force in the commonplace – as, for instance, the entrance, the passing across the stage, and the exit of Lear, Cordelia, and their forces. With the report of their defeat offstage, this emblematic tableau turns into a symbol, enacting a turn of fortune's wheel. In *tableau vivant* a coming and a going, a beginning and an end, are presented, compressing into a small space man's ultimate 'entrance' and 'exit,' his birth and death. Staging thus adumbrates theme, for *Lear* is about man's journey from birth to death, and the evils that plague him along the way.[8] But staging also reinforces the dramatic effect of arrest and balance. The convention that 'all the world's a stage' lies in the background of our awareness, to heighten artifice generally, and to invite reflection upon the entire play.[9]

Other commonplaces, aphorisms, and emblematic scenes in *King Lear* have similar thematic and dramatic functions. No one, it must be emphasized, would argue that this most moving play can be perceived as *only* a series of static emblems or emblems-in-motion, which altogether create an allegory. What *Lear* has that pure allegory or emblem books may lack – and this lack may have been one cause of their extinction – is, simply, stress on dramatic life. Emblem books force us to capture the meaning but we miss the experience. To remain *only* at the engaging level of psychological realism in *King Lear*, however, is to have the experience but miss the meaning: what Maynard Mack calls the 'emblematic mode'[10] works in this play to widen continually our perspective from the particular to the general, the person to the type, the historical to the allegorical, without blurring our point of focus on particular characters in immediate situations. The aphoristic expression of commonplaces is a Janus-like stylistic device that encourages both modes of perception, required for full response to the play.

That Shakespeare drew so freely on proverbial wisdom in *Lear* marks him as an artist of an earlier age, in which such traditions were cherished as the habit of aphoristic thought. From the ancients come many of the aphorisms themselves, as well as theories for their use. Aristotle calls them *gnomai*; Quintilian calls them *sententiae* or 'judgments' because they are 'collective' like the decisions of public bodies. In form and substance they were the *loci communes* or favourite topics of antique oratory, isolated, transformed, and incorporated into literature.[11] In his *Poetica*, Giangiorgio Trissino calls sentences 'wise sayings,' 'speeches short, moral, conclusive, and full of meaning.'[12] By Shakespeare's time it was a common practice to memorize sentences and commonplaces, to collect them, and to keep them at hand: Erasmus' famous *Adagia*, the classic collection of such sentences and aphorisms, was followed by many translations and collections of ancient saws, proverbs, and current lore. Though the *Adagia* and its imitations drew largely from classical sources, Christian tradition also made utmost use of *sententiae*, which in tracts, sermons, homilies, and essays in moral philosophy had their thematic, didactic, and stylistic functions.

Treatises and textbooks recommending the rhetorical and poetical use of *sententiae* were as common as collections of them. Renaissance theoreticians followed classical rhetoricians: Erasmus' *De Copia*, for example, urges the writer to use wise sayings in order to achieve variety and abundance of style; Thomas Wilson's *Art of Rhetorique* urges their use for amplification and argumentation. A student in the course of his general education in rhetoric, then, learned the uses of sentences, but he learned to handle them as well in his training in poetics. In *L'Arte Poetica*, Minturno takes his definition of *sententia* from Aristotle: 'A saying by means of which at a fit time a grave person, not ignorant of the things he speaks of, gives judgment not on any chance topic but on the course one should follow as excellent and good or flee as bad and wicked, generally and not particularly.' The choice of *sententiae* offers clues to literary character ('Through them the disposition and tendency of the mind, and the qualities and appetites of the man who speaks are revealed'), and 'sententiousness' itself is typical of certain characters: 'Sententious sayings are appropriate to the aged, as well as to those who do not lack authority and are not ignorant of the affairs of which they speak sententiously. Therefore aged men are brought on the stage in order that with sayings full of reason they may command, reprehend, admonish, comfort, and terrify.' They have, further, the dramatic function of engaging the audience's sympathies: 'The silent auditor agrees with them, understanding that something which is uttered as appertaining universally to life and morals is in conformity with his particular opinion.'[13] *Sententiae* are, then, vehicles for the wisdom of the ages: in their briefest form, they articulate a rule of life that has been tested by experience and transmitted across generations. In form and content, as Minturno and other critics suggest, they present many possible uses to the tragic poet and dramatist.

Shakespeare freely exploits *sententiae* for revelation of character. In *King Lear*, indeed, the sentence is a touchstone for the quality of a character's understanding of the profound truths of life. According to tradition and common sense, sentences are appropriate to old men because old men, wise in years, know whereof they speak. They reveal experiential rather than vicarious knowledge of the truth expressed; they generalize from a recognizably rich personal history. But sententiousness in a character (especially in a young person, such as Edgar soliloquizing on the heath) can express just the opposite (in line with Whitney's moral emblem) – superficiality and inexperience, instead of profundity of experience. As the familiar, inherited formulas for experience, aphorisms can be easily learned and facilely applied: rehearsed by a naïve speaker, they may betray mere copy-book knowledge of the truth expressed. The *puer* using sentences is *praecox*, but the *senex* has a right to such expression. In such cases, the general nature of a young man's utterance – for example, Edgar on the heath: 'When we our betters see bearing our woes, / We scarcely think our miseries our foes' (3.6.105–6) – exposes the distance between the knower and the thing known. Characteristically, though, Shakespeare has inverted the customary usage, as he has inverted so many of the conventional arrangements between the generations in this play; the *puer* has gained wisdom that the *senex* has missed. Furthermore, in *King Lear*, nearly everyone speaks aphoristically at one time or another, and many characters work variations upon the same commonplaces. Precisely in these variations lie important clues to the psychological and moral states of each character. The play makes very clear that only dramatic context allows us to judge the particular validity of the *sententiae*.

Two characters who are appropriately sententious types as prescribed in Renaissance poets and rhetoric are the elderly Kent, a good *consigliere*, and the young Fool, a *puer senex*. Consistent speakers of wise sayings, both are brought upon the stage to reprehend, admonish, and comfort the hero, but each has his distinctive style of proverbial utterance. Kent is the more formal and oratorical,

the Fool the more colloquial and riddling. Each, for instance, tries
to bring Lear to self-recognition with the commonplace that foolish
old men are like children. Kent's warning to Lear has a suggestion
of this commonplace:

> What would'st thou do, old man?
> Think'st thou that duty shall have dread to speak
> When power to flattery bows? To plainness honour's bound
> When majesty falls to folly. (1.1.146–9)

In the same act, the Fool counsels Lear:

FOOL If thou wert my Fool, Nuncle, I'd have thee beaten for being
old before thy time.
LEAR. How's that?
FOOL Thou should'st not have been old till thou hadst been wise.

(1.5.42–6)

The subsequent words and actions of Kent and the Fool demonstrate
that they speak this bitter truth out of love and loyalty, urging Lear
to recognize his condition and to assume responsibility for it.

Goneril and Regan, on the other hand, speak in bad faith the
bitter truth to their father. In the same act, Goneril says to Lear,
'As you are old and reverend, should be wise' (1.4.248); and Regan
in the next act reiterates her sister's opinion:

> O, Sir! you are old;
> Nature in you stands on the very verge
> Of her confine: you should be rul'd and led
> By some discretion that discerns your state
> Better than you yourself. (2.4.147–51)

They use the same commonplace as Kent and the Fool, but they urge
upon Lear not the assumption but the abdication of responsibility.
Previously, Goneril had excused her 'slack of former services,' her
disrespect of her father, with this commonplace, aphoristically expressed: 'Old fools are babes again, and must be us'd / With checks
as flatteries' (1.3.20–1). For Kent and the Fool, this very fact of
Lear's vulnerability justifies their continued, even increased service
to the old king.

These characters – Kent, the Fool, Goneril, Regan – are essentially static, and their sententiousness sets off the 'given' in their
natures. Lear, in contrast, is a dynamic character whose echoing of
this same commonplace reveals a stage in his own development. One
thing Lear learns is to see himself in the type; he comes to recognize
the painful truth that age has made him foolish, even though earlier

he had been unable to accept the Fool's or Kent's interpretation of his experience. His kneeling before Regan in act 2 parodies the recognition of truth his daughters would bring him to:

> Ask her forgiveness?
> Do you but mark how this becomes the house:
> 'Dear daughter, I confess that I am old;
> Age is unnecessary: on my knees I beg
> That you'll vouchsafe me raiment, bed, and food.'   (2.4.153–7)

His invocation to the heavens reveals that he still sees his age as duly majestical:

> O Heavens,
> If you do love old men, if your sweet sway
> Allow obedience, if you yourselves are old,
> Make it your cause; send down and take my part!   (2.4.191–4)

What Lear then says to Regan makes clear this self-image: 'Art not asham'd to look upon this beard?' (195). Here, as in Whitney's emblem, the beard is the symbol of the wisdom and reverence of age.

Lear must learn entirely alone the truth of his condition: on the heath the rude elements singe his white head, shake his white beard. At the sight of naked Tom, Lear removes his garb of false authority and wisdom to become the naked, vulnerable child he was once and has become again. His discovery is marked by the echo of another commonplace: earlier, he has said to Goneril and Regan, 'Man's life is cheap as beast's' (2.4.269); on the heath, he recognizes the truth of the thing itself: 'unaccommodated man is no more but such a poor, bare, forked animal' (3.4.109–10). Lear now sees that man's life, even his own, *is* cheap as beast's. Only on the heath, as Mack points out, is this discovery 'transformed now from a copy-book "sentence" (approved food for regal reflection) to agonized self-recognition.'[14] This recognition is embedded in the play's paradoxy. By his seeing himself as naked, in a sense Lear is no longer naked; the self-discovery that leads to wisdom is a kind of accommodation to the hard facts of life, the unrelenting rules of nature.

When Lear awakens in act 4 to find Cordelia, he is in this sense also dressed anew: 'all the skill I have,' he says, 'Remembers not these garments,' (4.7.66–7), and we know that he refers to more than his clean clothes. Echoing his earlier speeches and mirroring earlier actions, Lear once again kneels to a daughter, and in his own simple, deeply personal style reiterates the truth that others have tried to force on him:

> Pray, do not mock me:
> I am a very foolish fond old man,
> Fourscore and upward, not an hour more or less;
> And, to deal plainly,
> I fear I am not in my perfect mind.   (4.7.59–63)

His earlier parody of this gesture with Regan becomes something different with Cordelia: 'Pray you now, forget and forgive: I am old and foolish' (83–4). His self-discovery is again paradoxical – in this moment of recognition he transcends the type, for his wisdom, not his folly, sees foolishness in himself.

What does *sententia* reveal about Cordelia? She is remarkable in the first act not only for her silence, which initiates the tragic action of the play, but for her words, which provide a telling commentary on that action. Her parting words, to warn and admonish her sisters, take the form of a *sententia*:

> Time shall unfold what plighted cunning hides;
> Who covers faults, at last with shame derides.   (1.1.280–1)

At a psychological level, this sentence indicates (like Edgar's sententiousness on the heath) not ripe wisdom but naïve belief. Cordelia's precociousness, like Edgar's early in the play, has an edge of self-righteousness. But her words illuminate her character less than they do action and theme in the play. The epigrammatic form and the generalized, commonplace personification of Time in her rhymed couplet (typical of a concluding speech) take it out of the immediate dramatic context and hint at a veiled allegory of Time and Truth in *King Lear*.

For Cordelia's *sententia* is one version of the Renaissance commonplace *Veritas Filia Temporis*: Truth the daughter of Time. This and other versions, such as 'Time reveals all things,' and 'Time tries all things,' were commonly used as mottoes for personal emblems, devices, and *imprese* for printing houses.[15] Whitney's *A Choice of Emblemes* includes a version (Figure 2) in which Father Time, a winged old man, brings his daughter out of hiding in despite of the female figures of Falsehood. The motto and its illustration make explicit the concept of Time as a positive force that unveils, rescues, and rewards Truth. Time the Revealer[16] has a two-fold glory, Shakespeare writes in *Lucrece*, 'To unmask falsehood and bring truth to light' (940). In the many illustrated forms of this concept, the figure of Truth is naked or being unveiled; the figures of Falsehood are disguised as women or take the shape of monsters. Some emblems show the figure of Justice with her scales above the

THREE furies fell, which turne the worlde to ruthe,
Both Enuie, Strife, and Slaunder, heare appeare,
In dungeon darke they longe inclosed truthe,
But Time at lengthe, did loose his daughter deare,
    And setts alofte, that sacred ladie brighte,
     Whoe things longe hidd, reueales, and bringes to lighte.

Thoughe strife make fier, thoughe Enuie eate hir harte,
The innocent though Slaunder rente, and spoile:
Yet Time will comme, and take this ladies parte,
And breake her bandes, and bring her foes to foile.
    Dispaire not then, thoughe truthe be hidden ofte,
     Bycause at lengthe, shee shall bee sett alofte.

Figure 2, courtesy of The Huntington Library, San Marino, California figure of Truth, assuring her triumph; the Bronzino tapestry that Panofsky studied, for example, clearly connects Justice with Time the Revealer.[17] *Veritas Filia Temporis* acquired historical reality for Renaissance England when Mary Tudor, with hopes of renewing Roman Catholic dominion in her lands, chose it for her personal device, for the legend on her crest, the state seal of her reign, and her coins. Her sister, recalling that, cried out at her own coronation, 'And Time hath brought me hither!' – another revelation of Time's daughter, Truth.[18]

Cordelia's motto points to these traditions at work in the action of the play, for in *King Lear* Time does expose falsehood and reveal Truth. Cordelia's motto emphasizes the clothing imagery so crucial to the play: 'Time shall *unfold* what *plighted* [plaited] cunning hides.' One such 'garb' of falsehood is inflated rhetoric, as Sheldon Zitner's essay makes plain. Goneril's and Regan's dressed-up speeches about love disguise from Lear the absence in them of love itself. But Time exposes more – that Lear's daughters *are* monsters of falsehood. Beneath their 'woman's shape,' they are 'serpent-like,' 'dog-hearted,' 'tigers,' of 'wolvish visage.' Albany's *sententia* in act 4 points to the fulfilment of Cordelia's prophecy. Falsehood *is* uncovered, and Albany invites Goneril to self-recognition within her type:

> See thyself, devil!
> Proper deformity shows not in the fiend
> So horrid as in a woman.   (4.2.59–61)

> Thou changed and self-cover'd thing, for shame,
> Be-monster not thy feature.   (62–3)

> howe'er thou art a fiend,
> A woman's shape doth shield thee.   (66–7)

Lear's realization of his daughters' falsehood brings to his mind the exposure of more pervasive falseness: mad, but not mad, in the fields near Dover he sees that, in general, 'Robes and furr'd gowns hide all' (4.6.167).

Time brings not only the exposure of falsehood but the revelation that truth is naked. In act 1, Lear conspicuously misses one sign of truthful speech, expressed in such Renaissance commonplaces as 'Truth is plain,' 'Truth hath no need of rhetoric,'[19] when Kent says 'To *plainness* honour's bound' (1.1.148), and Cordelia can find no words, or few, to match her truthfulness. Lear learns not only that Cordelia has spoken truthfully and has been true; Time reveals more – that Cordelia *is* Truth. In that emblematic recognition scene

(4.7), Lear awakens to see himself as an old and foolish man. But he sees more, at last: he recognizes his daughter Cordelia.

> Do not laugh at me;
> For, as I am a man, I think this lady
> To be my child Cordelia.   (4.7.68–70)

Lear has seen the Truth, and that Truth is plain. The rhetoric of his dialogue with Cordelia is extremely simple, on her terms at last: Truth hath no need of rhetoric.

Cordelia's faith in Time is vindicated, as Justice is done to herself and to Lear. Time exposes Falsehood and reveals Truth. To have faith in Time is to believe that Justice will be done 'in due season'; Justice, thus, must be awaited with patience. The good characters in *Lear* share Cordelia's faith and her patience.[20] Edgar, for example, another figure for truth veiled, awaits the 'mature time' (4.6.277) to acquaint Albany with the plot against his life, and promises to reappear 'When time shall serve' (5.1.48). Kent (yet another figure for veiled truth) preserves his disguise until, he says, 'time and I think meet' (4.7.11).

Lear, however, is not patient. His sense of justice outraged, he invokes on the heath that ultimate moment of Justice, the Last Judgment:

> Let the great Gods,
> That keep this dreadful pudder o'er our heads,
> Find out their enemies now.   (3.2.49–51)

> close pent-up guilts,
> Rive your concealing continents, and cry
> These dreadful summoners grace. I am a man
> More sinn'd against than sinning.   (57–60)

Although Cordelia's sentence points to Time the Revealer, other *sententiae* and emblematic scenes, such as Lear's vision of the Apocalypse, point to a related but different concept, Time the Destroyer, a sense of Time that appropriately pervades this tragedy. Justice comes 'in time,' but injustice occurs through ill-timing; youth is cut off too soon, joy prevented; age is cut off too late, suffering prolonged. Nowhere in the last scene are the images of Time the Revealer of Truth triumphant.[21] Lear does not recognize Kent, now revealed as himself; Kent does recognize their lightless condition in his 'All's cheerless, dark, and deadly' (5.3.290).

Commonplaces about Time the Destroyer pervade the Renaissance arts.[22] In Shakespeare's sonnets, Time is the familiar scythe-swinging figure who diminishes everything without distinction. Other images in the sonnets, as well as in *King Lear*, however, suggest a broader force: Time is that inexorable and universal power that, in a cycle of procreation and destruction, governs all living things.[23] In Shakespeare's art, two motifs express the temporal condition of man – his life as a process of natural growth and seasonality[24] (as in Sonnet 15, for example) and his life as a journey from birth to death (as in Sonnet 60).[25] These motifs concur in *King Lear*.

Even as the good characters are servants of Time the Revealer in the play, so the evil characters are servants of Time the Destroyer. They are, literally, time-serving opportunists who seize the moment to wreak destruction.[26] Lear says to Regan, 'I gave you all –' and she rejoins, 'And in good time you gave it' (2.4.252) – meaning, in time for *her* good. Goneril plots with Edmund against her husband, Albany, '*You have many opportunities to cut him off ... time and place will be fruitfully offer'd*' (4.6.264–6). Clearly, the fruitfulness of the evil-doers depends on the unripeness of their victims. Gloucester, as we have seen earlier, is just such an unripe, unwise, vulnerable old man whom Edmund can exploit. Edmund's own views are revealed in those he imputes to Edgar: '*This policy and reverence of age makes the world bitter to the best of our times; keeps our fortunes from us till our oldness cannot relish them*' (1.2.47–9); and 'I have heard him oft maintain it to be fit that, sons at perfect age, and fathers declin'd, the father should be as ward to the son, and the son manage his revenue' (1.2.71–4).

Served by such villains, Time does destroy in *King Lear*. Cordelia's death epitomizes the unripeness of the good and the injustice of one kind of ill-timing. Lear comes too late – 'I might have sav'd her' (5.3.270). The irony of his ill-timing is the greater for his having once denied her in absolutes of time: 'Better thou / Had'st not been born ...' (1.1.233–4); 'we / Have no such daughter, nor shall ever see / That face of hers again' (1.1.262–4). Lear must suffer injustice for his injustice. All that finally remains for him is expressed in that inexpressible howl about time: 'Thou'lt come no more, / Never, never, never, never, never!' (5.3.307–8).

Lear's whole life has been plagued by ill-timing, so that he too is a servant of Time the Destroyer. He had been too quick to judge, too readily and enormously angered. Gloucester, too, had been guilty of ill-timing: the play begins with his casual joke about Edmund's illegitimate birth, he who 'came something saucily to the world before he was sent for' (1.1.21–2). The enormities they must endure in their old age, though, surpass justice, too; for from the

ill-timing that results from rashness, anger, and lust, these two old
men are punished more than enough. They are men, finally, more
sinned against than sinning: for the human folly of not realizing
that human folly has consequences that can be worked out only in
time, the 'time' of these two old men is made unbearable.

Time is the Destroyer in yet another way. Time-as-duration is
as painful and destructive as ill-timed birth or death. In *King Lear*
the duration is the slow and agonizing journey toward death, with
its ill-timed seasons of ripeness and rottenness. The duration is also
man's existence in history; he must suffer, too, the evils of the
'times.' Paradoxically, life as the duration, not death, is unjust;
death brings justice, and an ending to it all. Lear himself is plagued
by his ill-timing. His lifetime has not brought fruition in wisdom;
his old age manifests folly and decrepitude. ' 'Tis the infirmity of his
age,' Regan says, 'yet he hath ever but slenderly known himself';
and Goneril agrees that 'The best and soundest of his time hath
been but rash' (1.1.293–5). Thus Lear tragically misunderstands the
responsibility of the last phase of his life's journey:

> 'tis our fast intent
> To shake all cares and business from our age,
> Conferring them on younger strengths, while we
> Unburthen'd crawl toward death.   (1.1.38–41)

In shaking off too much, Lear makes himself vulnerable, and his
decline initiates the decay of his family and kingdom. The final
scenes of the play present this old king as a type, not just of childish
old man, but of *senectus mundi*.[27] Lear raves in the fields near Dover;
Gloucester's *sententia* provides the commentary: 'O ruin'd piece of
Nature! This great world / Shall so wear out to naught' (4.6.136–7).
By act 5, Lear has come to the end of his journey, as has Kent, who,
as he tells Lear, 'from your first of difference and decay, / Have
follow'd your sad steps' (5.3.288–9). The end is what Albany calls
'this great decay' (297).

Lear has discovered that he cannot crawl unburdened toward
death, that age brings its own burdens of responsibility and grief.
Though Kent has said to Cornwall, 'Sir, I am too old to learn'
(2.2.128), in this play, no one is too old to learn, least of all Kent.
For the old men who have suffered – Lear, Gloucester, Kent – not
the moment of death, but the duration, is tragic. They have experienced what Edgar ironically calls 'our lives' sweetness, / That
we the pain of death would hourly die / Rather than die at once'
(5.3.184–6). Kent and Edgar understand the grim justice in Lear's
death:

KENT Vex not his ghost: O! let him pass; he hates him
       That would upon the rack of this tough world
       Stretch him out longer.
EDG.   He is gone, indeed.
KENT The wonder is he hath endur'd so long:
       He but usurp'd his life. (5.3.313–17)

Only the young remain to obey 'The weight of this sad time' (323).

'This sad time' refers to the suffering of Lear's time and to the broader historical context hinted at in the play. To Gloucester, early in the play, the relinquishing of kingly responsibility and the cracking of filial bonds point to more general evils of his epoch. These evils, too, plague a man's journey toward death: 'We have seen the best of our time: machinations, hollowness, treachery, and all ruinous disorders follow us disquietly to our graves' (1.2.117–20). The Fool later predicts an unspecified future of world-upside-down: 'Then shall the realm of Albion / Come to great confusion' (3.2.91–2). These vague historical allusions transcend both the time in the play and Shakespeare's time. One clear emblem about all-time is created by the image of Edgar, disguised as Tom o' Bedlam, leading his old, blind father to Dover. Amidst the swirling movement of the play emerges a tableau of universal human history. Gloucester's *sententia* provides the motto: ' 'Tis the times' plague, when madmen lead the blind' (4.1.46).

This emblematic scene of a madman leading a blind man is complemented later in the act by that of a madman preaching to a blind man. Blind Gloucester meets mad Lear in the fields near Dover, and Lear preaches to him about the pain of life-as-duration:

Thou must be patient; we came crying hither:
Thou know'st the first time that we smell the air
We wawl and cry. I will preach to thee: mark. (4.6.180–3)

When we are born, we cry that we are come
To this great stage of fools. (184–5)

In his own sententious style, Lear echoes the Renaissance commonplace, 'We weeping come into the world and weeping hence we go.'[28] In an old Anglo-Irish lullaby, a mother sings that sad truth to her child in the cradle:

Child, lollai, lollai!
With sorrow thou com into this world,
With sorow ssalt wend awai.

Noting this similarity to Lear's speech, Chambers commented that

Lear, like the child in the song, must learn that 'sorrow is the law of life.'[29] A lullaby theme is appropriate to Lear and Gloucester, since both are 'child-chang'd' fathers – changed by their children, changed into children. We need not seek psychic authenticity in Lear's reason in madness here, for to do so would be to lose what Mack describes as its 'emblematic and morality-based dimension as meditation or oration in the tradition of *De Contemptu mundi*.'[30]

The lesson of Lear's homily is that we must be patient. We come crying hither because we anticipate the pain of life-as-duration, and, as Lear and Gloucester discover, we go crying hence. Our coming and going, Lear tells Gloucester, must be endured. His *sententiae* anticipate the aphorism uttered by Edgar in the next and final act: 'Men must endure / Their going hence, even as their coming hither: / Ripeness is all.' Lear too anticipates that *tableau vivant* in his metaphoric suggestion that he and Gloucester, like any man and Everyman, are playing out their parts on 'this great stage of fools.'

The implication of Lear's and Edgar's pleas for patience is the same. Their *sententiae* offer a defence against Time the Destroyer. They need such defence indeed, for their world is singularly marked by ill-timing: 'from hour to hour we ripe and ripe,' Jaques parrots in *As You Like It*, 'then from hour to hour we rot and rot' (2.7.26–7). The tragedy of Time, the times, and timing in *King Lear* is that decay comes before fruition, rottenness before death, and death before ripeness: that Time has to destroy so much to reveal the Truth. But Lear's and Edgar's *sententiae*, like Whitney's emblem about learning, suggest that the mind of man can be its own place, its own world, that Truth is timeless, and that wisdom can bring the courage and patience to endure. In imagery and theme, these formulations echo pagan and Christian consolation alike.[31] 'For every thing there is a season' is the wisdom of Ecclesiastes, 'and a time for every matter under heaven.' The wisdom of the ages lies enclosed in the aphorism: in a world of 'strange mutations,' as Edgar characterizes it, ripeness and readiness of mind are all a man has.

But the 'all' of Edgar's *sententia* has a haunting ambiguity, and the stasis created in action and emotion is only momentary. Edgar talks of patience, but has yet to witness the final going hence of his father, Cordelia, and Lear. Lear's homily, too, provides only the briefest pause in the play's action. Taken in full context, his plea for patience is pitifully ironic, for he has never been able to be patient. Further, he has yet, at that moment, to regain Cordelia, whom he then immediately loses again, this time forever. Although Edgar resolves that ripeness is all a man can achieve or have, the play as a whole – especially its last act – forces us to ask, *is* ripeness all a man needs? No *sententia* in *King Lear* can fully convince us that any man, young or old, foolish or wise, is ever ready to endure and accept what Lear endures but cannot accept before he dies.

Clearly *sententiae* and their tradition are immersed in the paradoxicality of the play. The tension is never fully suspended between sententious affirmation and the action or emotion that defies their rationality or renders it incomplete. Aphoristic formulations about experience thus never completely arrest the action or rationally accommodate the dramatic experience of the play. The play continually threatens to explode all inherited formulas and communal wisdom by showing the uniqueness and terrible isolation of individual suffering:

LEAR Howl, howl, howl! O! you are men of stones:
      Had I your tongues and eyes, I'd use them so
      That heaven's vault should crack. She's gone for ever.   (5.3.257–9)

      This feather stirs; she lives! if it be so,
      It is a chance which does redeem all sorrows
      That ever I have felt. (265–7)

      A plague upon you, murderers, traitors all! (269)

In the play's last dark scene Lear does not recognize Kent, whose sententious voice has marked him as a representative of rationality and communal wisdom. In rejecting Kent with the others, Lear rejects both a community of sufferers and a tradition of consolation.[32] In his madness he suffers alone.

The questions raised by this final scene cannot be ignored. Does the play here completely spring its stoical philosophic traditions, leaving only the devastating image of human isolation? Are the aphorisms affirming reason, faith, and patience thereby rendered hollow sententiousness? Three sententious voices suggest one answer – Kent's 'Is this the promis'd end?' Edgar's 'Or image of that horror?' and Albany's 'Fall and cease' (5.3.263–4). The promise that has been fulfilled is that Time will bring the horror of punishment. But the promise that has been *broken*, the promise of the proverb tradition appealed to throughout the play by these very characters, is that Time will also bring the reward of Justice.

This answer is somehow incomplete. The play does not end with Lear's impassioned, highly personal speeches, nor with his lonely death. Neither do all remaining on the stage 'Fall and cease.' The last speeches help to restore, but do not secure, the balance between nihilism and affirmation, between individual death and community life. After Lear's death, the community briefly moves to the foreground again: first Albany, in a public idiom characterized by formality and generality, orders the ritualized social actions of removing the bodies and public mourning: 'Bear them from hence. Our present business / Is general woe' (5.3.318–19). In the same mode, he confers upon Kent and Edgar the responsibility of governing the kingdom: 'Friends of my soul, you twain / Rule in this realm, and the gor'd state sustain' (319–20). Kent and Edgar now move from their private roles to the public one of sustenance and support, a role which makes explicit what their symbolic function has been throughout the play. Their sententiousness articulated faith in rational, traditional ways of coping with experience. They will now support the kingdom, as pillars and props of the community, even as their traditional beliefs support the larger human community within and beyond the play. Kent declines the public role because, although wise, he is old; the death of this *senex* is near. The rule passes to Edgar, the *puer senex*, young in years but old in wisdom: this *puer senex*, as ideal leader sustaining and renewing the community, is an old traditional in myth and literature.[33]

I follow the Folio in assigning the last lines in the play to Edgar:

> The weight of this sad time we must obey;
> Speak what we feel, not what we ought to say.
> The oldest hath borne most: we that are young
> Shall never see so much, nor live so long.   (5.3.323–6)

His speech, like Albany's, is formal, generalized, public. The rhymed couplets that enclose their final words return language itself to the conventional rhetorical order defied in Lear's lament. The references to 'The oldest' and the 'young' recall the types of age and youth evident throughout the play, and bring the wheel full circle: the transference from old to young of the weight of public responsibility, that Lear sought at the play's beginning, is now accomplished. The old order has passed, but the final speeches point to a new order in formation, one diminished by recognized loss but sustained by the old wisdom and inherited beliefs, now deepened into personal understanding by excruciatingly felt experience.

The final shift in focus from the individual to the type, from private suffering to public responsibility, suggests that in this play Shakespeare fully exploits the old tradition of communal wisdom. The key metaphor in the last speeches, of 'sustaining a weight,' tells something of Shakespeare's use of *sententiae* in *King Lear*. In the play's construction, aphoristic formulations do not frame the dramatic experience; they only help to support it. Rather than working toward the closure of systematic argumentation or explanation, *sententiae* afford necessary points of reference, fulcra of balance, in a rapidly moving, painfully involving play. Even Shakespeare's structural use of *sententiae* is, as it turns out, a traditional one: Julius Caesar Scaliger, in *Poetices Libri Septem*, wrote, 'Of sentences there are two sorts, [simple and extended], both the supports of the whole tragedy. They are like columns, or pillars, of the whole building ... They are to be managed and disposed however most quickly leads to the truth.'[34]

Working within artistic and philosophical traditions in *King Lear*, Shakespeare manages and disposes proverbial wisdom not to define any system of truths but to affirm the simplest truth, that men and their community need to believe in order to endure. Edgar, the new pillar of the state, suffers, believes, and endures. His formulations, with those of the other good characters, invite the audience to see reason in madness, light in darkness. One key to the timeless appeal of *King Lear* surely lies in Shakespeare's use of *sententiae* as a vehicle for the archetypal theme of human temporality. The triumph of his art is that in this least formulaic of plays so many familiar formulas are sprung into new and unforgettable life.

NOTES

1 William Elton *'King Lear' and the Gods* (San Marino 1966)

2 Geffrey Whitney *A Choice of Emblemes, And Other Devises, For the moste parte gathered out of sundrie writers, Englished, and moralized. And divers newly devised* (Leyden 1584) 173, Facsimile Reprint, Henry Green ed (London 1865)

3 Morris Palmer Tilley *A Dictionary of the Proverbs in England in the Sixteenth and Seventeenth Centuries* (Ann Arbor 1950) T320, A62

4 Ernst Robert Curtius *European Literature and the Latin Middle Ages* (New York 1953) 98–101

5 William George Smith ed. *The Oxford Dictionary of English Proverbs* (Oxford 1948) 472

6 Curtius *European Literature and the Latin Middle Ages* 101. Curtius notes that one translation of Lao-tzu is 'old child.'

7 In Jaques' speech, 'All the world's a stage' (*As You Like It*, 2.7), the world-as-stage convention takes the theme so important in *Lear* of man's 'history' (his journey in time) from childhood to 'second childishness.' This is but one similarity in the two plays that share the more fundamental pastoral pattern of extrusion, sojourn in a natural world, renewal, and return.

Maynard Mack 'King Lear' in Our Time (Berkeley 1966) 63–6, and Rosalie L. Colie, unpublished paper, ' "Nature's above Art in that Respect:" The Limits of the Pastoral Pattern.'

8 O.J. Campbell, 'The Salvation of Lear,' English Literary History, xv (1948) 107; Jan Kott, 'King Lear or Endgame,' in Modern Shakespearean Criticism, Essays on Style, Dramaturgy, and the Major Plays ed. Alvin B. Kernan (New York 1970) 372

9 Mack calls the world-as-stage convention 'one of the most notable ... of the Elizabethan theater for fostering a balance of engagement and detachment,' and discusses these principles in 'Engagement and Detachment in Shakespeare's Plays,' Essays on Shakespeare and Elizabethan Drama in Honor of Hardin Craig ed. Richard Hosley (New York 1962) 276–96

10 Ibid 276–7

11 Curtius European Literature and the Latin Middle Ages 69–70

12 In Tutte le opere (Verona 1729) tr. Allan H. Gilbert Literary Criticism from Plato to Dryden (Detroit 1962) 223

13 Antonio Minturno L'Arte Poetica (Naples 1725) in ibid, 293–300

14 Mack 'King Lear' in Our Time 53

15 Variations of these mottoes (Veritatem ... dies aperit, Tempus omnia revelat, Veritas odium parit) and their uses are discussed by Fritz Saxl, 'Veritas Filia Temporis,' Essays in Philosophy and History Presented to Ernst Cassirer ed. Raymond Klibansky (New York 1963) 197–222. That Cordelia's sententia is a cliché is demonstrated by the numerous English versions and analogues that Tilley gives: 'Time brings the Truth to light,' T324, 'Time tries the Truth,' T335; 'Time is the author of both truth and right, / And time will bring this treacherie to light,' Kyd, The Spanish Tragedy; 'Time will strip Truth to her nakedness,' Chapman, All Fools; 'Till truth make all things plain,' Shakespeare, A Midsummer Night's Dream; 'Time is the old justice that examines such offenders, and let the Time try,' As You Like It; 'As time in her just term the truth to light should bring,' Spenser, The Faerie Queene.

16 Erwin Panofsky, 'Father Time,' in Studies in Iconology (New York 1967) 83

17 Ibid 84–91

18 Saxl 'Veritas Filia Temporis' 207–8

19 Tilley A Dictionary of the Proverbs in England T593, T575

20 Elton 'King Lear' and the Gods 106

21 Saxl 'Veritas Filia Temporis' 199

22 Panofsky, 'Father Time,' 82–3. Shakespeare's epithets for Time the Destroyer are commonplace: 'Devouring Time,' 'swift-footed Time,' 'old Time' (Sonnet 19), 'Time's injurious hand' (63), 'Time's fell hand' (64), 'Mis-shapen Time,' 'carrier of grisly care,' 'Eater of youth' (Lucrece 925–9).

23 Panofsky, 'Father Time,' 82

24 Sonnet 15 *The Sonnets* ed. W.G. Ingram and Theodore Redpath, (London 1964)

> When I consider every thing that grows
> Holds in perfection but a little moment ...
> When I perceive that men as plants increase,
> Cheerèd and check'd even by the selfsame sky,
> Vaunt in their youthful sap, at height decrease,
> And wear their brave state out of memory:
> Then the conceit of this inconstant stay
> Sets you most rich in youth before my sight,
> Where wasteful time debateth with decay
> To change your day of youth to sullied night ...

25 Sonnet 60:

> Like as the waves make towards the pebbled shore,
> So do our minutes hasten to their end;
> Each changing place with that which goes before
> In sequent toil all forwards do contend.
> Nativity, once in the main of light,
> Crawls to maturity ...
> And Time that gave doth now his gift confound.

26 Elton *'King Lear' and the Gods* 106

27 Ibid 246–9

28 'I wept when I was born, and every day shows why,' Tilley *A Dictionary of the Proverbs in England* w889; 'The man that feeling knows, with cries first borne, the presage of his life,' Sidney *Arcadia* 1.3; 'Such is the state of men! Thus enter wee / Into this life with woe, and end with miserie,' Spenser *The Faerie Queene* 2.2.

29 'Weeping he comes into the world, and with good cause, for the world will be his foe as it has ever been the foe of his "eldron." His foot is in the wheel, and he is beginning a pilgrimage, at the end of which death out of "a wel dim horre" awaits him. It is the very cry of pagan Lear, as he feels the foundation of his life crumbling about him,' *Early English Lyrics* ed. E.K. Chambers (New York 1967) 284–5. The subject of Lear's homily, writes Mack, 'is the suffering that is rooted in the very fact of being human, and its best symbol is the birth cry of every infant, as if it knew already that to enter humanity is to be born in pain, and to cause pain,' *'King Lear' in Our Time* 11.

30 Mack *'King Lear' in Our Time* 69

31 Elton *'King Lear' and the Gods* 99–107

32 Lear's rejection of others reverses the commonplace (which, recalled in this context, is an astonishing understatement) given by Tilley as 'It is good to have company in trouble,' c571. This cliché, uttered by not a character

in the final scene, was rehearsed earlier in the play when Edgar sententiously – and naïvely – consoled himself on the heath:

> When we our betters see bearing our woes,
> We scarcely think our miseries our foes.
> Who alone suffers, suffers most i' th' mind,
> Leaving free things and happy shows behind;
> But then the mind much sufferance doth o'erskip,
> When grief hath mates, and bearing fellowship.
> How light and portable my pain seems now ... (3.6.105–11)

33 Curtius *European Literature and the Latin Middle Ages* 98–101
34 Cited and translated by Rosalie L. Colie from Julius Caesar Scaliger *Poetices Libri Septem* II xcvii (1561).

TEN

NANCY R. LINDHEIM KING LEAR as pastoral tragedy

THAT *King Lear* HAS SOME CONNECTION with pastoral literature is not altogether a new idea. Critics of *As You Like It* have long
noted various parallels between that play and *King Lear*,[1] and recently Maynard Mack has suggested *Lear's* relation to pastoral
romance. In Professor Mack's assessment, *King Lear* alludes to the
patterns of pastoral romance only to turn them upside down: 'It
moves from extrusion not to pastoral, but to what I take to be the
greatest anti-pastoral ever penned.'[2] What I wish to suggest instead
is that *King Lear* makes no apologies for taking its pastoral 'straight,'
and that pastoral is relevant to its germinating impulses. *King Lear*
derives its resemblance to *As You Like It* and to pastoral romance
from something which is basic to its conception. We have only to
reflect upon what the past thirty-five years or so have taught us
about the nature of pastoral – its vision and the questions it implies – to see why Shakespeare could have considered the combination of pastoral and tragedy a viable paradox.

The combination is viable because pastoral too deals with fundamental questions about man. By asking what is *natural* for man,

pastoral consciously and normatively explores man's relation with civilization, with nature, and even with the cosmos. For the Renaissance writer pastoral was clearly associated with the major poetic themes. Spenser, for example, turns to pastoral to examine time, death, and the natural order in the *Shepheardes Calender*, or to explore the roots of civilization and social cohesion in Book VI of *The Faerie Queene*.[3] Milton, too, conceives pastoral in this way, not only in the Eden of *Paradise Lost* but earlier in *Lycidas*, where tragic questionings implicit in pastoral elegy are insisted upon.[4] If for the moment we accept Frank Kermode's thesis that all serious pastoral is concerned with the contrast between art and nature,[5] this too has relevance to *King Lear*, for it lies at the core of Lear's discoveries about unaccommodated man: 'three on's are sophisticated; thou art the thing itself' (3.4.108–9). One of the thematic chains to which these words belong, the concern with gorgeous clothing and 'superfluity,' is in fact a traditional topos of the kind of pastoral Hallett Smith describes as extolling the values of the good life:

> Oh happy who thus liveth,
>> not caring much for gold:
> With cloathing which sufficeth,
>> to keep him from the cold.[6]

The muted generalities of these lyrics are wildly magnified and intensified in the storm scenes of *King Lear*, but certain themes in both can be identified: the concern for man stripped of all the accoutrements of society, the evils of that society itself when seen from the perspective of a man somehow purified, and finally the needs basic to all men that permit one to define what is minimally necessary for a genuinely human existence.

In Lear's anguished comments on the society he once ruled we meet a tragic satire that thus has its roots in pastoral as well. The connection between social or political commentary and pastoral, available at least since Virgil's First Eclogue, was one that Shakespeare apparently found useful. In *As You Like It*, for example, virtually an examination of pastoral conventions, Shakespeare introduces two satiric figures, Jaques and Touchstone, and a formal discussion of a satiric problem: the distance necessary for effective moral judgment. Among the questions opened in this interchange between Jaques and the Duke (2.7.44–86) is whether Jaques' libertine past disqualifies him from practising satire. In *King Lear*, all such considerations of personal infection (which remain relevant to tragic satire in *Hamlet*) disappear in the wake of the play's demand for feeling and experience. Lear's awareness of his responsibility for injustice in his kingdom ('O! I have ta'en / Too little care of this' [3.4.32–3]) is felt to lend even greater authority to his criticism of society. Jaques envies the Fool his motley, which he sees as a badge of his difference from ordinary people and his licence 'To blow on whom I please' (49); Lear's speeches are wrung from his newly awakened sense of identity with ordinary mankind ('Off, off, you lendings!'). *King Lear* may not rest in the equation of humanity with 'unaccommodated man,' but the identification seems logically necessary to substantiate Lear's discoveries. Though we may say that Lear is approaching a pastoral position by recognizing himself as an 'everyman' who is uninvolved in society's scramble for wealth and position,[7] nevertheless, his 'unaccommodated man' remains qualitatively different from the traditional shepherd who earns his authority as commentator by his purity and harmony with nature. It is an index of the kind of pastoral Shakespeare is working towards that this stripped figure should be defined not in terms of his moral purity, but as a forked animal who suffers and has suffered.

In *As You Like It* these perceptions (in so far as they are recognized) are held in disjunction; that is, they are strung along sequentially to make up the action. Jaques is a ridiculous figure, not, to be sure, because he is disqualified from making moral judgments by his libertine past, but because throughout the play he refuses to be fully human. And insufficient humanity, manifested doubly in his opposition to love and his inability to undergo the 'education and rebirth' offered by the pastoral experience,[8] is in this play a cardinal failing. The point is made beautifully in the very scene in which Jaques and the Duke discuss effective moral judgment (2.7) because Shakespeare will not underwrite Jaques' cynicism or pat formulations. Nor, indeed, will he underwrite the audience's expectations of pastoral. We begin with what seems another aspect of the contrast between court (city) and country; Jaques' desire to 'Cleanse the foul body of th' infected world' suggests the immense vulnerability of civilization and especially of the city, since he takes aim at 'the city woman' and him 'of basest function' who (illegally, immorally) wears gorgeous clothes. Yet this speech gives way to Orlando's entrance, and the terms of discourse suddenly alter, so that 'civility' and being 'inland bred' become signs of moral probity and the guarantors of humane behaviour:

If ever you have looked on better days,
If ever been where bells have knolled to church,
If ever sat at any good man's feast,

If ever from your eyelids wiped a tear
And know what 'tis to pity and be pitied,
Let gentleness my strong enforcement be.   (113–18)[9]

We may protest that this is merely Orlando's misunderstanding
of pastoral life – the first seven lines of the speech (106–12) assume
'savagery' from those who live in a 'desert inaccessible' and who
'Lose and neglect the creeping hours of time' – but the Duke repeats
these very words when he responds to Orlando's needs. The scene
in fact unfolds within an extraordinarily civilized context, reflecting,
it seems to me, the filtered influence of Æneas' entrance into the
temple of Dido's Carthage (*Æneid* 1. 446ff). The significant echo
occurs between the most important lines: Dido's 'non ignara mali
miseris succurrere disco' (630) and Æneas' famous 'lacrimae rerum'
speech form the basis of Orlando's 'If ever from your eyelids wiped
a tear / And know what 'tis to pity and be pitied' (cf. also the Duke's
'Thou seest we are not all alone unhappy' [136]). Virgil's emphasis
on the founding of Carthage, on the city as symbol of the desired
end both of personal trial and communal suffering, is also part of
the ambience of this exchange in *As You Like It*.[10] The Virgilian
echoes contribute to the decidedly urban, 'nurtured' cast of this
statement of values – which forms what is in effect the doctrinal
heart of the pastoral examination in *As You Like It*. Thus, even in
a play that we may consider an example of pastoral, Shakespeare's
handling of the relevant themes is extremely complex, oriented towards action rather than contemplation, so that impulses like pity,
which are normally pastoral expressions of purified human nature,
find their root justification as well in more complex civilization.
Shakespeare presents a similar ambivalence toward traditional
pastoral motifs in *Cymbeline* 3.3 (which also begins with a clear
reference to the *Æneid*, to Evander's 'aude, hospes' speech of
VIII.364f), where the two rusticated princes do not refute old
Morgan's statements about the corruption inherent in court and city
life, but insist that it is necessary for a fully human – meaning heroic
– existence: the princes complain, 'We have seen nothing / We are
beastly ...' (39–40).

It is perhaps in what I have suggested is its 'doctrinal heart' that
As You Like It shows its most important resemblance to *King Lear*
– in the insistence that the human condition requires one 'to pity
and be pitied,' to respond sympathetically to another person's suffering or to an outrage against one's sense of human value. The
first of these alternatives is more prevalent in *As You Like It*, where
repeated offers of sympathy or help to someone who is in need form

a central pattern of action in the play. The motif is usually expressed in terms of some bond or tie which impels it: Adam's decision to help Orlando because of loyalty to his old master, Celia's flight from the court with Rosalind because of their friendship, Orlando's determination to find food for the dying Adam (because of gratitude, honour, the reciprocal nature of the bond of service?), Orlando's rescuing of Oliver from the lion because they are brothers, Phebe's pity for Sylvius once she too knows the pains of love, etc. All these acts are generalized and epitomized in the central gesture with which the Duke responds when he is conjured to pity another, not because of particular attachment, but on the grounds of his civilized humanity.

One can, I think, scarcely overemphasize the importance of this same motif or gesture to *King Lear*, since it is the focus for Shakespeare's explorations concerning man and the minimally 'ideal' society. Shakespeare's strategy in the play seems two-fold: the first thrust is towards drastic reduction, towards the thematic word 'nothing'; the second is towards establishing the minimal essential 'something' that allows one to define man normatively, namely, feelings of pity and love. *King Lear* envisions possibilities of justice, equality, opulence which we may justifiably consider part of a maximally ideal society; yet the play, like pastoral, is really concerned with the basic and minimal. But paradoxically, what in political or social terms is only minimally ideal turns out to be, in personal terms, a kind of perfection: the love that obtains between father and child is sufficient to transform prison into something that the gods themselves throw incense on. However much the play makes of the theme of social justice, the 'minimally ideal society,' then, is not a political construct of any sort: its essence is the love between father and child, Cordelia reconciled to King Lear, Edgar reunited with Gloucester. In its fullest form the essential element is this special kind of purified love, but for purposes of 'definition,' the element that distinguishes man seems to be his capacity for pity. '... It is especially humane (and humanity is the virtue most peculiar to man) to relieve the misery of others ...': the authority is Sir Thomas More in his *Utopia*.[11]

The drive to reduce man to 'nothing,' to a state just *below* what we would accept as human, materializes in the figure of poor Tom, who is an objective embodiment of Lear's anguished imagination: 'Allow not nature more than nature needs, / Man's life is cheap as beast's' (2.4.268–9); 'Is man no more than this? ... unaccommodated man is no more but such a poor, bare, forked animal as thou art' (3.4.105, 109–11); 'I' th' last night's storm I such a fellow saw, /

Which made me think a man a worm' (4.1.32–3). But Shakespeare wants to do more than merely isolate this supremely negative figure; Edgar's decision 'To take the basest and most poorest shape / That ever penury, in contempt of man, / Brought near to beast' is taken apparently in part so that he may go through villages and 'Enforce their charity. Poor Turlygod! poor Tom! / That's something yet: Edgar I nothing am' (2.3.7–9, 20–1). The 'something' that poor Tom is, on the one hand, is a *role* (in contrast to which, Lear has lost his roles of king and father and Edgar is no longer a son), but on the other hand, more important for this discussion, it is an object of pity, a means by which other people are enabled to discover or manifest their humanity. Human reduction, the first motif, thus leads naturally to the second motif of pity. Lear's radical discovery about unaccommodated man follows such a moment of awareness of another person's suffering: 'Thou wert better in a grave than to answer with thy uncover'd body this extremity of the skies' (3.4.103–5). We recognize this as a statement about himself as well as about poor Tom; he too has been 'reduced' to a mere man. These perceptions of others are wrung from his own suffering: 'How dost, my boy? Art cold? / I am cold myself ... Poor Fool and knave, I have one part in my heart / That's sorry yet for thee' (3.2.68–9, 72–3). The mad speeches play variations on our sense of this identification: 'What! has his daughters brought him to this pass? ... nothing could have subdu'd nature / To such a lowness but his unkind daughters' (3.4.63, 70–1). Lear's inability to distinguish himself from other people is the mad counterpart of his new openness to feelings of pity and concern for others, and it culminates in his recognition of himself in the figure of 'man' he has just discerned: 'Off, off, you lendings! Come; unbutton here' (111–12).

The idea of compassion is so strong in *King Lear* that it seems to determine certain technical aspects of the play, one rhetorical in the large sense of the term, the other in the narrower stylistic sense. That the play 'notoriously overwhelms and exhausts us'[12] is Shakespeare's conscious intention, the result of an unprecedented insistence that the audience actively participate in the emotional experience of his characters. He does this by having the characters on stage constantly express their own emotional reactions, which calls attention to what the audience feels and certifies its response as proper before it can be stifled as 'unmanly.' On some such grounds we may account for Edgar's frequent remarks to the effect that 'My tears begin to take his part so much, / They mar my counterfeiting' (3.6.60–1) and 'I would not take this from report; it is, / And my heart breaks at it' (4.6.142–3), or Albany's 'If there be more, more woeful, hold it in; /

For I am almost ready to dissolve, / Hearing of this' (5.3.202–5).[18] It might be possible to attribute this emphasis on emotional participation both to the general rhetorical or affective bias of Renaissance poetic theory which had as its chief aim the moulding of audience response, and to the specific description that the Donatan tradition gave to tragedy: 'the primary effect of tragedy is sorrow or woe, of which pity is a species.'[14] Yet no other Shakespearean tragedy is so insistent in its allegiance to the theory – because in no other play is the concern with pity so central thematically.

The basis of the rhetorical scheme characterizing the expression of these themes is an implicit comparison of an extreme and an extremely negative character. Shakespeare restricts his usage of this rhetorical pattern to the Lear story, probably because the physical outrage of the Gloucester subplot makes any heightening of our responses there unnecessary. We hear it first in the very opening scene of the play, in Lear's assertion that

> The barbarous Scythian,
> Or he that makes his generation messes
> To gorge his appetite, shall to my bosom
> Be as well neighbour'd, pitied, and relieved,
> As thou my sometime daughter   (116–20),

where the comparison is still confined to human beings, though the Scythian is felt to be only marginally human, a figure who is morally 'nothing' to weigh along with the materially deprived figures who will later haunt the play. We hear it last just before the reconciliation scene, where it works in its more characteristic form, with animals:

> CORD.   Mine enemy's dog,
>   Though he had bit me, should have stood that night
>   Against my fire.   (4.7.36–8)[15]

In Albany's confrontation with Goneril the comparison becomes linked to the idea of filial bonds and the borderline dividing man, beast, and 'monsters of the deep':

> Tigers, not daughters, what have you perform'd?
> A father, and a gracious aged man,
> Whose reverence even the head-lugg'd bear would lick,
> Most barbarous, most degenerate! have you madded.   (4.2.40–3)

A 'head-lugg'd bear,' tortured to wildness, would show more pity – and piety – than Goneril and Regan have shown. The purpose of the rhetorical scheme is to help us realize the extent of the moral depravity, of the falling away from humanity, that is at the core of these actions. And in this play, 'to show the extent' of anything means to drive to the uttermost limits and then perhaps beyond, not just intellectually but emotionally. Gloucester's great speech condemning the sisters' behaviour most fully explores the hyperbolic tendency implicit in the scheme. He has disobeyed their order not to help Lear

> Because I would not see thy cruel nails
> Pluck out his poor old eyes; nor thy fierce sister
> In his anointed flesh rash boarish fangs.
> The sea, with such a storm as his bare head
> In hell-black night endur'd, would have buoy'd up,
> And quench'd the stelled fires;
> Yet, poor old heart, he holp the heavens to rain.
> If wolves had at thy gate howl'd that dearn time,
> Thou should'st have said 'Good porter, turn the key.'   (3.7.55–63)

Humanity has exceeded its upper and lower limits in the line containing 'anointed flesh' and 'boarish fangs,' just as the description of the sea suggests that the sufferings of this finite old man have exceeded what illimitable Nature could have endured without breaking her own laws. The wolves offer us a tonic return to the kind of rhetorical scheme we have been tracing; the extremity of the outrage it implies becomes underlined by association with the hyperbolic description of the sea. Most uses of the scheme point to the cruelty of the offence; here in Gloucester's speech Shakespeare gives equal emphasis to the magnitude of the suffering.

The affective mechanism of the rhetorical scheme itself contributes to the emotional exhaustion one experiences with this play. It is on the one hand powerfully expressive, yet it also points to a failure of expression because the tendency towards hyperbole implies that the speaker is without an adequate vehicle to convey the indignation he feels. In its full form it gives voice to the audience's sense of the enormity of the behaviour, the emotional and moral incomprehensibility of such personal yet cosmic evil. The expressiveness offers us some satisfaction at having recognized and condemned the outrage; the inexpressiveness keeps us tense and frustrated because ultimately it eludes our power as well as our intellectual grasp. It is exhausting too because it is pitched to such a key in order to evoke our astonishment as much as our pity or indignation; that is, Shakespeare is working with both halves of the Donatan formula and is trying simultaneously for woe and wonder, as the Renaissance thought tragedy should.

Shakespeare's desire to elicit the audience's emotional involvement and to keep passion at its apex is promoted by the way that the pure evil of the two sisters is manifested. Lear himself talks frequently of their stony hearts – one never forgets the question he hurls at the gods in the mock-trial scene, 'Is there any cause in nature that make these hard hearts?' (3.6.78–9) – and we are to follow this lead, I think, to understand their place in the economy of the whole. William Hazlitt's assessment is just: 'that which aggravates the sense of sympathy in the reader, and of uncontrollable anguish in the swoln heart of Lear, is the petrifying indifference, the cold, calculating, obdurate selfishness of his daughters.'[18] What shocks us most about them is their total lack of human feelings, especially pity. Lear is too complexly conceived to be defined by the single quality of his passion, but Goneril and Regan, and, later, Cordelia, are in fact largely determined by the quality of their feeling. (So that Lear's original question, 'Which of you shall we say doth love us most?' remains ironically central to the play, though the chamber in which it echoes changes from fairy tale to apocalypse.) The elaborate description of Cordelia in 4.3 reveals primarily a creature capable of feeling. She represents, if I may simplify, a middle term between the emotional outbursts of Lear and the absolute dearth of feeling in her sisters:

> KENT Did your letters pierce the queen to any
> demonstration of grief?
> GENT. Ay, sir; she took them, read them in my presence;
> And now and then an ample tear trill'd down
> Her delicate cheek; it seem'd she was a queen
> Over her passion; who, most rebel-like,
> Sought to be king o'er her. (4.3.10–16)

Shakespeare's imagination dwells most lavishly on the paradoxical play of feeling and restraint, making the balance also a transcendence:

> GENT.   patience and sorrow strove
> Who should express her goodliest. You have seen
> Sunshine and rain at once; her smiles and tears
> Were like, a better way; those happy smilets
> That play'd on her ripe lip seem'd not to know
> What guests were in her eyes; which parted thence,
> As pearls from diamonds dropp'd. (17–23)

This is surely a great deal of attention to give to a few tears in a play that encompasses so much and such violent action. Thematically, however, this is a moment of revelation, an outpouring of pity and love, but tempered by the quality of strength implied in 'queen'

and 'patience.' It would seem to be an answer to the problem of absolutes set up in the play's opening scene, where Cordelia's unbending
allegiance to Truth is almost inhumanly 'stoic.' The solution is not
a compromise with Truth, but an infusion of human feeling – of
pity for another's suffering as well as of love. An analogous change
takes place in the theme of 'service' or loyalty. In 1.1 Kent's Platonic
notion of service manifests itself as absolute fidelity to Truth (as
does Cordelia's understanding of her filial bond), but in the course
of the play the manifestations are all gestures of compassion, em-
phasizing human response rather than abstract principle: Cornwall's servant outraged by his master's attack on Gloucester, Gloucester himself seeking to aid the king, Kent's ministrations in the
storm, Gloucester's servants who help him after he has been blinded,
etc. Edgar's case binds the three motifs together because he becomes
his father's servant and 'saves' him, not through truthfulness, but
through the stratagem of pretending that Gloucester has survived
a leap from the Dover cliffs. The 'good' characters of the play are
defined by their capacity for this kind of human feeling; it is ultimately what makes Lear 'More sinn'd against than sinning.'

The followers of the wicked sisters, in turn, interpret 'pity' according to their own values. Regan tells the just-blinded Gloucester
that Edmund is 'too good to pity' him; in a later speech to Oswald
she reveals her Machiavellian understanding of feeling as only a
factor – real or feigned – in political manipulation:

> It was great ignorance, Gloucester's eyes being out,
> To let him live; where he arrives he moves
> All hearts against us. Edmund, I think, is gone,
> In pity of his misery, to dispatch
> His nighted life; moreover, to descry
> The strength o' th' enemy.   (4.5.9–14)

With Edmund we have the most telling statement of the evil camp's
relation to pity. In asking his captain to murder the imprisoned king
and Cordelia, he defines the new regime:

> know thou this, that men
> Are as the time is; to be tender-minded
> Does not become a sword ...   (5.3.31–3)

The officer's willing assent ironically hearkens back to the pastoral
definition of basic man that the play has been concerned with:

> I cannot draw a cart nor eat dried oats;
> If it be man's work I'll do't.   (39–40)

The two groups of people surrounding the king move in precisely opposing directions. Those in the evil camp move from a hypocritical profession of feeling (the sisters' declarations of love, Edmund's feigned compassion for Edgar and loyalty to his father) to a revelation of their coldness and Machiavellian opportunism; the good people are more complexly arranged, but they generally follow the pattern set by the king in moving from a relatively inflexible understanding of their roles to a new understanding based on or manifested by compassion (Cordelia and Kent as outlined above; Gloucester and Albany away from a kind of 'formalism' by which their allegiance for a while is given to wife or to constituted legal power; for Edgar the pattern seems to be increasing intensity of feeling rather than a qualitative change in direction). One of Shakespeare's methods in effecting these transitions is to fuse the metaphoric idea of knowledge frequently implied in sight imagery with the idea of suffering that potentially underlies 'feeling.' The best known of the fusions is probably Gloucester's 'I see it feelingly' (4.6.150), which echoes his earlier prayer,

> Let the superfluous and lust-dieted man,
> That slaves your ordinance, that will not see
> Because he does not feel, feel your power quickly.   (4.1.67–9)

These are expressions of the theme that explicitly connect sight (knowledge) and feeling (pity, suffering, touch); several other speeches work overtly with only one of the parts, but link it firmly to the other motifs of the play. The closely related prayer uttered by Lear during the storm, for example, works with 'feeling' and has its own reverberations in what we have seen to be pastoral motifs concerned with social justice and unaccommodated man:

> Expose thyself to feel what wretches feel,
> That thou mayst shake the superflux to them,
> And show the Heavens more just.   (3.4.34–6)

Even as Edgar's disguise as poor Tom answered the needs of the Lear plot by offering the reductive image of 'Man's life [as] cheap as beast's,' his statement of identity to Gloucester asserts the differentiating element which the play has been seeking:

> GLOU. Now, good sir, what are you?
> EDG. A most poor man, made tame by Fortune's blows;
>   Who, by the art of known and feeling sorrows,
>   Am pregnant to good pity.   (4.6.221–5)[17]

The fusion in this passage has suppressed the element of sight altogether and joined suffering directly with knowledge. That the tendency of the play in all its aspects is to insist upon the primacy of feeling has long been hidden by traditional interpretations of its dominant sight imagery which equate sight with insight. The reassessment offered in Paul J. Alpers' 'King Lear and the Theory of the "Sight Pattern" ' seems to me a much more accurate and sensitive reading of Shakespeare's use of sight and eyes in the play. Professor Alpers' argument is that references to the eyes in King Lear 'constantly draw our attention not to the perception of moral obligations, but to the actual human relationships that give rise to moral obligations'; eyes 'are characteristically represented as the organs through which feeling toward other people is expressed.'[18] He aptly quotes the final lines of Gloucester's 'I stumbled when I saw' speech – 'Might I but live to see thee in my touch, / I'd say I had eyes again' (4.1.23–4) – to affirm that 'what is important for Gloucester is not insight but a relationship for which the only possible metaphor is physical contact.'[19] Feeling in the play means not only emotion or suffering, but the actual sense of touch, just as seeing is often made more 'sensory' by being linked with the sense of smell (for example, Regan's 'Go thrust him out at gates, and let him smell / His way to Dover' [3.7.92–3]).[20] The double drive towards reduction and then differentiation discussed earlier is therefore contained within the double use of these words, for in addition to making use of overtones that suggest higher forms of apprehension (insight, compassion), Shakespeare employs the two key words 'see' and 'feel' to insist upon man as animal or creature, never letting his audience escape from the physical reality that underlies what is experienced in the play.

The slight possibility of relief offered by Gloucester's lines quoted above – that is, that embracing his son again would heal the anguish of his blindness – is echoed by Lear:

This feather stirs; she lives! if it be so,
It is a chance which does redeem all sorrows
That ever I have felt. (5.3.265–7)

As positive statements, both imply that the experiences that ultimately define one's life are those of pure love (agape not eros) rather than those of pain. Yet this is not, I think, our impression of the play. This hope of redemption is evoked only to be denied, not as 'truth' but as reality. 'Life' as defined by King Lear will not permit it. The dramatic embodiment of the possibility of redemption occurs in the reconciliation between Lear and Cordelia in act 4, but Shakespeare defied the 'Leir' tradition to have his play move on to the apocalyptic horror of act 5, beyond any experience of romance (for of course these moments of reconciliation are the stuff of romance, and of Shakespeare's later romances in particular) to a conclusion that in its painfulness is almost beyond the experience of tragedy itself. In fact, in terms of the audience's response, even the reconciliation scene between Lear and Cordelia can hardly be said to offer an oasis of relief. Its pathos is bearable only by contrast with the pain of having watched Gloucester's eyes being put out.

Our final impression of the play, as members of an audience even more than as readers, is dominated by a sense of physical pain, of life itself defined as torture: 'he hates him / That would upon the rack of this tough world / Stretch him out longer' (5.3.313–5). And again, we are expected to feel and give vent to our feelings. Lear's entrance with Cordelia in his arms is directed as much to us as to the people on stage:

> Howl, howl, howl! O! you are men of stones:
> Had I your tongues and eyes, I'd use them so
> That heaven's vault should crack.   (5.3.257–9)

(It is the old antithesis between persons with stone hearts and those capable of feeling, who have a sympathetic connection with nature and the cosmos.)[21] Kent's words at Lear's death are yet another cue for passion: 'Break, heart; I prithee, break!' Dr Johnson's famous comment upon the ending of *King Lear* is an emphatic statement of what we all feel in some measure – or the play has not done its job properly.

What we have been tracing here is, I think, the transformation of an essentially pastoral perception; but *King Lear* is not itself primarily a pastoral. The play uses pastoral structure to get at pastoral ideas – to arrive at basic man and a purified order of human values that encompasses public justice and private compassion – but once having arrived at the theme of human feeling, Shakespeare goes on to treat his material according to the tragic mode. The Aristotelian formula of pity and terror (underlying the Donatan woe and wonder) reinforced the propriety of the theme for tragedy, and the combined affective and didactic bias of Renaissance poetic theory channelled it into an attempt to stir up an analogous emotion on the part of the audience.

The pastoral-romance structure, like the reconciliation scene that is also from romance, is finally ironic, in the sense that both contribute to the meaningful pattern of life without ultimately having the power to define it. *King Lear* is tragedy, and neither pastoral nor romance, for all the use it makes of those modes. The last glimpse back to pastoral in the play (and it is fittingly to pastoral elegy) is a measure of the difference. One of the standard conventions of pastoral elegy is the comparison between the protagonist's death and the rebirth cycle of vegetative nature, a comparison which points to man's alienation from a nature that he is otherwise harmoniously part of and which formulates the anguish and tension that the final consolation of the elegy then overcomes. Another form this questioning frequently takes is 'Why this person and not someone less worthy?' There is an analogous moment in *King Lear* when Lear emerges with the body of Cordelia in his arms. The reduction motifs that culminated in the pitiable figure of unaccommodated man with whom Lear identified himself make the question of worthiness impossible for Lear to ask.[22] And there is no lush nature in our experience of the play to give the vegetative comparison resonance.[23] Instead, Lear's despairing cry is formed in terms of animals such as those which all along have been vehicles in the negative comparison that sought to define justice or humanity:

Why should a dog, a horse, a rat, have life,
And thou no breath at all?   (5.3.306–7)

The riddle, the incomprehensibility, the anguish are what we are left with. For King Lear there can be no final consolation.

NOTES

1 See, for example, Helen Gardner, '*As You Like It*,' in *More Talking of Shakespeare* ed. John Garrett (New York 1959) reprinted in *As You Like It* ed. Albert Gilman (New York 1963).

2 '*King Lear*' in *Our Time* (Berkeley 1965) 65

3 See Isabel G. MacCaffrey, 'Allegory and Pastoral in the *Shepheardes Calender*,' *English Literary History* 36 (1969), and Donald Cheney *Spenser's Image of Nature: Wild Man and Shepherd in 'The Faerie Queene'* (New Haven 1966) chap 5, for Courtesy's connection with Justice.

4 See the fine reading of *Lycidas* by Rosemond Tuve in *Images and Themes in Five Poems by Milton* (Cambridge, Mass. 1957).

5 *The Tempest* ed. Frank Kermode (London 1966) xxiv

6 *Elizabethan Poetry: A Study in Conventions, Meaning and Expression* (Cambridge, Mass. 1964) 30. The stanza is from William Byrd's 'The Heardmans happie life' *Englands Helicon* ed. Hugh MacDonald (London 1949) 144.

7 See William Empson *Some Versions of Pastoral* (Norfolk, Conn. 1960).

8 Walter R. Davis describes the pastoral romance pattern as one of 'disinte-

gration, education and rebirth' in W.R. Davis and R.A. Lanham *Sidney's 'Arcadia'* (New Haven 1965) 38.

9 *As You Like It* ed. Albert Gilman (New York 1963)

10 Note the further reference to Æneas in this scene when Orlando returns carrying old Adam on his back just as Æneas carried his father, Anchises. The words *pity* and *piety* were not fully distinguished in English until about 1600, and the confusion is part of the richness of 'Those pelican daughters' (3.4.75); cf. the phrase 'the Pelican in her piety.'

11 ed Edward J. Surtz, sj, (New Haven 1964) 93

12 Paul J. Alpers, '*King Lear* and the Theory of the "Sight Pattern," ' *In Defense of Reading: A Reader's Approach to Literary Criticism* ed. Reuben A Brower and Richard Poirier (New York 1963) 145

13 Similar to these in attempting to evoke and channel our pity are Lear's repeated remarks concerning his own tears, endurance and old age: 2.4.192–5, 274–5; 3.2.20, for example.

14 Both points are made in J.V. Cunningham *Woe or Wonder: The Emotional Effect of Shakespearean Tragedy* (Denver 1951) 99.

15 Actually, about half the number refer to human beings, half to animals, but the latter tend to be more striking. Other examples occur at 2.2.136–7, 3.1.12–15 (where oddly the animals seem right out of pastoral romance), 4.7.30–1, perhaps 4.6.205–6.

16 *Characters of Shakespeare's Plays* (1817) reprinted in *King Lear: Text, Sources and Criticism* ed. G.B. Harrison and R.F. McDonnell (New York 1962) 88. Just after this Hazlitt suggests that Shakespeare uses the Fool as comic relief for the audience's tension; the emotional effect of the scenes with the Fool seem to me quite the opposite. For the remarks of Goneril and Regan that are especially cruel in the way indicated, see 2.4.203, 219, 304ff.

17 Cf. Dido's 'non ignara mali miseris succurrere disco.'

18 P. 135. Note that in the final lines of the play, 'see' has been rechannelled towards feeling rather than knowledge: 'The oldest hath borne most: we that are young / Shall never see so much, nor live so long' (5.3.325–6). 'See' has little to do with moral perception here, but is another form of endurance or experience, parallel in meaning with 'borne' and 'live.'

19 Ibid 144

20 Alpers discusses this and the two related speeches of the Fool (1.5.19–23 and 2.4.68–71) on pp. 136 and 142. See also his fine treatment of another scene that has an overwhelming emotional impact, 4.6 on pp. 146–7.

21 The bond between Nature and Lear shown in the storm scene and between Nature and Cordelia suggested in her invocation to the 'unpublish'd virtues of the earth' to cure her father (4.4.15–18) are of course related to pastoral convention.

22 A comment made about the mad Lear in the negative rhetoric discussed

above also links the implications of the rhetorical pattern with the reduction motifs: 'A sight most pitiful in the meanest wretch, / Past speaking of in a King!' (4.6.205–6). Here pity is generated first for the marginal figure, then applied to the king, reversing the pattern of the play, where we first understand the suffering of the king himself and then apply it to man in general. The movement of the play forces greater and greater generalization, but the identification at the heart of it is truly reversible, so that there is no possibility of Lear's asking finally why should this happen to his daughter and not some more ordinary person. The issue is not one of worth, but of mere human life.

23 Note that the 'shadowy forests ... with champains rich'd, / With plenteous rivers and wide-skirted meads' described in the opening scene (1.1.64–5) become in our experience a place where 'for many miles about / There's scarce a bush' (2.4.303–4).

ELEVEN

ROSALIE L. COLIE reason and need: KING LEAR and the 'crisis' of the aristocracy

No; he's a yeoman that has a gentleman to his son; for he's a mad yeoman that sees his son a gentleman before him.   (3.6.12–14)

When every case in law is right;
No squire in debt, nor no poor knight ...   (3.2.85–6)

Prithee, tell him, so much the rent of his land comes to ...   (1.4.140–1)

Love cools, friendship falls off, brothers divide: in cities, mutinies; in countries, discord; in palaces, treason; and the bond crack'd 'twixt son and father.   (1.2.110–14)

... unnaturalness between the child and the parent; death, dearth, dissolutions of ancient amities; divisions in state; menaces and maledictions against King and nobles; needless diffidences, banishment of friends, dissipation of cohorts, nuptial breaches, and I know not what.   (1.2.151–6)

THESE COMMENTS from *King Lear* show some of the topsy-turvyness in the social order that informs the play, which has often been criticized as if its tragedy sprang from the simple disruption of an hieratic, orderly, customary society in which each man knew his place and responsibilities and kept to them both, in which duty and deference were expected and exacted in proportion to a man's known social and political status. According to one interpretation of *Lear* (as of many Shakespearean and other Renaissance dramas) the plot itself, with its manifold difficulties and sufferings, results from the deliberate abrogation of responsibility by the ruler. This Love-jovian or Tillyardian view has ruled for some time in criticism of the English Renaissance,[1] and only recently has it begun to be criticized, both by literary students who find in the abrogations of degree, priority, and place a less than necessary cause for tragic, or even significant action; and by historians who have consistently found the English Renaissance (like any other historical 'period') full of inconsistency, anomaly, disorder, and disruption.[2] Without quarrelling deeply with the Tillyardian notion of *the* Elizabethan world-picture, I want to pillage from quite a different historical scheme to illustrate some aspects of the social tensions involved in *King Lear*; that is, from Lawrence Stone's *Crisis of the Aristocracy, 1558–1641*, a rich, suggestive analysis of a major social class over a long period of time.[3]

Mr Stone's 'crisis' was a prolonged affair,[4] during which the aristocracy, although it never lost its favourable position in English society, lost its relative importance and was forced to alter its own self-image from that of an entrenched chivalric and 'feudal' group, with particular military obligations of service and general obligations of largesse, to that of a group involved in private lives and obligations precariously facing the problems of an expanding economy and a society increasingly articulate. Although the Tudors elevated themselves above their erstwhile peers, they came out of the aristocratic class and shared, as a family, some of the social and personal problems of that class.

Yet they sought to identify themselves with their state and its administration. Thus public policy underlined their differences from the nobility rather than their likenesses, and the English nobility found itself, like its European cousins, increasingly threatened by the centralizing efforts of the state. Chiefly, the court set out to gentle the armigerous aristocracy, to disarm them in all kinds of ways – by charming the nobles to live at court and to involve themselves in a growing bureaucracy;[5] by cutting the number of armed servants and thus the private military power long enjoyed by local noblemen; by educating the nobility to the gentle pursuits of humanistic learning and artistic patronage; by allowing and even encouraging the greater participation of women in social life – especially at its centre, the court itself. In many ways, central governments sought to domesticate the aristocracy; the aristocracy, too, found some pleasure and satisfaction in domesticating itself – in building houses according to new patterns; in making collections of paintings, sculpture, furniture, and books.

Withal, the aristocracy was faced with the particular problem of self-definition. Those who had given up the sword for the chamberer's graces found their relation to the sovereign somewhat altered: under Elizabeth and James, noble courtiers accustomed to deference themselves had to learn the importance of deferring to a monarch. The greater the family from which a courtier came, the greater the deference the monarch seemed to require. The more opulent a subject's house, the more he was expected to put it at his sovereign's service. In various rather touching ways, noblemen attempted to show their difference from other men. The great 'prodigy houses,' most of them built by Lords Treasurer, of whom Stone so amusingly speaks,[6] were for a while a major proof of class grandeur. With their ancient outlet in militarism gradually being closed off, noblemen and gentlemen tended to substitute the code of honour for the chivalric values. The older system of armigerous behaviour was superseded not only by modern technology and ordnance, but also by modern social arrangements: there was less and less place for the serious tournament or the trial-by-combat, as judicial settlements were otherwise reached. So a nobleman's word came to be defended and upheld by a complicated system of swordsmanship, based on the peculiar anomaly of the long, showy, dangerous rapier, which belonged neither to the old world of weaponry nor to the new. The rapier duel was an invention of a group of men trying to set themselves off socially from the 'others'; the weapon itself, carrying on a social tradition of archaism, was brilliantly and obviously nonfunctional as a practical weapon in an ordnance world.[7]

Another method by which noblemen set themselves off was dress. As Stone puts it, the acid test of living nobly was to have the money to spend liberally, to dress elegantly, and to entertain lavishly.[8] The portraits of the royal favourites, Leicester, Essex, Ralegh, and Buckingham, give some proof of the expense involved in looking the peacock courtier or the 'compleat' Queen.[9] Against such expenditure, even the conservative authors of the homilies sounded their injunctions: preachers never ceased to bewail the ruinous and frivolous preoccupation of the rich with their apparel.[10]

> Thou art a lady;
> If only to go warm were gorgeous,
> Why, nature needs not what thou gorgeous wear'st,
> Which scarcely keeps thee warm   (2.4.269–72)

Lear says to Goneril, whose costume we can imagine from the opulent ladies portrayed in Renaissance pictures; and Kent's rage at Oswald – 'a tailor made thee!' – records his anger at the upstarts who imitated their social betters.

Conspicuous expenditure and consumption were frequent causes of ruin for aristocratic families: 'Put not your finger in mortar,' Coke wrote, having observed the financial difficulties incurred by many great builders. Critics of gorgeous apparel noted that men 'weare their lands upon their backes.'[11] Yet these particular modes of setting themselves off from other men did not protect the aristocracy from imitation by social inferiors: noble ladies were offended by the liquefaction of merchant capital that could be heard in the rustle of city wives' skirts. Satirical literature of the period is full of upstarts, crow and popinjay, 'nobodies' who deck themselves in the costumes and manners of their betters. Ralegh himself, though an intermittent profiteer from the arbitrary system of favourites, was in effect such a 'nobody': he rose by his wits, his imagination, and his *sprezzatura*, and he fell for the same qualities. Ralegh had exceptional talent and exceptional personality; the Osrics, Oswalds, and Parolleses of Shakespeare's world are permitted no such virtues. Their showiness is just that: they are the froth thrown up by a roiled social system. Clearly, then, garb and retinue were insufficient protections from social intrusion, and dressed-up nobodies offered a real critique of the methods by which noblemen defended themselves against encroachments upon their rank and exclusive privileges. One can recognize at once the superficiality of distinctions as separate from function, while acknowledging that as function declined, such distinctions seemed ever more necessary. Barred from the automatic recognition conferred by its old sumptuary monopolies,[12] the aristocracy had to find in just such attitudes, attributes, and costumes a substitute means of self-definition, even of self-identification. The sociological importance of the nobility's self-concentration is obvious – and it carried economic implications as well, as shoals of craftsmen, jewellers, tailors, silkworkers, cabinetmakers, stonecarvers, architects, and so on, were called upon to support the aristocratic self-image in England.[13] The lavish expenditure characteristic of the medieval noble way of life was simple, as many commentators remarked,[14] compared to the new ways a nobleman might spend his money – the new commerce, the New World, and the aristocratic need for show accounted for remarkable outlays of income.

Although these signs of aristocracy were important and obvious at the time, they were by no means the only problems an aristocrat faced. Over the long span of time from the accession of Henry VII to the outbreak of the Civil War, there was obviously a slackening in the deference automatically due to a lord: the war itself is one gross measure of the change in aristocratic weight in the nation's social world. Other changes took place as well: for one thing, as Stone stresses, even among the aristocracy there was a considerable decline in paternal authority. Very few children adopted the social views Edmund attributed to Edgar, that 'sons at perfect age, and fathers declin'd, the father should be as ward to the son, and the son manage his revenue' (1.2.72–4), but the case of poor Sir Brian Annesley, whose daughters sued to declare him insane that they might get his estate,[15] is relevant to the general problem and perhaps even to the play of *King Lear*. In spite of marked deference shown parents by their children in England, it is clear that over the century and a half of the Renaissance, fathers lost their unquestioned authority in the disposition of their children's lives and fortunes. Legal requirements came to protect, particularly, daughters. In other cases, fathers took a more active interest in their children's individual personalities and welfare, in particular permitting them to marry with greater attention to need and temperament; often, too, fathers provided so generously for daughters and younger sons (in some cases, for bastards as well) that support for entailed estates was severely jeopardized.[16] As general respect for the individual came to be recognized, paternal authority counted for less; as ideals of social egalitarianism grew more widespread, aristocratic authority counted for less too. All the same, the class was, and remained, particularly privileged. Their crisis, such as it was, was as nothing to the difficulties suffered by the rural and urban poor, some of whom were not even privileged to recognize a 'crisis' in their affairs: life was certainly problematical for many segments of what is now called the middle class. But the nobility did face changes that unsettled many individuals within the class, if not the class itself. Against this particular set of problems, especially in their psychological manifestations, I want to look at *King Lear*. It is a play deeply rooted in its own period, a play which draws some of its power from the playwright's insight into the peculiar aristocratic situation of the time in which it was written, the situation Lawrence Stone has been at such pains to delineate.[17]

Before beginning on that task itself, I must assert something else, obvious enough. This play will not provide a proof-text for the aristocratic crisis (if that is what it was). Indeed, the adjustments described in Stone's book are too drawn out to have been compressed into one literary work – although, for a critic dissatisfied with a 'crisis' lasting for nearly a century, perhaps the concentration of the play more nearly justifies the use of that term. There is, of course, much in the general aristocratic social situation that is *not* in *King Lear*: for one thing, the play does not dwell topically on a major problem occupying the nobility and their advisers, namely, education; for another, though it exploits the question in its metaphors, it does not overtly deal with economics. In the play, actual economics are vague: the curious anachronisms of this play are uncompromised by discussions of pounds, shillings, pence, guineas, rose-nobles, and so on: but it is difficult not to read from this play a profound critique of habits of quantification induced by a commercial revolution. Though certainly questions of deference, of privatism, of personal and class ethos are of the utmost significance, *King Lear* is something very much greater, very much more complex, than a mere sketch in play-form of the psycho-social problems of new-style sovereigns and magnates. As these essays exist to proclaim, *King Lear* is made up of so much that to isolate one strand of its meaning is dangerously to oversimplify its multifoliate richness. The play is only in the highest sense an historical 'source,' testifying but fitfully to the problems historians must face head on. Indeed *King Lear* handles what might be called sociological materials very unevenly; at some points, the text is amazingly allusive, vague, and generalized; at others, remarkably direct and precise. The problem of being 'noble' is no less complicated than many of the purely literary problems this book deals with: the poet is sometimes astonishingly exact in what is here taken as data, and at other times hazy. But the playwright is nonetheless remarkable for what he saw in his society – and furthermore in a segment of society not naturally 'his' – and in his efficient translation into *literary* structures of the social structure of these problems. Indeed, he used many social paradigms in the terms of his given literary schemes and paradigms: he was able to treat his society, then, as he treated many other non-literary materials, as something to be rendered in the terms of his craft. What is remarkable, too, is that the playwright dealt analytically, even-handedly, and problematically with social problems, even as he consistently did with literary problems, and, thus, with the same striking insight and originality. If one may turn things about somewhat, the hypothesis might be offered that the play gives us, in its own laying out of social problems untouched by the benefits of modern analytical techniques, one bulwark to Lawrence Stone's massive analytic reconstruction of aristocratic society.

Within the play, historical structures are oddly treated. First of all, English 'history' is telescoped. According to chronicle-myth, the troubles of the Lear family did not end with the king's death; his daughters quarrelled fatally, and Cordelia's sons (imagine Cordelia with her sons!) did too. A train of Celtic king-figures had to reign before the historical Edgar could join the kingdom under a single strong rule.[18] The very names of the major figures in this play serve to fuse the layers of the English past – Lear and his daughters come from the catalogue of British royalty; Edgar and his wicked brother bear Anglo-Saxon names, one of them of the greatest significance in the roster of English kings; Gloucester was a Plantagenet royal title until the fifteenth century and would again become a royal title; the earls of Kent were local noblemen who had died out early in the sixteenth century; the title revived under Elizabeth in 1572. Albany and Cornwall were imaginable titles in the English Renaissance;[19] the earls of Cornwall had been both Plantagenets and Piers Gaveston; the kings of Scotland descended from a darkling Duke of Cornwall, and Albany was one of James I's titles as well.[20] The names 'Albany' and 'Cornwall' are realistic enough, then, but they recall something as well of Arthurian intermarriage. These names reverberate symbolically with English historical meaning; they do for the vertical range of time past what Edgar and Kent between them do for the horizontal range, across the social estates, of English speech, as those figures shift their dialects to offer a schematic section of the local and class languages of the nation. But Shakespeare was careful, too, in his use of title: he observed the rules of precedence, so that the blood royal takes precedence over all others, dukes take precedence over earls, and earls over the rest of the play's population.[21]

By such simple means, then, great implications are suggested. For all its moments of exact social observation and commentary, *King Lear* is surrounded by questions neither directly met nor directly answered. The action is mysteriously sited both in time and in place. The great rituals of the first scene echo with reverberations of something far deeper than specific reason or policy. We never know the practical details about the kingdom Lear rules and divides. Where does Lear hold court? Where was his palace before he went to lodge with his daughters in turn? That palace vanishes like Prospero's: indeed, except for Dover, we never know where anything takes place.

In *1 Henry* IV, the rebels divide the kingdom precisely, even arguing about its boundaries – Lear simply draws on a great map we never see. Obviously Gloucester's 'little' house (apparently a small castle of the old nobility rather than a great house of the new, but even so, peculiarly situated: 'for many miles about / There's scarce a bush' [2.4.303–4]) lies within the district allotted to Regan, for Cornwall becomes, Gloucester says, his 'patron.' Where Regan's house is in relation to it, or Goneril's in relation to either, we do not discover: simply, Lear's palace dissolves with his power, and the 'court' is concentrated on where power subsequently is rather than in a specific town or at a specific seat.

Other things are odd, too. Letters pass at an amazing rate from hand to hand – but there is no hint of how they do so. Nor do we know why the Gentleman (evidently the messenger between Cordelia and Kent) so readily trusts Kent on the heath; simply, we must accept that two good-hearted people, devoted to the king and Cordelia, trust one another on sight and do each other's offices willingly for that trust. All we know is that letters and people pass from here and there to Dover; even a beggar can lead a blind man to that critical port.

As with geography, so with other things: much is left unclear. Did Oswald do the act of darkness with Goneril, and if he did, why was he so willing to act as go-between for his mistress and Edmund? What happens to the Fool in fact and (more critical even) what kind of 'journey' must Kent go on, at the end of the play? Albany is left sole ruler of the kingdom, a position to which, judging from the first speech of the play, he had aspired; but without explanation or anything like the ritual fuss of the first act he resigns his rule first to Lear, then to Edgar. Most important of all, does Lear die thinking Cordelia dead or alive – can we tell, or should we try to tell? Within these areas of non-definition, of vagueness and mystery, the lives of King Lear and his three daughters, of the Earl of Gloucester and his two sons, of Kent, the Fool, and the rest are nonetheless lived to an extraordinary degree within the terms of sixteenth-century English society. Maynard Mack has pointed to one thematic and poetic gamut operating in this play, that from morality abstraction to naturalistic imitation of actions; the play moves along another gamut, from ritual and myth to an extremely practical and accurate grasp of local affairs.[22] There are things in this huge, difficult, and shocking play that become a little clearer when we apply to it some of the categories laid out by Stone's paradigm of the English aristocracy in the Renaissance.

Indeed, the more we look at the play, the more clearly we can see in it Stone's schema for the problems of the aristocracy. As he put it, 'the aristocratic ethic [*sic*] is one of voluntary service to the State, generous hospitality, clear class distinctions, social stability, tolerant indifference to the sins of the flesh, inequality of opportunity based on the accident of inheritance, arrogant self-confidence, a paternalist and patronizing attitude towards economic dependents and inferiors, and an acceptance of the grinding poverty of the lower classes as part of the natural order of things.'[23] These values are striking illuminations of the value-system of the play. For one thing, Kent's extraordinary loyalty to the king is a mark of his commitment to the aristocratic ethos. His behaviour within the play, evidently, is no less consistently loyal than his behaviour before the play began:

> My life I never held but as a pawn
> To wage against thine enemies. (1.1.155–6)

As a private person Lear assumes the hospitality and generosity of his daughters; and Gloucester's touching confidence that Cornwall cannot mean either his extreme rudeness to the old king or his cruelty to Gloucester's own person is based on his view of the unchangeable relation between host and guest – 'You are my guests,' he says (3.7.31) and 'I am your host' (3.7.39). The class distinctions of the play are clear enough, although the play's action in part consists in showing how tenuous they are when faith is bad. Gloucester's tenant comes on stage, it seems, solely to demonstrate how greatly Gloucester's landlordism attached the loyalty of his dependents; Lear shows gentleness, even on the heath, to his dependent, the Fool. Gloucester's repetitious *sententiae* about the breaking of social bonds are one measure of the limitations of his imagination – he recognizes that social bonds are being broken around him, but not why that is so. For him, as for the composers of the homilies, the social order 'ought' to remain constant, even when he sees it fall into disruption. Hence Gloucester's defencelessness against the deceptions of his son and the brutality of his lieges. Both Gloucester and Kent, adherents of the old aristocratic mores, are tolerant of the sins of the flesh, as we learn in the play's opening interlude; the Fool conforms to the manners of his social betters when, at the end of act 1, he suggests his love-play with the castle maids.

The problems raised by the inequality of inheritance are twice dramatized and very differently stressed. Lear takes a 'modern' solution to his predicament, the absence of a male heir: he divides his kingdom justly among his co-heiresses, attempting to prevent strife later. Gloucester, on the other hand, acts as the old aristocrat would, not noticing, until he thinks himself betrayed by Edgar, the injustice of what Stone calls 'the winner-take-all doctrine of primogeniture';[24] Edmund's bastardy-speech is, in fact, not a paradox only: it bespeaks a new and fairer view of individual worth in rejecting the automatic second-classness of bastards. These aristocrats are all arrogant, in different personal idioms; Kent never entirely forgets who he is, even when he is stocked for his apparent presumption to Cornwall. Cornwall is wantonly confident of his own power and safety among his servants, as he mutilates his elderly, aristocratic host. Goneril and Regan are high-handed with all others; both Lear and Cordelia are extravagantly high-minded and proud. As Sigurd Burckhardt has beautifully pointed out, Lear's absolute trust in his own and other people's 'word' is an outmoded social habit, but one entirely appropriate to his rank and style.[25] Of the noblemen, only Edgar demonstrates his independent awareness of the plight of the kingdom's poor – and yet this same Edgar, companion of poverty, becomes the champion of the whole kingdom, on whose swordsmanship the national virtue must be risked. He ranges along the whole social scale, from beggar and Bedlamite, doubly outcast, to the rituals of high-born conflict.

As against the 'paternalistic and patronizing attitude toward economic dependents and acceptance of the grinding poverty of the lower classes as part of the natural order of things,' one must note that Stone's aristocrats were also astonishingly open-handed.[26] Their testamentary charities may not have reached the standards set by the middle class[27] in this period, but their daily and weekly support of the poor and of other odd folk was both steady and generous.[28] In his dealings with the Fool and with Tom, Lear shows some of that characteristic paternalism – in his case, the more poignant because of his personal problems as a father. From his behaviour to the Fool, we can realize both Lear's automatic aristocratic kindness and his personal gentleness:

> My wits begin to turn.
> Come on, my boy. How dost, my boy? Art cold?
> I am cold myself. Where is this straw, my fellow?
> The art of our necessities is strange,
> And can make vile things precious. Come, your hovel.
> Poor Fool and knave, I have one part in my heart
> That's sorry yet for thee. (3.2.67–73)

Finally, in the king's awareness of the plight of the truly poor in his kingdom, lies his achievement of a responsibility which, without his tribulations, he might never have won. There is nothing in the past life of King Lear – indeed, nothing in the play itself – to suggest that 'the people' were important in either the private or the public economy of the nation or of its rulers. Of all Shakespeare's political plays (in which I include all his late tragedies), this one most overtly closes off considerations of subjects, populace, and the non-noble life. In the history plays, in the other tragedies, there is much reference made to the people, English, Scottish, Danish, Roman, even Cypriot; in both *Hamlet* and *Macbeth* we are ever aware of potential rebellion against the centres of power. In *King Lear*, though, the great ones fight out their battles within their own class, and such realization as the audience has of other groups is skimpy and schematic. The more remarkable, then, that from this background and in this setting, King Lear, having renounced his kingdom, comes to realize, at the stretch of his extremity, what it means to be really poor. In his 'houseless poverty' speech ring the echoes of a common configuration of ideas of poverty, charity, clothing, and food:[29]

> Poor naked wretches, whereso'er you are,
> That bide the pelting of this pitiless storm,
> How shall your houseless heads and unfed sides,
> Your loop'd and window'd raggedness, defend you
> From seasons such as these? O! I have ta'en
> Too little care of this. Take physic, Pomp;
> Expose thyself to feel what wretches feel,
> That thou mayst shake the superflux to them,
> And show the Heavens more just.   (3.4.28–36)

As in so much else, Gloucester echoes both the king's predicament and his insight; in his blindness, exposed to the miseries the Bedlam beggar illustrates for him, he says, too:

>   Heavens, deal so still!
> Let the superfluous and lust-dieted man,
> That slaves your ordinance, that will not see
> Because he does not feel, feel your power quickly;
> So distribution should undo excess,
> And each man have enough.   (4.1.66–71)

Both old men began the play securely enclosed in their own convictions of rightness and security; both undergo indescribable psychological torment, Gloucester paying with his eyes for not having 'seen' aright, Lear with his reason for not having understood how to be a proper parent. Both emerge from their class-bound view to 'see feelingly,' as kings and aristocrats were generally spared from seeing and feeling, what it meant to be a plain poor man in the kingdoms of this world. Both men are remarkably modernized by their sufferings, enlarged from the conscriptions of their social status. It comes with some irony that these undefended old men reach their new insights, their astonishing sympathies, under the guidance and by means of the emblematic beggar who seems to them 'the thing itself; unaccommodated man,' but whose unaccommodated state is simply a disguise.

To say that Lear and Gloucester achieve some of their greatness because they break out of the limitations of high-born assumptions does scant justice to the richness of their experience. Yet no more than in real life can this play be presented by some abstraction or social paradigm. In different ways, Lear, Gloucester, and Kent are old-fashioned aristocrats, theirs the noble ethos in the process of erosion during the Renaissance; equally, Albany, Cornwall, Goneril, Regan, and Edmund are domesticated in a 'new' world of power and might, which they intend to keep well within their own control. But just because we prefer Lear, Kent, and Gloucester to the scheming members of the next generation, we cannot explain the play by the glib assumption that Shakespeare asserted his characteristic conservatism by the play's means, praising an old if outmoded way of life for its moral symmetry and beauty; nor can we claim that human virtues are assigned to the old way, vices consigned to the new. Like Shakespeare's other great plays, *King Lear* deals in problems and problematics: neither way of life is sanctified, neither is regarded as an unqualified success.

This play begins with the situation feared by all men, kings and noblemen alike, with an inheritance to leave behind them, the absence of a male – that is, an obvious – heir. The number of noble families that died out in the period between Elizabeth's accession and the outbreak of the Civil War was frighteningly large.[30] Of royal families, the Tudors themselves died out, and in spite of Henry II's quiverful of sons, the Valois died out too. For a time Philip II feared to die without a male heir; the Stuarts survived by the puny breath of James VI; the nearly-royal Oranges twice just escaped heirlessness, both times at a period critical to the Netherlands' turbulent history. Great families had to worry about male issue, and kings more than others. Shakespeare followed his sources in providing King Lear with no male heir, but he stressed that critical fact not at all, though his sources, including the earlier play, make much of it. We see, then, the king coping with his problem and deciding to deal with his three daughters as co-heiresses. This is not an English or French royal habit – or, at least, not a modern habit, though Charlemagne had split his kingdom three ways long before Lear treats his girls in a thoroughly modern manner, as noblemen and commercial grandees without sons had begun to treat their daughters. Shakespeare followed these same sources in making the king relinquish sovereignty before his own death, and Lear's reason for doing so makes political sense in either a primitive or an early modern kingdom. Lear wanted to be sure, before he died, that his division of the kingdom was acceptable both to his beneficiaries and to the subjects over whom, after all, the girls with their husbands would rule. The division was proclaimed in public, before the lords and with the acquiescence of daughters and sons-in-law, 'that future strife / May be prevented now' (1.1.44–5). As a generation of students has written in criticism of this play, Lear's unwisdom is 'proved' by just this gesture – no king 'ought' to relinquish rule before it has formally ended with his mortal death. Historical rulers were not so obedient to this regulation as critical orthodoxy would suggest – against the rule there are several counter-cases. Not only was there no rule against abdication – Charles v, after all, voluntarily gave up his great Empire; Mary Stuart had perforce abdicated; though Shakespeare's Richard II may have been an anointed king, the playwright does not conceal his unfitness to rule, all the same – but also Lear was unlucky. In cases where a male heir lacked, was young, or was weak, political disruption could be expected, as Machiavelli taught; it could be argued that in trying to secure assent to the division of his kingdom, Lear showed foresight of an unexpected sort.[81]

Although Lear never complains of having only daughters, his assumption that continuance is crucial emerges clearly from his speeches to his daughters: he says to Goneril, 'to thine and Albany's issues / Be this perpetual' (1.1.66–7), and to Regan, 'To thee and thine, hereditary ever, / Remain this ample third of our fair kingdom' (1.1.79–80). The significance of his later cursing Goneril with sterility becomes even more profound when we consider his preoccupation with issue.[82] Apparently, too, Lear was less satisfied with one son-in-law than with the other. In the first words of the play, Kent says, 'I thought the King had more affected the Duke of Albany than Cornwall' (a preference which does the king credit, after all); later we hear of 'inevitable' dissent between the sons-in-law. But, as Gloucester says, Lear had resolved for strict justice between the dukes –

It did always seem so to us; but now, in the division of the kingdom, it appears not which of the Dukes he values most; for equalities are so weigh'd that curiosity in neither can make choice of either's moiety. (1.1.3–7)

In the first scene, the emotional weight of Lear's imposition of the competitive declarations of love for him tends to overbear the fact that, in spite of his psychological inequity, his division of the kingdom was 'just.' He divided the land into three rich parts, intending for his favourite child a third evidently not larger, but 'more opulent,' than those assigned her sisters. There is in the ritual charting of the new rule more than the suggestion that, before he allowed his psychological needs expression in the competition, Lear had taken thought for the political needs of the nation: he was not, in fact, dividing his kingdom solely in response to his daughters' declarations of devotion.

Looked at in the context of contemporary behaviour, Lear's solution for his kingdom was in line with modern aristocratic providence about rule, and with modern aristocratic treatment of daughters, by which the strongly paternalist father strove to provide generously for their futures.[33] The difficulty with Lear's situation is that it did not allow for the roles both of ruler and of father; he did not recognize his situation as unique – though Charlemagne, another dimly historical ruler in Elizabethan imaginations, divided his kingdom into three, British and English rulers customarily did not. But there is an interesting record of aristocratic division of wealth: consideration of daughters' material prosperity often contributed to the financial difficulty of noble families, some of which collapsed at the centre because of generosity in dowries and jointure-arrangements. By treating his kingdom as if it were simply 'his land,' an estate, Lear threatened his land, his 'country,' at its centre, too. It might be said that Lear's kingdom *figuratively* came to grief just because of his generous division of it among his heiresses. To say this, though, is to offer material substitutes for eventuations in the play sufficiently grounded in character and psychology, to say nothing of the ritual folklore of the deed itself. We do not need to know that, as a matter of economic and social fact, great holdings were often dissolved by division among children, especially female children, to realize that there is something fatal in Lear's act of division; but the modern relevance of that problematic gesture deepens the play's reference to a felt reality. One simplistic observation might be that in making Lear regard his kingdom as his property, Shakespeare made his profoundest comment on kingly misapprehension of rule and on ancient modes of governing.

Just the same, in at least two ways, Lear's disposition of the kingdom *did* observe modern rules of prudence and justice. In many ways doubtless more important, Lear must be ranged with the conservative noblemen of the play as an adherent, even a blinkered adherent, of the old ethos, dependent upon its values and profoundly endangered by their abrogation. His notion of *himself*, if not of his daughters and his kingdom, is entirely in terms of the old modes: though divesting himself of 'the sway Revenue, execution' of kingship, Lear chooses to retain 'only,' as he says, 'The name and all th'addition to a king' (1.1.136). In practice, what this means is that Lear wants to spend his latter days surrounded by his familiar household and the signs of his former greatness (in this case, a retinue of a hundred armed knights, a clever Fool, and whatever servants he may require for his personal needs), domiciled with his daughters by turn, on a perpetual royal progress. Under normal circumstances, this arrangement could very well have been made for an old patriarch and even for a self-retired king, at his life's end turning in legitimately upon private and familial pleasures. Furthermore, a great social figure would have had a household – witness Catherine of Aragon after her repudiation, or Mary Stuart in her detention – distinguished by a train of retainers. Retainers were not only a sign of an aristocrat's prestige but a defence of his prerogatives.[34] The sovereign often attempted to cut down on retaining because of its potential danger, but no ex-king could imagine himself entirely without retainers, simply to show his rank. One deep theme of this play is the *meaning* of deference to those who expected it as their due. The significance of *King Lear* would be greatly lessened if we could not understand what it meant to the king, to his children, to his nobles and servants, that men were deferred to according to their rank in society. From the vantage-point of the aristocratic ethos, there was nothing odd about Lear's wanting to maintain the 'exhibition' of his former greatness, even after he had delegated its great function to others. From the point of view of the new functionalism, equally, there was nothing peculiar about Goneril's and Regan's attempts to cut down their father's retinue: Elizabeth never allowed Mary Stuart a quota of *armed* servants.

Since so much of the struggle between early modern rulers and their nobility was over the monopoly on violence, it is obvious that retainers were looked at darkly by the sovereign.[35] The physical inconvenience and danger surrounding a retinue was one thing, the *psychological* importance of such a train was another. Rulers intent on their own security were unlikely to tolerate a mighty subject surrounded by proofs of his power; a retinue was, as Lear called it in that quantitative language so characteristic of his utterance before the storm, the 'addition' by which a grandee could reckon his importance.

Thus when Goneril says, 'His knights grow riotous,' Elizabethans would scarcely have found her remark incredible – if they knew of Sir Richard Cholmley's liveried retainers, who sneaked into the kitchen and speared the meat out of the pot with their daggers,[36] they might well have sympathized with her. On the face of it, her complaint carried weight; her insistence on the retainers' 'rank and not-to-be-endured riots' was hardly different from Henry's or Elizabeth's. Goneril was, by her father's donation, sovereign in her portion of the country, and certainly in her house. As sovereign, she simply acted the efficient ruler striving for order in her palace and, by extension, her kingdom:

> A hundred knights!
> 'Tis politic and safe to let him keep
> At point a hundred knights; yes, that on every dream,
> Each buzz, each fancy, each complaint, dislike,
> He may enguard his dotage with their powers,
> And hold our lives in mercy.   (1.4.332–7)

Later, as the size of Lear's retinue is ruthlessly cut down (only thirty-five or thirty-six of his knights join the king's forces at Dover), Regan states the general argument against a mobile retinue in a speech far more neutral and sensible, in social terms, than it is usually considered:

> what! fifty followers
> Is it not well? What should you need of more?
> Yea, or so many, sith that both charge and danger
> Speak 'gainst so great a number? *How, in one house,*
> *Should many people, under two commands,*
> *Hold amity? 'Tis hard; almost impossible.*   (2.4.239–44; italics mine)

The objections the daughters raised against the knights were those of a practical, modern, civilizing, rationalizing social orderliness; their objections were, in fact, received opinion. Further, from Goneril's remarks about Lear's servitors, we realize what sort of household *she* kept:

> Hear me, my Lord.
> What need you five-and-twenty, ten, or five,
> To follow in *a house where twice so many*
> Have a command to tend you?   (2.4.262–5; italics mine)

From this hint, we may assume that Goneril's house was – in contrast to Gloucester's isolated little house, typical of the parochial older nobility – a truly 'great' house, a palace, a prodigy house; she had a staff of at least fifty servants, from whom a sufficient number could always be spared to tend to her father's needs.[37] With this glimpse into Goneril's milieu, we suddenly see the degree of pride, of self-indulgence, involved in the lives lived by 'these daughters and these sisters.' They have their modern ways of conspicuous consumption no less grandiose than their father's old-fashioned train – and far more centred on themselves, on their own comforts and the projected image of their own greatness. Coupled with the fact that Shakespeare makes us witnesses to Goneril's complotting with Oswald to offend the king ('Put on what weary negligence you please' [1.3.13]), this glimpse into her values and manner of living makes us realize that her objections to Lear's knights are *not* simply those of a sovereign lady intent on maintaining civil peace. Indeed, just as with Edmund, at first sympathetically presented and only later revealed as the cheat he is, the playwright is careful to deny Goneril her claims to justification in this respect. So also with Cornwall, commanding that Kent and Oswald put up their swords – 'Keep peace, upon your lives: / He dies that strikes again' (2.2.48–9) – his words are those of any sensible ruler concerned for civil order.[38] We might take them at face value if we were not in the next act to see how Cornwall behaves when he thinks the monopoly on violence securely his. Shakespeare never leaves us long in doubt about these 'new' statesmen.

That Lear's knights *were* troublesome, we have only Goneril's authority; when we hear Regan linking Edgar and the knights, an association clearly false, we must wonder about the knights' behaviour altogether. Of Lear's 'riotous' train, only a single gentle figure says anything at all, and what he says is, it seems, a remarkable understatement of the actual situation:

> My Lord, I know not what the matter is; but, to my judgment, your
> Highness is not entertain'd with that ceremonious affection as you were
> wont; there's a great abatement of kindness appears as well in the
> general dependants as in the Duke himself also and your daughter.
>
> (1.4.60–5)

'Ceremonious affection' is entirely absent from this house, as we know from Goneril's planning with Oswald to withhold deference from her father. Gradually we realize the symbolic importance of withholding the ceremony normally due a father and a king: Goneril seeks to destroy the old man's sense of himself long before king-killing becomes part of the action.

Goneril and Regan were, of course, afraid of something other than mere inconvenience; they were afraid that their father, invested with his military power, might discover their aims and seek to stop them by turning that power against them. Their eagerness to strip Lear of his symbols of personal greatness is one thing; but it was quite another matter, a matter of pure power, to want out of the way those hundred knights who might have made up a Lear faction. Since the remnant of the retinue *did* join Cordelia at Dover, if Oswald's words are accurate, we may assume that at least those knights knew the proper duty of their allegiance and followed it.

One problem of the Tudor monarchs was that, like King Lear, they lacked soldiers. In times of crisis, Elizabeth had to depend upon a very mixed army, composed of trained bands, pressmen[39] (some little better than the crew gathered by Falstaff), and the cohorts of her great lords contributed as private trains, in the old-fashioned way, to the sovereign's cause.[40] During the period studied by Stone, loyalty was never entirely diverted from the great lords to the Crown, for all of Henry VIII's statutes and propaganda of the 'Faerie Queene'; the dutiful behaviour of Lear's knights was still quite understandable to a Jacobean audience. As far as the play itself is concerned, though, the knights barely appear; they are a shadow-retinue, whose importance depends entirely upon the director's, not upon the playwright's, injunctions. Their behaviour is undefined, largely attributed them by the daughters' unreliable words. Lear is effectively stripped of his strong bodyguard, left destitute and alone save for his Fool and a disguised servant. He has not forgotten the orthodox meaning of his retinue, however, as on the heath he recruits the Bedlam beggar as its replacement – 'You, sir, I entertain for one of my hundred' (3.6.80). That his retinue wore his colours is evident from his next remark to Tom, famous for its beautifully learned associations: 'only I do not like the fashion of your garments: you will say they are Persian; but let them be chang'd' (3.6.80–3). It is important to notice throughout these scenes, the great gentleness of the king. While he has control of his retainers, he never thinks to call them in his own defence against the extraordinary behaviour of his daughters, never thinks of himself as the leader of a band of *armed* men. For all his childishness, his irascibility, his arrogance, Lear is a civilized man, thinking himself in a civilized country. He lets his defenders slip away from him as if their 'real' function had never crossed his mind. Indeed, for him, the knights *were* simply a means of signalling his dignity to himself and others, never defences against his nearest kin.

The astonishing breaches in decorum in this play are not so immediately obvious to us as to an audience trained in the deference society. When Oswald refuses to stop at the king's command, when he identifies the king as 'My Lady's father,' the shock was almost as severe to the audience as to the defenceless and unprepared Lear. That Oswald 'would not' do the king's bidding utterly shatters Lear; when he finds his servant stocked, he says,

> They durst not do't,
> They could not, would not do't; '*tis worse than murther,*
> To do upon respect such violent outrage.   (2.4.22–4; italics mine)

Lear's awareness of criminal degree is imperfect, one might say; because, as Kent sits outside the house in which Gloucester's mutilation is soon to take place, we shortly realize how insignificant, beside that crime, the stocking of the king's servant is. But at the time, that punishment is part of the ruthless imposition of their will and rule on Lear and his kingdom that the daughters' party puts into effect. Lear must learn that he is no longer sovereign in Britain; his daughters undertake to teach him.

Of course Lear was arbitrary. Sovereigns were – and could count on absolute deference, even in their tantrums. Hence Lear's fury at Kent's gainsaying him, his attack on Kent in terms of the feudal bond – 'Hear me, recreant! / On thine allegiance, hear me!' It is one measure of Shakespeare's art that we come to see Lear's autocratic demands for his dinner naturalistically, as the signs of the childish greed in an old man, rather than as one automatic prerogative of royal position.[41] Goneril has, after all, commanded that dinner be made ready; why should not the king, hungry from hunting, have it when he likes? That Goneril orders her *servants* to slight the king shows how far she was willing to go, disgracing him, her kin, her father, before outsiders; Regan, literally, went further to show Lear incivility. When he rushes from Goneril's house to hers, Lear could expect (as any sovereign could) to be received. But Regan did what only a few landowners dared to do to Elizabeth; she left her house empty, so that the king was unable to rest on his progress. That she could do such a thing, unthinkable either to a father or to a sovereign, makes it less incredible that Regan could take such an active part in the blinding of her host shortly after.

In terms of the deference society, Kent's behaviour is interesting. He is round with the king, but obviously loyal and dutiful. With Oswald he is violent, outraged that a 'clotpoll' should so treat a king, outraged that his clotpoll should so flout *him*, even when he is in disguise. When Cornwall makes to stock him, Kent cannot believe that such a punishment, from which noblemen were securely exempt, could possibly be meted out to him; both he and Gloucester remonstrate with Cornwall in vain, urging him not to punish the king's servant.[42] Kent's reaction, like his overreaction to Oswald, is a remnant of his own aristocratic experience. Such things simply cannot be done to a man like him. That they are somehow prepares us for the outrage done Gloucester within doors.

Indeed, in spite of the control he achieves at stress-points, Kent's reactions are not always under his own control. His outburst against Oswald is that of the old aristocrat, against the falsity of a cowardly, braggart 'new' man, a nobody, a butterfly made by a tailor – 'That such a slave as this should wear a sword!'[43] Kent too lacks deference, lacks 'reverence' for those apparently his superiors; his gorgeous rudeness to Cornwall may endear him to the audience, but it brings him to suffer punishments expressly forbidden to be applied to aristocrats. Still, no servingman Caius could speak as Kent spoke to the Duke and Duchess of Cornwall. For all his willing self-degradation in the service of his degraded king, Kent has difficulty in maintaining his servant role, although the violent language he uses to Oswald is certainly matched by other historical noblemen and gentlemen.[44] That difficulty shows in one very interesting context: Kent evidently did not share his master's fellow-feeling for the Bedlam beggar, who later says of him that he, 'having seen me in my worst estate, / Shunn'd my abhorr'd society' (5.3.209–10). When he comes to recognize in the beggar his old friend's son, Kent is joyously reconciled to Edgar – but a remnant of his fastidiousness remained during their time of common disguise.

The question of rank is relevant also to the 'punishment' of Gloucester. Though noblemen could be, and were, put under attainder and executed for treason, they could not be hanged, as Regan suggested, and certainly could not be blinded. Neither were they properly subject to the summary 'justice' meted out by Cornwall (who was himself uneasy about it [3.7.24–7]). The blinding of Gloucester is shocking dramatically, humanly, and socially: the First Servant's reaction to the deed sprang from his outraged sense of decorum as well as from his shock at the cruelty of the deed. The Servant is interesting: he dares give an order to his lord –

> Hold your hand, my Lord.
> *I have serv'd you ever since I was a child,*
> But better service have I never done you
> Then now to bid you hold.   (3.7.71–4; italics mine; cf. 4.2.73–8)

'Ever since I was a child': the Servant's devotion to Cornwall, which should have been automatic, could only be broken by the horror of what he was forced to witness, this wanton brutality against an old man, a peer, and his master's host. To Regan the Servant speaks as boldly,

If you did wear a beard upon your chin
I'd shake it on this quarrel, (3.7.75–6)

which causes Cornwall, in turn stunned by the disruption of received decorum in his train, to cry, 'My villain!' Unthinkable – 'My villain!' Obviously Cornwall and Regan, recognizing their youth, power, and strength, think themselves immune from opposition and above social regulations; but that they too live within the conventions of deference is shown by their shock that a 'peasant' should 'stand up thus!' Regan is never more herself than when she stabs the man, and from behind. For Regan, as she makes plain later, is sovereign and intends to make the most of her independence. She and her husband simply take over Gloucester's house; later, in the rivalry for Edmund, she plays her advantageous widowhood against Goneril. Her 'rights' are in her own gift, and she can 'invest' Edmund with them so that he then 'compeers the best' (5.3.69–70). Regan knows her power and uses her precedence for her own ends.

The rise of Edmund, the bastard, the nobody, the new man, is indeed spectacular. He appears at the beginning, acknowledged but unprovided, a victim of his father's callousness to his predicament. Gloucester says of him, quite calmly, 'He hath been out nine years, and away he shall again,' never thinking that a nice-looking young man (who also happened to be his son) might prefer to stay 'in,' at court.[45] To Cordelia's and Edgar's disinheritance Edmund stands as emblem: we see in Gloucester's carelessness toward this child of his flesh (whose mother he does not even name) a failure of paternity which slightly prepares us for the king's abrupt rejection of his child and for Gloucester's speedy rejection of Edgar later. Cordelia is, of course, incapable of policy altogether, and Edgar's dissimulations trouble him; Edmund's nature, on the contrary, mates with his condition to make of him a natural machiavel, a new man, outside the customary values, as careless of privileged lives as his father had been of Edmund's unprivileged existence. Edmund follows his version of 'nature,' an impartial naturalistic goddess who, with other gods unnamed, stands up for bastards. At first, it seems to be only 'land,' or position, that he wants – and Edgar's, not his father's. That is, as a bastard he wishes simply to stand in his brother's legitimate place, content at the time simply to be his father's heir.[46] That Gloucester took it for granted that an heir he must have, is evident from his remarks to Edmund at Edgar's supposed treachery. Like King Lear and like Henry VIII (who, despairing of a legitimate son, for a while considered legitimating the Duke of Richmond), Gloucester knew the importance of male issue. Thus he can say, almost without thinking, 'of my land, ... I'll work the means / To make thee capable' (2.1.83–5), acknowledging both the need for an heir and the legal difficulties involved in such a transfer of rights. It turns out that Edmund need not – perhaps could not – wait out his father's natural life; perceiving the means, he betrays Gloucester, and Cornwall takes over the punishment of the old man's 'treason,' sequestering his estates and awarding them to Edmund, who by his father's attainder becomes Goneril's 'most dear Gloucester.' The young simply cancel out the older generation; later, we can read Albany's re-alliance from his refusal to accept Edmund's new title and his references to the old Earl as 'Gloucester.' Once an earl, why not more? So Edmund makes his loves to the two queens, evidently indifferent to their relative charms.[47] As the example of the Earl of Essex attests, if one is granted private privileges by a ruler, it is an easy temptation to fancy one's self as ruler. When Edmund sees the two women dead before him, he says with a pardonable pride but an unpardonable self-centredness, 'Yet Edmund was belov'd' – with never a word to spare for them.

Edmund brutally illustrates the ambitious ethos of the new man (in this respect he is unlike Essex and his aristocratic crew, rather men failed in their ranks than new men aspiring to greater noble position); Edmund is the natural talent unsupported by background who makes his way into the chancy world of Renaissance opportunity. Without respect for the privileged, he nonetheless covets their privileges; his parallel at a lower rank is the opportunist Oswald, a clothes rack, a mock-man, a braggart soldier, a go-between. Whatever can be done for his advancement, Oswald does, in ways that have their real analogue in the disoriented men of Essex's train. Oswald's view of the world as made for him emerges from his horrible remarks just before he blunders upon his own death. Seeing the blind Gloucester, on whose head a price has been set, he cries:

> A proclaim'd prize! Most happy!
> That eyeless head of thine was first fram'd flesh
> To raise my fortunes.   (4.6.227–9)

'To raise *my* fortunes'! After this, the audience can see him dispatched without the least qualm. 'Advancement' and 'fortune' are associated with this whole party: Goneril promises Oswald advancement; Edmund purchases the murder of Lear and Cordelia. To his tool, the Captain, he says,

> One step I have advanc'd thee; if thou dost
> As this instructs thee, thou dost make thy way

> To noble fortunes; know thou this, that men
> Are as the time is; to be tender-minded
> Does not become a sword; thy great employment
> Will not bear question; either say thou'lt do 't,
> Or thrive by other means.   (5.3.29–35)

Actually, the 'other means' of thriving is illustrated in the play. When he asks Tom to direct him to Dover, Gloucester gives him a purse, at that point speaking of aristocratic charity not as an automatic duty, but in terms of social justice (4.1.70–1); when he believes himself on the point of dying, he gives Tom another purse, 'in it a jewel / Well worth a poor man's taking' (4.6.28–9). At the end of his 'every inch a king' speech, Lear in turn gives money to the blinded Gloucester, whose condition he recognizes – 'No eyes in your head, nor no money in your purse?' (4.6.146–7) – before he admits to recognizing the man himself: 'I know thee well enough; thy name is Gloucester' (4.6.179). The almsgiving of both Lear and Gloucester has become something more meaningful than that largesse traditional to aristocrats: Gloucester at least begins to speak in full awareness of what destitution means, and to realize in personal terms what money can do for a beggar (4.1.76–7), and Lear has made his astonishing remarks about his poor subjects, about those denied justice by their poverty, and about 'the thing itself.'

For the old men, the realization that some men are poor comes as an immense revelation. Unlike them, and in spite of his naïveté about his brother's motives, Edgar possesses remarkable social experience for a young aristocrat. His description of Bedlam beggars may argue a mere sightseeing visit to a madhouse, but his knowing how beggars 'Enforce their charity' (2.3.9–20) and are 'whipp'd from tithing to tithing, and stock-punish'd, and imprison'd' (3.4.137–9) suggests that he has already paid considerable attention to contemporary customs outside the normal purview of the heir to an earldom. This sort of knowledge, got we know not how, argues for Edgar's ultimate fitness to rule the kingdom: he will not, one assumes, take 'Too little care of this.' As king he will be, it is implied, a just judge, a 'justicer' in reality for whom 'Robes and furr'd gowns' shall not 'hide all,' fulfilling the ancient duties ascribed to an earl, or 'Iudex.'[48]

Edgar may seem surprisingly democratic in this respect, but he is impeccably trained in the old aristocratic ethos – his training offers one explanation, indeed, of how he was so easily duped by his half-brother, from whom he could not imagine treachery; and why he was unable to do his father hurt, sorely though that father had hurt him. Edgar's nature makes him the ideal *preux chevalier* to challenge

Edmund; in that short episode of trial-by-combat, when Edmund receives his mortal wound, much is involved. First, Edmund is arrested for 'capital treason' on a charge familiar enough in sixteenth-century England, adultery with the Queen. Second, he is to prove himself by an old-fashioned and quintessentially aristocratic method, the formal trial-at-arms outmoded in the late sixteenth century as a customary proof. The modern equivalent of this sort of combat was the duel, a far more private affair than Edgar's challenge to Edmund; treason trials were judicial, carried on *in camera*. The anachronism stresses the play's archaism; further, it sets the struggle between factions into a simple morality-context, where virtue must be victorious. With this episode we are back in the world of chivalry of which we have heard nothing in the play and to which, under normal circumstances, Edmund the bastard could never have aspired. The new man, intent only on the main chance, ought to have looked on such an outmoded, hazardous process with contempt – but Edmund found himself subtly flattered by being party to such a procedure, the signature, after all, of the aristocratic life which he had usurped.[49] From his answer to Edgar's formal challenge we can hear how attracted Edmund was to the idea of himself as a 'real' aristocrat, the true inheritor of this beautiful, dangerous, elaborate ritual:

> In wisdom I should ask thy name;
> But since thy outside looks so fair and war-like,
> And that thy tongue some say of breeding breathes,
> What safe and nicely I might well delay
> By rule of knighthood, I disdain and spurn ...   (5.3.141–5)

Edmund adapts his language to the archaic formalities of chivalric address; his behaviour assimilates to that of the nobleman born. In this hour of his greatest danger, Edmund is at least offered a chance to act with the full dignity of the high-born, to take up the class-legacy his father did not leave him. Evidently, too, there is something purgative about this gesture; though he speaks to Edgar with a condescension disallowed by the real facts ('If thou'rt noble, / I do forgive thee' [5.3.165–7]) he admits his guilt and acknowledges the ironic justice of fortune's wheel, to which he was bound from the beginning (5.3.173–4). He resolves to do 'some good' by sending to stop the execution of Lear and Cordelia, and is borne off to die with some dignity before that terrible *pietà* of parent and child takes place.

Beside the bodies of Goneril and Regan, the bodies of Cordelia and Lear come to lie. Before our eyes, the greatest family in England is brought to its end. What every patriarch feared – even Lear, who could invoke sterility upon Goneril – has come to pass. From 'the promis'd end,' or 'image of that horror' the survivors must build back to some restoration of order, of justice. Kent refuses the commission of the kingdom, resigning his share to Edgar; Albany, who has begun the play ambitious for rule, is glad to relinquish its responsibility; Edgar, who never wished any such thing, lives to rule, his father's surviving son and godson to the dead king. A dynasty has ended, and a different rule is about to begin.

We do not know what the reign will be like: we can only assume that Edgar, having profited from knowing 'The worst' in his own experience, his father's, and his godfather's, having travelled the long road from the heath to the combat at Dover, from destitution to sovereignty, will rule as a Lear 'improv'd.' Just as at the play's beginning we are given no hint of what went before the day of division, at the play's end we are given no warranty of the future, but are simply asked to commit ourselves to Edgar's experience, sense of justice, and human-kindness. As the play began, *in medias res*, without explanation or motivation offered, to present us with the agonizing exemplum of the complexity of human life and human intents, inexplicable often even to the actors themselves, so it ends without explanation, prophecy, or promise.

That contemporary social problems were analysed and exploited to make up much of the substance of this play may strike us as astonishing, although readers of Shakespeare's history plays will not be surprised at this further link between them and *King Lear*. Some of the elements of the aristocratic 'crisis' – for example, primogeniture, retinue and service, exhibition of power, and actual power – are obvious enough in plot and theme; but other aspects of the problem, on their face less apparent in society, as well as less prominent in the play, turn out to be crucial. I have spoken of the importance of deference to both old and new aristocrats; Stone regards the decline of respect to the nobility as one of the major social changes that class had to face,[50] and, obviously, monarchs had to come to terms, after 1647, with the regicidal ideas subjects could afford to entertain. Stone gives many reasons for the decline of automatic deference to aristocrats – the passing of aristocratic military power, the relative rise of the gentry and the commercial classes with respect to the nobility, the creation of a 'rival' ethos involving prudence and frugality rather than openhandedness and magnificence, the venality of some noblemen and the wickedness of others, together with a communications system that permitted open criticism of such foibles and faults. Shakespeare, of course, concentrates, translates, and transvalues this process of devaluation in dramatic and symbolic rather than realistic or reportorial terms. For example, the terrible poignancy of the play's situation is heightened by the fact that it is Lear's daughters who, instead of jealously guarding the prerogatives of their rank and family (as would have been the normal 'real' behaviour of even unloving daughters), so calculatingly rob Lear of the deference due him. But 'rule' enforces high stakes: in his private capacity, Lear might expect family solidarity, but as ruler he risked great dangers particularly from members of his family.

A rather silly way of speaking of this play is to suggest that it dramatizes, as no other piece of literature in the period does, the actual decline of paternal authority that Stone has tried to measure in the English Renaissance.[51] Some of the power noble fathers exercised over their children, as we have seen, they themselves relinquished, and did so gladly for the children's sake. Some of the decline in parental authority is related to the gradual softening of behaviour between the generations, as noblemen allowed themselves a greater preoccupation with private pleasures and satisfactions. This tendency toward privatism – symbolically crucial in the play, and ironically expressed in Lear's joy at the prospect of sharing his prison with Cordelia – is apparent also in his early speeches, when he clearly looked forward to retirement in his daughters' houses, especially Cordelia's: 'I lov'd her most, and thought to set my rest / On her kind nursery' (1.1.123–4). Unlike Richard II, whose preference for private pleasure brought an end to his rule, King Lear had evidently fulfilled his public obligations during his reign; but that he could take such pleasure in withdrawing from public power is one mark of the period in which this play was written, rather than the primitive period in which it is supposed to have taken place. Obviously, Lear thinks that he has come to deserve the delights of retirement on his own terms.

In England, a mark of respect paid parents by their children was kneeling for their blessing: in a sermon of 1629, far later than this play, Donne wrote, 'Children kneele to aske blessing of Parents in England, but where else?' Still later, Evelyn commented on the childish dutifulness of grown children before their parents.[52] Against such a background, Lear's cursing his daughters (Cordelia, 1.1.108–20; Goneril, 1.4.284–98; 2.4.147, 163–9), and his denial of benison to Cordelia (1.1.264–5) gain great force, and bring the play out of its Celtic pre-christianity into the sixteenth century; so also does his bitter mockery of the forgiveness Regan counsels him to ask of Goneril:

> Ask her forgiveness?
> Do you but mark *how this becomes the house*:
> 'Dear daughter, I confess that I am old;
> Age is unnecessary: on my knees I beg
> That you'll vouchsafe me raiment, bed, and food.'
>
> (2.4.153–7; italics mine)

The king's gesture of kneeling to his children is not just a momentary criticism of the children's behaviour to him, but also a confirmation of the Fool's sharp words, that he has made '[his] daughters [his] mothers,' and must kneel to them to supplicate the elemental support that fathers without question provide for their children and can in turn expect from them.[53] From Cordelia, much later, he does receive raiment, bed, and food: she becomes his real mother, on whose kind nursery he can set his brief rest. Not only that, Cordelia asserts her daughterhood the while, by asking the blessing he had withheld from her when they parted –

> O! look upon me, Sir,
> And hold your hand in benediction o'er me,   (4.7.57–8)

she says, cancelling out the harshness of that last exchange. And Lear, as befits the moral and social dependent, kneels to her, a gesture which her dutiful daughterhood cannot permit: 'No, Sir, you must not kneel' (4.7.59). He is still her father and, for her, still king as well (4.7.44). The significance of these gestures of reconciliation sticks in Lear's mind, so that when Edmund's guard carries him and Cordelia off to prison, he welcomes the respite from warlike life and plans, in the safety of the birdcage endlessly to recapitulate his reunion with Cordelia:

> When thou dost ask me blessing, I'll kneel down,
> And ask of thee forgiveness: so we'll live,
> And pray, and sing, and tell old tales, and laugh
> At gilded butterflies ...   (5.3.10–13)[54]

The old man's union with his child is, in fact, their fusion: each as parent blesses the other, who asks blessing as a child. The paternal and filial functions, so long misused, skewed, and uncommunicated in the play, finally interchange to become one. When it is too late to do more than assert their value, the old bonds are confirmed and made stronger than ever.

Lear becomes reconciled to his child, and to his own paternity. Stable values are corroborated as he comes to rest, for a tragically brief moment, confident of the security of Cordelia's 'bond.' In other ways, Lear shows traces of 'modern' attitudes toward sexuality and paternity, some pleasant and some unpleasant. Although the play's skilful arrangements with its secondary plot both corroborate and counterpoint the main plot, in one social respect Lear and Gloucester, so often alike, differ markedly. Betrayed as he is by the fruit of his adultery, Gloucester might have been expected to denounce aristocratic licence. Not so, however; the harshest comments on sexuality come from Edgar, puritanical in his view of his father's behaviour, and from Lear, who suffers an extra-ordinary revulsion from sexuality altogether. Although, presumably, aristocratic tolerance of sexual laxity remained greater than that of other social classes, it too underwent some stiffening over the period of the Renaissance, in part because marriages had more to do with love than hitherto, in part because women emerged as a stronger social force within the class, and in part because real pressure was exerted on the nobility by chaplains, ministers, and disapproving puritan commentators on sexual habits.[55] Lear's attacks on Goneril's sexuality, his comments on the 'rascal beadle' standing in for lustful humanity at large, and his backhanded encomium of adultery and luxury all testify to his obsession with his own begetting, but also represent the greater preoccupation of noblemen with the question of sexual standards, earlier rarely considered at all. As a whole, the play condemns sexual licence and casts doubt on the values of sexuality: Gloucester suffers extremely for his early adultery, and their sexuality is one mark of the monstrousness and inhumanity of Goneril, Regan, and Edmund.

In quite a different range of language, another major theme of *King Lear* is tied to the problems of an aristocracy caught between an old ethos of unreckoned generosity, magnificence, and careless-ness, and new values stressing greater providence, frugality, and even calculation. The economic alterations characteristic of the period struck the aristocracy, as everyone else; noblemen made various kinds of compromise with new economic exigencies – dowries and jointures, for example, were initiated as prudential arrangements; some noblemen were faced with choosing between imposing higher rents and receiving still the unqualified reverence of grateful tenants. Old-fashioned aristocrats tended to maintain old ways, with their concomitant bonds of service, in the teeth of economic difficulty; newfangled lords often put their relations with their dependents upon a businesslike basis unknown earlier.[56]

We might well expect Goneril, Regan, and Edmund to think quantitatively – to fractionate and even annihilate Lear's retinue, to set prices on Gloucester's head and Lear's and Cordelia's lives; we might expect, too, that Oswald and the Captain should seek their material advancement by the deaths of these great ones. Such people represent and act out their lives in terms of the material values of both power and accounting. They can always go one arithmetical step farther – 'What need one?' 'Till noon! till night, my Lord; and all night'; 'Hang him instantly.' – 'Pluck out his eyes.' They know the minimum and the maximum – Goneril calculates to the last, assuring her mortally wounded lover that he had not had to answer the challenge of 'An unknown opposite.' Their naked calculation reduces all human values to quantitative measurement and thus easily loses sight of the 'need' underlying such values, to slip easily over into the utmost barbarity. But the fractionating by Goneril and Regan of their father's train, after all, echoes the same habit of mind and spirit exercised by the king himself, who set a price on his daughters' love and divided his kingdom in relation to their assertions of quantitative devotion. Again and again, characters take account, reckon their own and others' emotions: even the saintly Cordelia (perhaps pedagogically) speaks to her father of bonds and fractions – half her love for her husband, half left with her father. Gloucester tells Kent that Edgar is 'no dearer in [his] account' than Edmund; Kent speaks metaphorically of fee, as does the Fool later. For Lear, bestowing his disinherited daughter as a bad investment, Cordelia's 'price is fallen'; for France, brought up to admire magnanimity, 'She is herself a dowry.' Later, when Goneril's husband tells her she is not 'worth the dust which the rude wind / Blows in your face' (4.2.30–1), we realize how much he has begun to learn of calculation's values. Finally, the language of number is dissolved into paradoxes of 'all' and 'nothing,' thereby running out into areas of meaninglessness and incalculability. Need cannot be reasoned, or measured – nor can love, fidelity, or truth. It takes Lear a long time to come to that lesson: on his way to it, he can still say to Goneril,

> Thy fifty yet doth double five-and-twenty,
> And thou art twice her love, (2.4.261–2)

only to hear Regan ask a moment after, 'What need one?' Reduced to nothing, he has reached the point of non-support implied when the Fool asked Kent, 'Prithee, tell him, so much the rent of his land comes to' (1.4.140–1) – that is, to nothing. Lear, like Gloucester, passes through a stage of thought involving 'distribution' and 'superflux,' the language of justice in which he arraigns his daughters and criticizes the exercise of authority. He must evidently pass through that stage, which is after all simply another kind of reasoning of need (exposed in Goneril's hard statement of power, 'Who can arraign me for't?')[57] to realize that there are senses, good and bad, in which 'None does offend, none, I say, none' (4.6.170) – and in which even those with cause to harm or punish reject the bargaining code implied by the concept of 'cause': 'No cause, no cause.'

In all kinds of ways, in many ranges of expression and of art, this play passes through ordinary human experience to insist upon the greatness and the abyss of human life. From the simplest, and often the silliest, aspects of human behaviour, its morality is made to open upon an almost metaphysical amplitude. The play forces upon us a realization of the limitations of being human, as well as of humanity's potentiality for transcending and even transvaluing itself. In one particular literary type, the figure of the Fool, we have an example of this transfiguration from naturalistic representation to reverberating symbol. Fools, as the books assure us,[58] were typical appendages of both medieval and Renaissance courts. Interestingly enough, in England James I (famous for his fools and his foolishness, though perhaps not yet for the latter when this play was first put on) was the last English monarch to patronize professional fools; they too went out in the peculiar, muted modernization of life resulting from the War and the Interregnum. Of the figures in the play, the Fool most of all moves along the gamut from morality to naturalism: the Fool speaks both *in propria persona* and in the stylized persona of the official fool, sometimes 'all-licens'd' and satirical, sometimes sad and despondent, sometimes mixing modes of actuality and metaphor. His 'prophecy' is one such mixture (3.2.81–95); at first he seems to project a utopian world 'When priests are more in word than matter,' at other times a world upside down in unpleasantness – 'When brewers mar their malt with water.' From that point on, the prophecy jumbles ideal with deformed elements, and we are never sure what the measuring-rod is. Why should it be better, or worse, if 'No heretics' are 'burn'd, but wenches' suitors'? Though it would indeed be utopian if 'No squire' were 'in debt, nor no poor knight,' and if usurers could 'tell their gold i' th' field' secure from theft, still it is an imperfect England that harbours usurers at all; there is, too, no particular virtue in bawds' and whores' building churches. The world of the Fool's prophecy is no schematic world of handy-dandy, where evil systematically replaces good or good evil: the Fool recognizes, even in this utterance, that the world in which he lives is deeply confused.

His words to Kent in the stocks, too, both the prose comment on fortune and favour and the little poem reiterating the theme, seem to say that wise men ought not to follow declining patrons; yet he calls those who fly such patrons 'knaves' and insists with pride upon his own 'foolish' loyalty to his powerless lord. The Fool knows the ways of Goneril and Regan – and rejects them. Perhaps it is not so grotesque, after all, that he is one of the justicers of the crazy King's Bench which arraigns Goneril, the joint-stool in a symbolic gesture whose meaning the real woman could never recognize. Like Erasmus' Folly, Lear's Fool knows truth from fiction, and knows their complicated interdependence as well.

The Fool disappears – from the play as from English courts, and for just the reason Lear's Fool gives: 'Lords and great ones' usurp his monopoly. The Fool's comment is extremely shrewd. For a time folly was the monopoly, granted by monarchs, as the exclusive privilege of fools, but as the social distinctions upon which such regulated mockery depended fell away, so everyone 'snatched' at all privilege, even the dubious one of folly. Along with the gentleman and yeoman of the riddle, even a king can be a fool. When that happens, deference offers no defence against folly, and professional fools must be got rid of.

Lear becomes, by his own admission, a fool – an old king, caught in the conflict of one ethos with another, trying to be fair by the new standards and yet relying on the privileges granted by the old, becomes a child again, with all the nonsense and the clarity of a child. He fails in the impossible task of doing right by a double standard he cannot even define, but after he *has* failed, he comes to understand, reject, and transcend those standards to assert a vision even truer than the normal ones, a reason purer than the customary assessments of either need or logic, and a charity greater than even royal munificence could show. One way we can perceive Lear's poignant predicament and accomplishment is to reckon it by the real problems that faced his peers, as Stone's book enables us to do. Shakespeare has not let Lear off easily; as so often, the playwright, for all that his heart lay with the old mores of abundance, kindness, and carelessness, scrupulously shows the problems and limits of such a code. Magnanimous noblemen were careless of costs, wasted human potential in their easy acceptance of the old customs. Ambitious 'new' noblemen may have corrected some of the errors of their conservative elders – but the cost of their correction, as this play demonstrates, is prohibitive. We are forced to acknowledge that there is a crisis of values in this play, and that neither ethos will do – and, though there is no doubt which side the playwright preferred, he was too scrupulous to present the problem simply as a morality, or simply as a conservative argument for 'order' and 'degree.' He saw both the practical rightness of the position Goneril, Regan, and Edmund abused, and the social grace of the position Lear and Gloucester exploited. But however we come to love and pity the old aristocrats, we know that their unconsidered acceptance of their own values was too expensive, in terms of their own families. Those lapsing fathers counted on unexamined social custom for protection against everything, even against the mysteries of hard hearts and calculating brains. The moral weight of the play comes down decisively with the advocates of old values, but not without having hesitated long enough to show how crucially those values fell short.

NOTES

1 E.M.W. Tillyard *The Elizabethan World Picture* (London 1943); A.O. Lovejoy *The Great Chain of Being* (Cambridge, Mass. 1936); E.W. Talbert *The Problem of Order* (Chapel Hill 1958)

2 For example, Sigurd Burckhardt *Shakespearean Meanings* (Princeton 1968) 117, 137, 150; Nicholas Brooke *Shakespeare's Early Tragedies* (London 1968) especially pp. 8–10; Wilbur Sanders *The Dramatist and the Received Idea* (Cambridge 1968); and Herbert Howarth, *The Tiger's Heart* (New York 1970) 165–91, especially 168–73 for *King Lear*. As for 'historians,' *all* serious students of the period accept, even embrace, its anomalousness.

3 (Oxford 1965); see my brief review, *Renaissance News* xix (1966) 48–54.

4 Stone's notion of so long a 'crisis' has been criticized; for my purposes, that criticism proved helpful in showing how the play's focus demonstrates such a crisis more schematically and intensely than historical documents covering a hundred-year period. That is, 'crisis' may be the wrong word for Stone's book, but it *is* the right word for *King Lear*.

5 Stone *Crisis* chap 8; and G.E. Aylmer *The King's Servants* (London 1961) chap 5

6 *Crisis* 549–55; and in a still-unpublished lecture on English country houses

7 *Crisis* 242–50; Sheldon P. Zitner, 'Hamlet: Duellist,' *University of Toronto Quarterly* xxxix (1969) 1–18. See also Vincentio Saviolo *His Practice* (London 1595); and George Silver *Paradoxes of Defence* (London 1599).

8 *Crisis* 50

9 Ibid 562–6; *A Discourse of the Common Weal of England* ed. Elizabeth Lamond (Cambridge 1929) 82–3; *The Household Papers of Henry Percy, Ninth Earl of Northumberland* ed. G.R. Batho (London 1962) 63, 108, 114

10 *Certaine Sermons* (London 1595) Part II, 6: 'Against excesse of apparell'; see also Lawrence Humfrey *The Nobles, or the Nobilitye* (London 1563)

III: 'Of Apparel'; Philip Stubbs *The Anatomie of Abuses* (London 1585) 6–7, 16–38; Robert Greene *A Quip for an Upstart Courtier or, A quaint dispute between Velvet breeches and Cloth breeches* (London 1620); William Harrison *Description of England* ed. F.J. Furnivall (London 1877) I, 168–72. For appropriate illustration, see Roy Strong *Portraits of Queen Elizabeth I* (Oxford 1963); and *The English Icon: Elizabethan and Jacobean Portraiture* (London and New York 1969).

11 James Cleland *Propaideia, or the Institution of a Young Noble Man* (Oxford 1607) 214–17

12 Stone *Crisis* 28–9

13 Ibid 184–8, 547–86

14 Hieronimus Osorius *A Discourse of Civill, and Christian Nobilitie* (London 1576) 27ff; *Cyvile and Uncyvile Life* (London 1579) 12; Gervase Markham *A Health to the Gentlemanly Profession of Servingmen* Roxburghe Library ed. 1868 (London 1598) 126–31

15 *King Lear* ed. Kenneth Muir, xliii, n1

16 Stone *Crisis* 170–5

17 See *Renaissance News* XIX (1966) 48–54. I do not want to seem to take the play as reportage on current political and social conditions: see the debate between Allan Bloom and Harry Jaffa on one side, and Sigurd Burckhardt on the other, in *American Political Science Review* LIV (1960) 130–66, 457–73.

18 See F.T. Flahiff, below.

19 Stone *Crisis* 99, and personal communication to the author

20 Thomas Milles *The Catalogue of Honor* (London 1610) 20

21 See Sir William Segar *Honor, Military, and Civill* (London 1602) 113, 122, 220.

22 *'King Lear' in Our Time* (Berkeley 1965) 47–8, 56, 166–8; W.B.C. Watkins *Shakespeare and Spenser* (Princeton 1966) 83; William Frost, 'Shakespeare's Rituals and the Opening of *King Lear*,' *Hudson Review* X (1958) 577–85.

23 *Crisis* 9

24 Ibid 182

25 *Shakespearean Meanings* 239–40

26 *Crisis* 42–9, 50, 187ff

27 Ibid 44–7, referring to W.K. Jordan's voluminous work. As Stone points out, although noble testamentary charities were relatively smaller than those of the merchant class, or the whole 'middle' class, there was some reason for this apparent limit on almsgiving by the facts of noble inheritance. All noblemen, in effect, had fixed heirs with respect to the bulk of their estates, and middle-class patriarchs, with no such restrictions on legacies, were free to dispose of their estates as they wished, or as they thought God wished.

28 See ibid 47–8, for some samples of noble support to others.

29 *Cyvile and Uncyvile Life* 35, for charity properly bestowed on beggars; Humfrey *The Nobles* II, on liberality; III, on apparel, and on beggars

30 Stone *Crisis* 167–9, 171

31 The division is all the same ambivalent, though: apparently Lear had already divided his kingdom among his co-heiresses, reserving simply the part 'more opulent' for his favourite daughter. Otherwise, principally to prevent potential strife between these sons-in-law, the division appears to have been conceived as just. The relation of the rhetorical contest among the daughters, then, to the original political division remains, like so much else in the play, mysterious and irrational.

32 See Stone *Crisis* 167, 197.

33 Ibid 170–5

34 Ibid 201–17; *Cyvile and Uncyvile Life* 34–9; Markham *Health* passim; Harrison *Description of England* lxxi, 134–5.

35 Stone *Crisis* 238–57; Wallace MacCaffrey *The Shaping of the Elizabethan Regime* (Princeton 1968) 330–71; see also Humfrey *The Nobles* III, for distinctions between necessary and unnecessary servants; and Harrison *Description of England* 134–5, for idle servingmen.

36 Stone *Crisis* 211–12

37 Stone *Crisis* 549–65; Harrison *Description of England* 267–77, for princes' palaces

38 Stone *Crisis* 201, 215–50

39 See Lear's remark, 'There's your press money' (4.6.86–7), which suggests that, however dimly, he knew he needed some defence.

40 For cohorts, see Stone *Crisis* 203–6.

41 For royal meals, see Aylmer *King's Servants* 26–32.

42 Stone *Crisis* 54 speaks of aristocratic punishment; *King Lear* ed. Muir, 77, note to 2.2.133 for punishments to servants in great households.

43 It is worth noting that Kent does not actually fight with Oswald, but uses his sword only to beat him. He is ready, however, to take on Edmund, 'goodman boy,' who enters with his noble rapier drawn.

44 See Stone *Crisis* 224 for examples.

45 For a sensitive reading of Edmund's nature and role in the play, see Julian Markels *Pillar of the World* (Columbus, Ohio 1968) 104–6; also H.A. Mason *Shakespeare's Tragedies of Love* (London 1970) 184–94; Arnold Kettle, 'From Hamlet to Lear,' in *Shakespeare in a Changing World* ed. Arnold Kettle (London 1964) 158–71.

46 For some of the disabilities of bastards, see B.G. Lyons, above; and John Ferne *The Blazon of Gentrie* (London 1586). A bastard might not inherit from his father without the father's specific and deliberate designation by gift or by testament; even a legitimated bastard might not sit at his legitimate brother's table except by invitation. These regulations had

become old fashioned by 1586, however, and in many noble families bastards were generously treated.

47 Although her behaviour indicates more feeling for Edmund than do her words, Regan's argument for marrying him rests on the fact that it is more 'convenient' for her to do so than for the still-married Goneril.

48 Segar *Honor* 220 on earls: '*Elderman, id est, Iudex*'

49 Ferne *Gentrie* 308–12; Segar *Honor* 113

50 Stone *Crisis* 747–53

51 Ibid 591–3

52 Quoted in ibid 592

53 See, for example, Robert Cleaver *A Godlie Forme of Household Government* (London 1598) for the duties of parents to children and of children to parents.

54 This quotation actually has one of the few direct references to 'the court' – 'Who's in, who's out' – in the entire play.

55 See Stone *Crisis* 660–9; and *Certaine Sermons*, homily against adultery.

56 Stone *Crisis* 273–334, for estate management

57 F.T. Flahiff has written, in an unpublished paper, about the separation in this play of judgment and power: Lear's arraignment of his daughters on the heath is purely symbolic, and the blinding of Gloucester is done without the ceremony of justice.

58 Enid Welsford *The Fool* (London 1935); Barbara Swain *Fools and Folly during the Middle Ages and the Renaissance* (New York 1932)

TWELVE

F.T.FLAHIFF

edgar, once and future king

IT IS NOT DIFFICULT to understand why generations of readers, like the Folio editors before them, have rejected the Quarto description of *King Lear* as a *'True Chronicle Historie.'* In the play's final scene alone, with Lear dying after his children have died, without an heir, with an unaccountable Edgar as his successor, we witness violations of recognized historical sources that leave us little choice but to dismiss as fanciful any claims concerning this play's historicity. *King Lear* does not invite us to speculate about antecedent actions, and, as it ends, we are, I think, impressed less by what remains, by the relationships of characters and events to subsequent history, than by what is ending; an old king struggling to undo a button commands our attention in a way in which the fate of his kingdom does not. As happens so often in this play, in its last scene Lear's private concerns overwhelm public matters; his final agony threatens to annihilate everyone and everything that is not himself. The fact remains, however, that the Quarto does describe *King Lear* as a *'True Chronicle Historie,'* and I propose that we entertain as a possibility that this title, by which the play was known in

Shakespeare's lifetime, makes a statement about the play that we would be foolish to ignore.[1]

There have been other kings in drama who have died and some, like Henry IV, who have misjudged their children; of course, in other plays Shakespeare has intertwined domestic and political affairs. But *King Lear* is different, and what distinguishes it – in part at least – from those other plays and the king himself from his counterparts is not only the power of Lear's person, but the kind of power that enabled him in the first instance to impress upon his kingdom the shape of his own preferences. Whatever the other characters think of his judgment, no one questions his right to do what he does at the beginning of the play.

The fact of this power, the likes of which is possessed by no other English king in Shakespeare's works, accounts for much that is peculiar in the play. It provides, as F.D. Hoeniger has observed,[2] a primitive basis for the social order of Lear's kingdom. When the king exercises his power in order to give it away, when his heirs use this awful legacy, they act without reference to any structure of traditional precedent. In other plays dealing with English history, there are legal and institutional assumptions to define the nature and authority of the king: one has only to think of the reflections of Richard II and Henry V on these matters. In *King Lear* the nature of royal power is obscure, for its limits are defined by its exercise. This is apparent in the ambiguous status of Lear's heirs at the beginning of the play as well as during it. Because there is no mystique attached to their father's crown, there is no focus for their ambitions, and because there is no ritual of coronation there is no definition of their rights and responsibilities. This ambiguity is due in large measure to the confusion surrounding Lear's granting of power. As subsequent events demonstrate, he had no very clear idea what he was doing in that first scene, but because of his extraordinary, undisputed authority, he could perform an arbitrary, paternalistic, and primitive act.

The nature of Lear's first actions has led some critics to assume that Shakespeare's concern here is with prehistory, a conclusion supported by the personal rather than social nature of motives and actions in the play. Lear acts in dividing his kingdom in the name of a father's love and according to a father's whim. Throughout the play, whether selfishly or selflessly, characters respond to events in intensely personal ways. This is clear enough in the actions of those who are members of the two central families, but others, like Kent, the Fool, the Servant who slays Cornwall, and the old Man who at first leads the blinded Gloucester, act as they do because of their relations with particular characters. The most problematic of these, the Servant who kills Cornwall, performs his one action in fulfilment of his obligation to his master: 'better service have I never done you' (3.7.73). It is only at the end, when there are no families left, that Albany's injunction to Kent and Edgar to sustain 'the gor'd state' (5.3.320) makes us aware of an entity larger than a person or a family that must have first claim on those who would rule.

Although consciousness of the state emerges only very painfully and gradually in the play, the society before the end is not without its civilized and civilizing forms, of which the trial on the heath and the combat between Edmund and Edgar are evidence. But these forms of justice are so charged with private meaning (father against daughters, half-brother against half-brother) that they have the quality more of personal acts than of means by which detached and impartial justice can be realized. The decisions in the trials of Richard II and Katharine of Aragon may be as inevitable as the judgment in the trial on the heath, but the elaborate articulation of ritual, the awareness, however perverted, of a common good, and the sense of traditional social obligations lend weight and solemnity and significance to these occasions that are absent in Lear's court. By the same token, the combat between Henry Bolingbroke and Mowbray, presided over by Richard II, demonstrates the perfection of a form that is only imperfectly realized in Edgar's encounter with Edmund. These more sophisticated judicial forms are not guarantees of justice, but even when they are abused their symbolic force and their impersonality remind us of values that transcend a particular occasion.

The symbolic power and impersonality that accrue to words and gestures and actions as they develop from primitive beginnings into public ritual are stripped away in *King Lear*. The result is more skeletal and cryptic than anything we find in Shakespeare's other histories. At the same time, the histories provide a gloss upon this play in their detailed and naturalistic exploration of the language of politics and social order. King Richard II's forced abdication and his deliberate and ceremonial putting off of the regalia and prerogatives of kingship – 'for I must nothing be' (4.1.201)[3] – are in effect a commentary upon Lear's willingness to give power to his daughters and their husbands as well as upon his obliviousness to the true meaning of his action. Richard's 'must' points up his awareness of the necessary consequences of stripping power from himself, awareness that is echoed in quite a different context in Edgar's 'Edgar I nothing am' (2.3.21) but which comes only very gradually and partially to Lear: 'they told me I was every thing; 'tis a lie, I am not ague-proof' (4.6.106–8). There is none of Richard's consciousness – 'Now mark me how I will undo myself' (4.1.203) – in Lear's 'Pray you, undo this button' (5.3.309), yet the fact of his being unbonnetted and his desire both here and earlier (3.4.112) to unbutton recall Richard's readiness 'To undeck the pompous body of a king' (4.1.250). Lear's gestures are less deliberate and less self-conscious than Richard's, but at the same time they suggest elemental human conditions which are the origins of ceremonial acts, but which origins, as Henry v realized (4.1.250ff), ceremony can obscure.

This unaccommodated quality exists on all levels in the play. Lear's 'Thou'lt come no more, / Never, never, never, never, never!' (5.3.307–8) echoes Constance's lament in *King John* when she hears of her son's imprisonment: 'therefore never, never / Must I behold my pretty Arthur more' (3.4.88–9). Parents rage against their own powerlessness, although Constance does so in an altogether more coherent, allusive, and formal way than Lear. And she possesses a kind of consolation, 'That we shall see and know our friends in heaven' (3.4.77), for which there is no equivalent in *King Lear*. There is no escape from Lear's 'no more' and 'never', and this is underlined by his attempts to find one: 'Look on her, look, her lips, / Look there, look there!' (5.3.310–11). King John realized that despite his power, he could not 'hold mortality's strong hand' (4.2.82): John of Gaunt repeated this sentiment as a warning to Richard II, that while a king can take a life he cannot 'lend a morrow' to a dying man (1.3.228). We are nowhere more aware of the limits of a king's power than we are in this drama about the most powerful of kings. Lear can avenge Cordelia's death, he can have his authority restored, but he can never breathe life into one who has 'no breath at all' (5.3.307).

James I wrote: 'By the Law of Nature the King becomes a naturall Father to all his Lieges at his Coronation.'[4] What later kings became through custom and ceremony, Lear is. Metaphors, conceits, assumptions, and policies have a terrible literalness in this play. The king is indeed 'a naturall Father,' his godson is a godson, the Bastard is a bastard, and the Fool a fool. An adversary's fanciful description of Henry IV as 'the unfirm king / In three divided' whose 'coffers sound / With hollow poverty and emptiness' (2 *Henry* IV, 1.3.73–5) is deprived of its fanciful dimension here and is presented as fact. Falstaff's 'the laws of England are at my commandment' (2 *Henry* IV, 5.3.139–40) has its dreadful because true counterpart in Goneril's 'the laws are mine' (5.3.158). And when Falstaff prepares to play king and Prince Hal observes, 'Thy state is taken for a joint-stool' (1 *Henry* IV 2.4.423), the episode anticipates a much darker situation in which a king prepares to play king (3.6). The literal as distinct from the metaphoric fabric of the play reinforces its extraordinary concentration. Just as the absence of background, of antecedent causes, prevents us from escaping the action before us, the literalness of this action and of the play's language denies us the consolation of supposing or concluding that things are not as they appear. *King Lear's* preoccupation with nakedness and plainness extends into the way in which customs and rituals and clichés are stripped of their figurative meanings, their 'lendings,' that something altogether more fundamental and unaccommodated can stand revealed.

Near the end of 2 *Henry* IV, when the king lies dying and his son, believing his father already dead, has taken the crown and put it on, Henry is moved to prophesy (as Gaunt had before him) the ruination of his kingdom:

> England shall give him office, honour, might;
> For the fifth Harry from curb'd licence plucks
> The muzzle of restraint, and the wild dog
> Shall flesh his tooth in every innocent.
> O my poor kingdom! sick with civil blows.
> When that my care could not withhold thy riots,
> What wilt thou do when riot is thy care?
> O' thou wilt be a wilderness again,
> Peopled with wolves, thy old inhabitants. (4.5.128–36)

What Henry sees as the fate of England, Gloucester, in the second scene of *King Lear*, sees as the present state of Lear's Britain: 'in cities, mutinies; in countries, discord; in palaces, treason' (1.2.111–13). Gloucester's bleak though accurate evaluation of the state of things is provoked, like Henry's prophecy, by his belief that the bond "twixt son and father' has cracked. Each has allowed himself to be persuaded that his heir desires to succeed him before his time. We have known for sometime how wrong is Henry's estimate of Hal, and we soon learn how mistaken Gloucester is about Edgar.

The time past, with its wild dog and wolves and rule by riot, whose return King Henry fears *is* the time present of *King Lear*. The later king's bitter fancy anticipates an earlier kingdom, 'sick with civil blows,' whose rulers, like dogs, bark at their father, where women (and men) are wolfish in nature, and a good man must assume the shape of a beast in order to survive. The relationship of Henry's prophecy to *King Lear* is, I think, specific; I wish to propose a source common to the two plays, present in the closing lines of Henry's speech, more complexly present in *King Lear*. But first, and by way of providing a setting for this source, I want to return to a problem I raised at the beginning of this essay, the problem posed by Lear dying after his daughters, to be succeeded by one for whom there is no counterpart in earlier versions of the Lear story. Whatever other effects Shakespeare sought or gained by this curious manipulation of his sources, we can, I think, appreciate the shock and surprise of his first audiences when they did *not* witness Lear's happy restoration to his throne, his peaceful death, or his succession by Cordelia. Presumably, they had been invited to attend Shakespeare's reworking of familiar history and what they did witness was his exploration of a quality of the human condition that would appear to have no place in history, the quality of unpredictability. In short, they witnessed Shakespeare's disaccommodation of history.

In order to illustrate this process of disaccommodation as it applies to Shakespeare's handling of the history of King Lear – a process which, as I have suggested, has its echoes in his handling of language and action in this play – I wish to consider the soliloquies spoken by Prince Hal at the end of the second scene of *1 Henry* IV and by Edgar in the second act of *King Lear*. There are obvious similarities between these characters: each is a consummate actor, each is misjudged by his father and proves himself with, in the eyes of some at least, unexpected bravery and dignity by defeating and slaying an adversary who to a degree has usurped his place in his father's regard. Still the differences between Hal and Edgar are so striking as to obscure these similarities, and these differences are obvious when we compare the first soliloquy spoken by each. Both speeches are concerned with disguise deliberately assumed: Hal will continue to 'permit the base contagious clouds / To smother up [his] beauty' (1.2.220–1), so that when he is called upon to 'pay the debt [he] never promised' (231), he will emerge 'like bright metal on a sullen ground' (234), 'to be himself' (222). His 'reformation,' or so he predicts, will appear like a rare accident, enabling him to redeem 'time when men think least [he] will' (239). Edgar's disguise, on the other hand, is quite simply his response to the situation at hand: 'I will preserve myself' (2.3.6). The kind of control that Hal exercises over his own image sets him apart from Gloucester's son, who must assume 'the basest and most poorest shape' (7) because he has been unable to control the effects of Edmund's misrepresentation of him. In time, of course, Edgar too becomes his own master, maintaining his disguises long after his father's wrath is a threat to him, less for his own safety than as a means of preserving that same father and ultimately of restoring to Lear his kingdom.

That Edgar comes to act with cunning and deliberateness reminiscent of Hal's cunning and deliberateness is a measure of the differences between these characters and between the plays in which they figure. In a stroke that one critic has described as a quality of lyric drama,[5] Shakespeare chose to endow Hal at the outset with a sense of his own abilities and destiny that reflects his actual place as a king's heir and himself as an historical figure. Edgar's development is unpredictable because when he assumes his disguise he is without place or expectations. When he first appears, so much the thing of Edmund, he is a nonentity: in a special sense he comes into existence within and by means of the drama, his own nature developing and realizing itself as he responds to or merely copes with situations that he neither invited nor caused.

We see in Hal and Edgar two sides of a coin. In time each will be called upon to sustain a 'gor'd state.' It is a prospect that shapes everything Hal does and thinks, what he calls 'the debt I never promised.' Edgar becomes king accidentally and unwittingly. When Albany abdicates and Kent turns back into the play in search of his master, Edgar alone is left, because he is there and because at the end he is what he has become in the course of the drama. Edgar's lack of ambition (unlike Hal, and Lear and Edmund for that matter, he is not given to declarations of far-reaching purpose, although he does speak four of the play's eleven soliloquies), the very limited nature of his prospects (at best he can hope to regain his rightful place as Gloucester's heir), and his absence from earlier versions of the Lear story make his succession something unexpected. But if Shakespeare violated the Lear story by altering its conclusion, in a curious way he drove the sources of the *Henry* IV plays into those plays. He did this by endowing Hal with prescience and self-consciousness that are, as I have suggested, reflections of the historical knowledge or historical consciousness of his audience. In the beginning Hal knows his end even as his audience knows that he will become Henry V and the victor at Agincourt. The relationship between Hal and his audience is intimate and peculiar; together they observe with some detachment those – his father, Falstaff, and Hotspur, for example – who see no promise of a sun behind the ugly mists that form the prince's disguise. No such detachment is possible for the audiences of *King Lear*; our memories simply do not provide us with prescience, with that sense of control we enjoy (however vicariously) when we witness the shapes of familiar careers and actions. Shakespeare has not permitted us the satisfaction of predicting from what we know of the past. He has made the familiar unfamiliar; he has brought us, as he brought Edgar, into history, not as it *has* been recorded, but as it *is* being woven upon Time's loom.

History *informs* the plot of *King Lear*; it does not, as Coleridge suggested, merely subserve it.[6] Set as it is in a time more remote than the time of *Cymbeline*, this is literally Shakespeare's first English history play. In so far as it contains primitive, unaccommodated equivalents of forms and actions in the other histories, it can be said to stand at the beginning of Shakespeare's chronicle of England. It is as if in writing *King Lear* Shakespeare went back to the time of the wolves (that time whose return King Henry IV dreaded) in order to search out precedents for a later social order, and in his depiction of the establishment of these he presupposed his audience's knowledge of what was to follow. The historical future exists in the play in much the same way 'that fair field / Of Enna' exists in Milton's Eden, as a reminder of our indebtedness to the past and of the real source of patterns that have never been lost.

And what of Edgar and his role at the end of the play? Is his unpredictable presence as Lear's successor evidence that Shakespeare abandoned the outlines of history in order to comment on something other than history? On the contrary, the emergence of Edgar forms a part of a very important statement about the nature and facts of British history. Coleridge proposed that for a drama to be 'properly historical' it must be 'the history of the people to whom it is addressed.' He continued: 'The events themselves are immaterial, otherwise than as the clothing and manifestation of the spirit that is working within. In this mode, the unity resulting from succession is destroyed, but is supplied by a unity of a higher order.'[7] In a more literal and compelling sense than Coleridge himself realized, *King Lear* verifies his conclusions about the nature of the history plays. It is indeed '... a collection of events borrowed from history, but connected together in respect to cause and time poetically, by dramatic fiction.' Coleridge was right, I think, when he observed: 'the history of our ancient kings – the events of them, I mean – are like stars in the sky: whatever the real interspaces may be, and however great, they seem close to each other. The stars, the events, strike us and remain in our eye, little modified by the difference of their dates.'[8] Stars that are light years apart are made to seem close: events borrowed from history are connected by dramatic fiction. The fiction, the poetry, lies in the connection and not in the events. What Coleridge called 'the unity resulting from succession' (literally, and in this context, Cordelia succeeding Lear) is

replaced by 'a unity of a higher order.' Shakespeare's Lear is succeeded by one who is, as we are told by Regan (2.1.91–2), his godson and whom Lear himself named Edgar. It is a Saxon name, the
name in fact of one of 'our ancient kings' whose reign was indeed
separated by vast interspaces of time from the reign of Lear, but
a king whose memory was kept in Shakespeare's day, who was
described by Thomas Heywood as 'the first that could truely write
himselfe an absolute Monarch of this Island'[9] and who was hailed
by Michael Drayton as 'the flower and delight of the *English*
world.'[10]

Earlier I suggested that *King Lear* has a source in common with
Henry IV's backward glance to a time of wolves. If you recall, Henry
feared that his son's accession would cause his kingdom to revert to
a primitive state of 'wilderness,' 'Peopled by wolves, thy old inhabitants.' His was the perspective of one who lived at a time when
there were no wolves in Britain, when they were viewed as 'old [in
the sense of *former*] inhabitants.' Britain rid of wolves, like Ireland
rid of snakes, is a part of national folk history. According to Ralph
Higden in the *Polychronicon*, it took four years to rid Britain of
wolves, and the four years occurred sometime between 959 and
975.[11] These years marked the reign of King Edgar, who, Holinshed
recorded, set about to 'rid the countrie of all wild ravening beasts,'
but who succeeded only in disposing of wolves, and that, by the
simple device of demanding an annual tribute of three hundred
wolves;[12] and 'in the fourthe yere,' Higden wrote, 'mygte nevere a
wolf be founde.'[13]

The times that Henry IV fears his son will restore are just those
times that King Edgar brought to an end: Hal, according to his
father, will undo what Edgar accomplished. How justified are we
in attributing to Henry so sharp an historical consciousness? And
what bearing does his prediction have upon *King Lear*? To answer
these questions, I shall turn to a work with which Shakespeare was
very likely familiar, from which – according to some commentators
– he took details of Hal's early exploits,[14] a work that the Arden
editor has cited as a possible source for Edgar's reflections on ripeness and maturity[15] – *The Gouernour* of Sir Thomas Elyot.

In the second chapter of *The Gouernour*, Elyot introduces an
important assumption of his work: 'the best and most sure gouer-
naunce is by one kynge or prince, which ruleth onely for the weale
of his people to hym subiecte.'[16] He illustrates his thesis from history, comparing the prosperity of those societies ruled by 'one
soueraigne gouernour' (the Jews by Moses, the Greeks at Troy by
Agamemnon, Rome under Augustus) with the disorder of divided

leadership. His distrust of the multitude is, of course, proverbial, Athenian democracy appearing to him 'a monstre with many heedes,' its counterparts giving rise to nothing so much as handy-dandy worlds wherein, according to Elyot, 'beddes, testars, and pillowes' appear in halls, and 'carpettes and kusshyns becometh the stable.'[17]

I do not think it necessary to dwell upon the consequences of divided authority in *King Lear*, nor am I proposing that Shakespeare was much influenced by Elyot's discussion of this matter. His sentiments were, after all, commonplace. What does concern me about this chapter of *The Gouernour* is Elyot's view of history, more specifically, of British history. Having considered the fates of various Hebrew and classical societies (always, of course, enforcing his thesis about the necessity for 'one soueraigne gouernour') Elyot then turns to what he calls 'sufficient examples nere unto us.' Very briefly he compares the calamities that beset Florence and Genoa 'for lacke of a continuall gouernour' with the well-being of Ferrara governed by a duke and of Venice ruled by an earl. Then he invokes 'an example domesticall, which is moste necessary to be noted.'[18] It is the penultimate example he cites, the final evidence for his argument being the England of his own day, ruled by 'his highnes, equall to the auncient princis in vertue and courage,' Henry VIII.

Elyot's 'example domesticall,' the only British sovereign before his own he places in the tradition of great governors of history, is King Edgar. Like Moses and Agamemnon and Augustus, he brought order and decorum to an 'odiouse and uncomly' society. Elyot's own account of pre-Edgarian Britain speaks for itself:

> After that the Saxons by treason had expelled out of Englande the Britons, whiche were the auncient inhabitantes, this realme was deuyded in to sondry regions or kyngdomes. O what mysery was the people than in. O howe this most noble Isle of the worlde was decerpt and rent in pieces: the people pursued and hunted lyke wolfes or other beastes sauage: none industrie auayled, no strength defended, no riches profited. Who wolde then haue desired to haue ben rather a man than a dogge: whan men either with sworde or with hungre perisshed, hauynge no profit or sustinance of their owne corne or catell, whiche by mutuall warre was continually distroyed? yet the dogges, either takynge that that men coulde nat quietly come by, or fedynge on the deed bodies, whiche on euery parte laye scatered plenteously, dyd satisfie theyr hunger.[19]

This surely is the time of the wolves referred to by Henry IV, when the wild dog fleshed 'his tooth in every innocent' and riot had care of the kingdom. It was a time that came to an end with the accession (first in Wessex and then in all of Britain) of the destroyer of wolves:

> such iniquitie semeth to be than, that by the multitude of soueraigne gouernours of all thinges had ben brought to confusion, if the noble kynge Edgar had nat reduced the monarch to his pristinate astate and figure: whiche brought to passe, reason was reuiued, and people came to conformitie, and the realme began to take comforte and to shewe some visage of a publike weale: and so (lauded be god) have continued ...[20]

Elyot's own king could hardly have been surprised to find Edgar included in this noble catalogue. The greatest monument to the memory of Edgar – the Chapel bearing his name located behind the high altar of the Abbey Church at Glastonbury – was begun in the reign of Henry's father and was completed only after he himself had come to the throne.[21] That Elyot did not feel obliged to justify his choice of Edgar ('an example ... moste necessary to be noted'), that he made no further reference to him, in short, that he depended upon his readers' familiarity with his achievements is evidence enough of the regard in which Edgar was held, at least in the third decade of the sixteenth century. And Elyot was by no means alone in seeing King Edgar as an historical figure of peculiar significance. Earlier in this essay, I quoted Thomas Heywood's description of Edgar as 'the first ... absolute Monarch of this Island.' Heywood made this claim some 106 years after the publication of *The Gouernour*, in a treatise celebrating the launching of a most extravagant ship, 'Royal Sovereign of the Seas,' that Charles I had built at Woolwich. The ship, 'not paralleled in the whole Christian world,' had carved upon its beak-head the image of 'royall *King Edgar* on horsebacke, trampling upon seven kings.'[22] I mention the Heywood references as evidence that a figure who appears to have slipped from the popular historical imagination, whose reputation has been overshadowed by the reputation of Alfred and by the lengthening shadow cast by Arthur, enjoyed an extraordinary reputation in Tudor and Stuart England.

The values Elyot attached to Edgar's reign were commonplaces in the period. Where his account is of particular interest, however, is in the place he gives Edgar in his survey of history from Moses to his own time and in the crucial words with which he ends this brief account of his achievements: 'and so (lauded be god) haue continued.' Clearly Elyot saw Edgar's reign as some kind of beginning, or rather, as *the* beginning of civilization and social order in post-Roman Britain, an order presided over by 'one soueraigne

gouernour,' based upon reason, conformity, and some sense of the
public weal. While admitting that Edgar did not usher in the mil-
lenium (England subsequently 'nat beinge alway in like astate or
condition') Elyot nevertheless invoked him as a model for Henry VIII,
who he hoped ('god so disposynge') would, like his ancestor, reduce the realm 'unto a publike weale excellynge all other.' For a
variety of reasons, and upon a variety of occasions, Edgar was similarly held up as a model for Elizabeth, for James I, and for Charles I.[28]

I have already observed that in a literal sense *King Lear* stands
as the earliest of Shakespeare's British histories. I proposed that the
play's position is more complex than this simple fact implies, that,
having written his other British histories (save *Macbeth, Cymbeline,*
and his part in *Henry VIII*), Shakespeare went back in time to search
out the origins of ceremonial acts and policy in this drama of the
erosion of a primitive and paternalistic social order. At the same
time, I have acknowledged the overwhelming sense of ending that
is a quality of this play. But ending should not be confused with
annihilation or apocalypse. Lear's world ends because by the close
of the play it has *passed.* Only one character survives its rueful,
destructive attraction. The closing lines of the play seem almost
cursory: Lear dies without knowing he is dying (an oddity in
Shakespeare) and Edgar succeeds matter-of-factly. So many are
dead by the end and only three remain. But of the three, two die in
the sense that they are drawn back into the play by what can only
be termed the centripetal power of Lear himself. Early in the final
scene, Edmund provided as his justification for imprisoning Lear,
this shrewd estimate of Lear's influence:

> I thought it fit
> To send the old and miserable King
> To some retention and appointed guard;
> Whose age had charms in it, whose title more,
> To pluck the common bosom on his side,
> And turn our impress'd lances in our eyes
> Which do command them.   (5.3.46–52)

This power 'To pluck the common bosom on his side' remains even
after Lear's death, obviously in Kent's refusal to rule in order to
follow his master's call, more darkly in Albany's proposal to divide,
once again, the kingdom. Sensitive as he is to the responsibilities at
hand ('the gor'd state' must indeed be sustained), Albany, like Lear
before him, chooses to remain 'Unburthen'd,' and he recalls the
precedent set by Lear's first awful act in order to ensure this. Edgar
alone is able to survive the end of Lear, to assume responsibility, to

obey the weight of sadness. It is he who distinguishes with compassion between 'The oldest' and 'we that are young,' and who realizes that whatever comes after will differ from what has gone before:

> we that are young
> Shall never see so much, nor live so long.   (5.3.325–6)

And what will come after for the kingdom? If we know nothing of post-Lear Britain we do know something of its prospects. They are less unpredictable than Edgar's succession might lead us to believe. In fact, they are precisely those prospects of renewal and consolidation that Sir Thomas Elyot saw realized in the reign of King Edgar. The values of Shakespeare's Edgar are there to be seen. His sentiments concerning personal responsibility ('we must obey' merely echoes his earlier 'I come to cope' [5.3.124] as well as his inexorable judgment upon his father's blindness [5.3.170–3] and his appearance on the heath as one for whom there is no discrepancy between guilt and suffering [3.4.85–102]), his sentiments concerning maturity, even those concerning his responsibility for the state (when he challenges Edmund, after all, he accuses him of being a traitor: 'Conspirant 'gainst this high illustrious Prince' [5.3.135]), these are more than mere sentiments. In this play in which sentiments have a way of being hypocritical, in which language is imperilled by a king rewarding words and disregarding actions and by his subsequent insistence upon using a king's rhetoric even after he has given away a king's authority, in this play that has as one of its central concerns the dreadful gulf that can develop between word and act, Edgar's actions are consistent with the values he expresses. He is not alone, of course, in his honesty, but unlike the play's other honest characters, he survives.

If I am correct in what I have been suggesting about the presence of King Edgar in the Edgar of *King Lear*, then the prospects for Lear's kingdom are contained in Edgar's name. It is difficult to argue for the connotative power of a name in a time as distant as Tudor England is from our own; it is difficult for some of the same reasons that Sir Thomas Elyot's most famous descendant maintained that 'We cannot revive old factions ... / Or follow an antique drum.'[24] Still, if Shakespeare had named Lear's godson and successor Arthur, and had given him a half-brother named Uther, and had introduced a servant named Merlin (or Lancelot, or Galahad), something of what I am maintaining would by now be taken for granted. This hypothesis (and the examples I have cited) is not so far-fetched as it might appear. Shakespeare has introduced 'christian' names into the Lear story, the names of Edgar, Edmund, and Oswald. They are un-

like the given names of Lear and his daughters in that they are Saxon
names, and, willy-nilly, they occur in the history of King Edgar. His
father's name was Edmund, and one of those who figured promin-
ently at his coronation was Oswald, Archbishop of York. He had,
moreover, a wicked brother, Eadwig, who preceded him as king of
Wessex, and who so alienated his subjects that they forced him to
divide his kingdom with the younger Edgar. Upon Eadwig's death,
Edgar was, according to Roger of Wendover, 'elected by all the
people' to reign over a reunited Wessex.[25]

I am not proposing that Shakespeare's Edgar is Elyot's King
Edgar, any more than I could maintain that Shakespeare's Lear is
the Lear of the chronicles. The names Shakespeare inherited with the
Lear story contained a tale, a drama, a succession of actions that he
did not hesitate to change; the names of Lear, Cordelia, Goneril, and
Regan do not dictate the play's outcome. What had been familiar to
many in Shakespeare's audience must have become unfamiliar as the
cup of their deservings passed from character to character according
to a pattern dictated not by history but by dramatic necessity. And
perhaps a contrary movement is also at work in the play, calculated
to draw the audience back from the newly-unfamiliarized to something recollected and predictable – to history.

I have assumed what I attempted to demonstrate earlier, that
King Lear is the most skeletal and literally conceived of Shakespeare's plays, its climactic vision, Lear's vision upon the heath, 'the
thing itself.' Edgar in the guise of Tom was indeed 'the thing itself';
undisguised, he stands as the play's ultimate reductive force, realizing as he does others' fancies: 'here's three on 's are sophisticated;
thou art the thing itself' (3.4.108–9). Upon reflection, we are only
too aware of ironies darker than even Edmund intended in his introduction of Edgar into the play:

> pat he comes, like the catastrophe of the old
> comedy: my cue is villanous melancholy, with a
> sigh like Tom o' Bedlam.   (1.2.141–3)

But the ironies in Edgar's final accomplishments are not contained by
Edmund's fancy. The mock combat he contrived in order to discredit
Edgar assumes, for Edmund at least, an awful reality in the play's
last scene when Edgar does in fact wound him, and mortally, thus
accomplishing for himself (though selflessly) what Edmund had
aspired to. By the same token, the roles imposed upon him by the
maddened Lear – 'philosopher' and 'justicer' – prepare us for what
he becomes. And his identity as Lear's godson, so evocative of cere-

monial and symbolic values, becomes so literally his nature, that he succeeds his godfather as ruler of the realm. It is really in this light, of the nature of Edgar as he is conceived and realized in the play, that I propose a literal, factual, historical prototype and source for him. If at the end Lear does not quit himself like Lear, Edgar at least does quit himself like Edgar.

And finally, in the most curious scene in which he figures – a scene I take to be a paradigm for this most curious play – Edgar leads his blind father to the edge of 'Dover cliff.' So far as Gloucester knows, the place is real: 'Set me where you stand,' he urges (4.6.24). But Edgar has led his father into a landscape of flat ground that he has misrepresented in order to evoke an action (the suicidal leap) the landscape thwarts. Edgar's design is like Shakespeare's in writing *King Lear*; he deceives his father as Shakespeare deceived his audience, leading them into a familiar setting (the Lear story) only to frustrate their expectations. What Edgar accomplished by his manipulation of place and space, Shakespeare has accomplished by his manipulation of sources and time. Like Gloucester's leap that was no leap at all but was so much more profound a leap than ever he intended, our experience in *King Lear* is of an unpredictable history, in which the Lear of the chronicles becomes unfamiliar, and an unaccountable Edgar becomes historical, in which by means of an anachronistic baptism, we are confronted with something very like the history of history itself.

NOTES

1 Of titles listed in the Stationers' Register, A.P. Rossiter observed, 'It is arguable that the players would be reasonably careful to put down the right titles, and that (though Shakespeare may have had no hand in it) what we can read *was* what the plays were called,' 'Shakespearian Tragedy' in *Tragedy: Modern Essays in Criticism* ed. Laurence Michel and Richard B. Sewall (Englewood Cliffs, NJ 1963) 183. The entry for 26 November 1607 reads: 'Master WILLIAM SHAKESPEARE his "*historye of Kinge LEAR*" ...' The Quarto title is more elaborate and of some significance to my argument: 'M. William Shak-speare: / *HIS* / True Chronicle Historie of the life and / death of King LEAR and his three / Daughters. / *With the unfortunate life of* Edgar, *sonne* / and heire to the Earle of Gloster, and his / sullen and assumed humor of / TOM of Bedlam ...'

2 See F.D. Hoeniger, above.

3 All references to Shakespeare's plays other than *King Lear* are to the Oxford edition, ed. W.J. Craig (London 1943).

4 'The Trew Law of Free Monarchies,' *The Political Works of James I* ed. C.H. McIlwain (New York 1965) 55

5 Milton Wilson *Shelley's Later Poetry* (New York 1959) chap 1

6 *Coleridge's Essays & Lectures on Shakspeare & Some Other Old Poets & Dramatists* ed. Ernest Rhys (London n.d.) 111

7 Ibid 108

8 Ibid 109

9 Thomas Heywood *A True Description of His Majesties Royall Ship, Built this Yeare 1637 at Wooll-witch in Kent. To the great glory of our English Nation, and not paralleled in the whole Christian World* (London 1637) 30

10 His note to line 349, Song XII of *Poly-Olbion*

11 ed. J.R. Lumby (London 1858) VI 467

12 Raphael Holinshed *Chronicles of England, Scotland and Ireland* (London 1807) I 695

13 Higden *Polychronicon* 467

14 Allan Chester in the Introduction to the Penguin edition of *Henry IV, Part Two* (Baltimore 1957) 17

15 See Muir's note for 5.2.11.

16 *The Boke Named The Governour* ed. Ernest Rhys (London n.d.) 8

17 Ibid 6

18 Ibid 13

19 Ibid 14

20 Ibid

21 Accounts of this Chapel and its brief history can be found in the following works: Armine Le Strange Campbell *The Glories of Glastonbury* (London 1926); Christopher Hollis *Glastonbury and England* (London 1927); Hugh Ross Williamson *The Flowering Hawthorn* (New York 1962).

22 Heywood *A True Description of His Majesties Royall Ship* 29

23 John Dee reminded Queen Elizabeth that 'the Queenes Maiesties royaltie over the British Ocean sea' was traceable to Edgar, and that his example in remaining vigilant over the coasts of Britain, even in peace time, was the only precaution to be taken by an island nation: John Dee *General and Rare Materials pertayning to the Perfect Arte of Navigation* (London 1577) 59. Upon at least three occasions, Francis Bacon cited Edgar's laws as precedents for James I: Sir Francis Bacon, 'The Argument of Sir F.B., Knight, His Majesty's Solicitor-General, in the case of the Post-Nati of Scotland,' *Three Speeches of the Right Honorable, Sir Francis Bacon Knight* (London 1641) 10; 'A Proposition to His Majesty, by Sir F.B., Knight, His Majesty's Attorney-General, and one of His Privy Council; Touching the Compiling and Amendment of the Laws of England,' *Law Tracts* (London 1737) 8; 'An Offer to King James of a Digest to be Made of the Laws of England,' *ibid* 19. Heywood claimed of Charles I, '... whatsoever his *sacred Maiesty*

challengeth concerning his absolute dominion over the *foure Seas,* hee
justly and with an unquestionable Title claimeth from this King *Edgar,*
being his true and lawfull hereditary Successor': Heywood *A True Description of His Majesties Royall Ship* 39
24 T.S. Eliot, 'Little Gidding,' 11. 185–7
25 Roger of Wendover *Flowers of History* tr. J.A. Giles (London 1849) I 259

afterword

ROSALIE COLIE died just as this – her most characteristic project – was accepted for publication. Her essays contained here are of
a piece with her other work. The volume itself celebrates the kind of
scholarly and critical co-operation that she describes in the Preface
and that her friends and colleagues will recognize as her hallmark.

We who have been cajoled and encouraged by her appreciate that
this is – *quintessentially* – her book.

contributors

Martha Andresen *Pomona College*
William F. Blissett *University College, University of Toronto*
Maurice Charney *Rutgers University*
Rosalie L. Colie *late of Brown University*
F.T. Flahiff *St Michael's College, University of Toronto*
F.D. Hoeniger *Victoria College, University of Toronto*
Nancy R. Lindheim *Trinity College, University of Toronto*
Bridget Gellert Lyons *Rutgers University*
John Reibetanz *Victoria College, University of Toronto*
Thomas F. Van Laan *Rutgers University*
Sheldon P. Zitner *Trinity College, University of Toronto*

This book
was designed by
WILLIAM RUETER
under the direction of
ALLAN FLEMING
and was printed by
University
of Toronto
Press